THE SKILL OF LIVING

*The Buddha's Path
for Developing Skillful Qualities*

By

PETER DOOBININ

TABLE OF CONTENTS

"We must learn to reawaken and keep ourselves awake, not by mechanical aids, but by an infinite expectation of the dawn, which does not forsake us in our soundest sleep. I know of no more encouraging fact than the unquestionable ability of man to elevate his life by a conscious endeavor. It is something to be able to paint a particular picture, or to carve a statue, and so to make a few objects beautiful; but it is far more glorious to carve and paint the very atmosphere and medium through which we look, which morally we can do. To affect the quality of the day, that is the highest of arts."
(Thoreau/ *Walden*)

INTRODUCTION

At the age of 35, I found myself in a place of suffering, emotional pain. I was in a downward spiral. My life seemed worthless, meaningless. Realizing my plight, I began to look for a way out.

I don't know that my story is all that different from anybody else's; I think we're all looking, at some level, for a way out. A way out of suffering, pain, anxiety, stress, fear, depression, despair. A way out of the meaninglessness that strangles contemporary life.

We're all looking, the Buddha says, for happiness. We're all looking for a road to travel, a path to happiness.

It was my good fortune, when I was 35, to find the Buddha's path. For the last twenty plus years I've been a student in the Theravada Buddhist tradition. The Theravada form derives from the core teachings of the Buddha, as found in the Pali Canon, the earliest surviving record of what the Buddha taught. Within Theravada Buddhism there are various lineages, streams. In my practice, I follow the style of the Thai Forest tradition. Specifically, the teachings of Ajaan Lee, a 20th Century Thai master, and Thanissaro Bhikkhu, abbot of Metta Forest Monastery. The teachings offered in this book are largely a reflection of the Thai Forest lineage, the teachings of Ajaan Lee and Thanissaro Bhikkhu.

This is a book about developing the skillful qualities of generosity, ethical conduct, renunciation, truthfulness, effort, determination, discernment, lovingkindness, patience and equanimity. Although a primary element of the Buddha's path, developing skillful qualities isn't emphasized by most western dharma teachers. But it's terrifically important. In my own practice, I've come to understand with increasing clarity the critical role that the development of skillful qualities plays in the unfolding of the path. In teaching the dharma, as I've been doing in New York City for more than a decade, I've seen that it's essential for students to make developing skillful qualities an integral component of their practice. If students don't develop skillful qualities, they won't get very far along the path.

My practice is a householder's practice. I'm not a monk. I don't live or work at a meditation center. I live in, of all places, New York City. For the first ten years of my practice, I held a job in the publishing industry. Accordingly, I've always had an interest in learning how to follow the Buddha's path while living amidst the complexities of contemporary life. As a dharma teacher my task, as I see it, is to help students cultivate the path within the context of their householder's lives.

Most of the emphasis in offering Theravada, or Insight Meditation, teachings to western students has been put on providing opportunities for silent retreat practice. Students take time away from their lives, go on retreat, practice meditation, then return to their lives. Retreat practice has value, but it's just one segment of the path. The path goes much further; the Buddha's way out, at heart, is a way of living. A way of living skillfully. A way of living joyfully. A way of living in which we know freedom. It's essential, therefore, that we learn to follow the path as we move through the landscape of our lives, through the undulating terrains of our relationships, our work, the day-to-day events of our lives.

At Downtown Meditation Community, we attempt to follow the path as we go through our days and nights, as we encounter the range of human experience, the ups, the downs, all of it. We've had students who've followed the teachings as they've prepared for the birth of a child. And students who've practiced the dharma as they've moved through the stages of dying. And everything in between.

It's been a process of discovery, figuring out how to do this, how to teach students to keep to the path while living in the modern world. This book represents some of what I've learned during this process. It offers a practical map for following the Buddha's path, for developing skillful qualities, and it offers a way to implement these teachings in our everyday lives.

I've been blessed to be able to pass on the dharma as the guiding teacher of Downtown Meditation Community, to share the teachings with people who've taken them to heart, who've made a great effort to practice the dharma. The students at DMC have certainly helped to show me the way. This book is dedicated to them.

OPENING WORDS

FINDING THE BEGINNING

In the things of life, we look for a place to begin. This is a mark of wisdom. We find the beginning.

It might not be the place we'd like to begin. We might prefer to begin further down the road. We might prefer to skip ahead. We'd like, perhaps, to bypass these opening words, get to the meaty parts of the book. In practicing the dharma, we may find we're inclined to forsake the groundwork. We may be inclined to look for shortcuts. We may be interested strictly in the big stuff, nirvana, enlightenment, whatever you want to call it.

This book, then, will not be about enlightenment.

Or maybe it will be.

The truth is, there's significant pain in trying to get somewhere we're not ready to get.

And the truth is, there's a joy in finding ourselves right here, at the beginning.

There are different ways to view the Buddha's path. A good way to think about it is as a path in which we develop three things:

1-Skillful Qualities
2-Concentration
3-Insight

The path begins with developing skillful qualities. When the Buddha taught new students, this is where he began. Children growing up in Asian Buddhist cultures begin their training right here, by developing skillful qualities.

We make an effort, from the start, to cultivate each of the three elements: skillful qualities, concentration, and insight. But it's important to realize there's a cause and effect relationship at work as we develop these basic aspects of the path. The growth of skillful qualities gives rise to the growth of concentration; the growth of concentration gives rise to the growth of insight. There isn't any possibility of developing concentration and insight, to any reasonable degree, without developing skillful qualities. The Buddha was clear about this. He understood the cause and effect relationship among skillful qualities, concentration, and insight. In following the path, we have to understand the cause and effect process. We have to respect the process.

It's said that the Buddha, in his past lives, cultivated ten skillful qualities (sometimes known as the Ten Paramis or Ten Perfections). These ten skillful qualities are generosity, ethical conduct, renunciation, truthfulness, effort, determination, discernment, lovingkindness, patience, equanimity. The Buddha, the story goes, cultivated these skillful qualities before he took birth as Siddhartha Gotama, and by the time he took that birth these skillful qualities were well developed. As a result, he was in position to cultivate concentration and insight, and consequently find true happiness. Whether we believe in the notion of past lives is not important. We can learn by the Buddha's example. These skillful qualities must be developed.

Following the Buddha's map, we develop the skills we need to make the journey toward a greater happiness in our lives. We cultivate joy, self-confidence, inner strength. We put ourselves in position to build concentration, gain insight. When we're suffering, struggling, there may be the tendency to think we'll be able to lessen our pain by practicing meditation, by putting more effort into meditation, but in order to meditate, in order to establish that kind of face-to-face encounter with ourselves, we need certain skills, we need to be developed in certain skillful qualities. Our capacity to meditate depends on the degree to which we've developed these skillful qualities.

If we don't develop these qualities, we won't be able to build a strong meditation practice. We won't get very far along the Buddha's road. We'll stall. Our practice will break down like an old Chevy abandoned on the side of some forlorn interstate. All the talk about enlightenment will be just that, talk.

Developing skillful qualities is a place to begin. It's a wise place to begin. It's a compassionate place. It's compassionate because everybody can develop these qualities. Everybody. No matter where you are in your life, in your spiritual life, in your dharma practice, you can develop generosity, ethical conduct, renunciation, truthfulness, effort, determination, discernment, lovingkindness, patience, equanimity.

COMING TO SEE FOR YOURSELF

If you develop the skillful qualities, you'll realize significant benefits. You'll move through life more effectively. You'll build self-esteem. You'll know greater joy. You'll find you're able to grow a much stronger meditation practice; you'll deepen in concentration and insight.

But you shouldn't take my word for it. It's something you'll have to come to see for yourself.

This isn't a practice that asks blind obedience. It isn't dogma.

Generally we subscribe to dogma. We unhesitatingly believe what we're told. We go along with what we're told by parents, teachers, friends, people on TV, the culture. As dharma students, however, we don't do what others tell us to do simply because they tell us to do it. We follow the path, we develop skillful qualities, not because somebody, the author of the book, the teacher, or even the Buddha, tells us that we should, but rather because we've come to see for ourselves that there's value in it. We've seen that it's a good path, a path that leads to happiness.

In his teaching to the Kalamas, the Buddha makes this important point:

"Now, Kalamas, don't go by reports, by legends, by traditions, by scripture, by logical conjecture, by inference, by analogies, by agreement through pondering views, by probability, or by the thought, 'This contemplative is our teacher.' When you know for yourselves that, 'These qualities are skillful; these qualities are blameless; these qualities are praised by the wise; these qualities, when adopted & carried out, lead to welfare & to happiness' — then you should enter & remain in them." (AN 3.65)

In order to bring about change, in order to find true happiness, you have to act in ways that you determine, through firsthand experience, are good for you, in your best interests. You have to come to see for yourself what supports your ability to live a more joyful life. You have to come to see for yourself what has to be done.

We need teachers, wise beings, to point us toward true happiness, but ultimately we have to see for ourselves what we have to do in order to find it.

It's by understanding the benefits of certain actions that you become inclined to take these actions. Seeing the benefits, you're motivated to keep doing what you're doing. Seeing the benefits in your skillful actions (and the drawbacks in your unskillful actions) is a key aspect in fostering skillfulness.

As you practice, you'll begin to understand, to know, in your heart, the benefits of developing skillful qualities.

It's through practice that you'll learn to cultivate the skillful qualities, the same way you learned to ride a bicycle. You didn't learn to ride a bike by listening to somebody tell you how to do it. You learned by getting on the bike yourself.

At the end of each chapter there will be a set of "Practice Suggestions." They offer ways to learn to cultivate generosity, ethical conduct, renunciation, truthfulness, effort, determination, discernment, lovingkindness, patience, equanimity. When I teach courses on this facet of the path, I give students practice suggestions at the end of each class. In the ensuing week, before the next class, they have an opportunity to cultivate the skillful qualities. This "homework," I stress, is the most important part of the course. In this spirit, I recommend taking some time, perhaps a week or so, after reading each chapter to work with the practice activities. Give yourself a chance to learn how to cultivate these qualities. This is where the learning takes place. In the doing.

The skillful qualities are functions of your goodness. You have an inherent capacity for goodness, but you have to develop it. As a dharma student, that's your job. You have to put effort into developing your goodness. You have to take action.

It will require effort to develop the skillful qualities. It may be more than we bargained for. Perhaps we'd rather just read, in hopes of finding answers in the book. But answers aren't found in books; they're found in doing. Dharma practice isn't about sitting back, putting up our feet. It's not passive. It's a path of action.

It's a path, like any true path, that we have to walk.

RESTRUCTURING THE WAY YOU SEE

In developing skillful qualities we learn to restructure the way we see. We learn, specifically, to restructure the way we look at our actions.

It may be our habit, when we consider our actions, to think in terms of "good" and "bad" or "right" and "wrong." As dharma students, however, we're asked to take a different approach. In studying our actions we're asked to discern whether they're "unskillful" or "skillful."

It's critical that we learn to make this shift, that we learn to recognize our actions as "unskillful" or "skillful."

When we talk about action, we're referring to three kinds of action:

1-Physical action (what we do with our body)
2-Verbal action (the way we speak)
3-Mental action (the way we think)

In developing the path, we pay attention to all three kinds of action.

Paying attention, we discern whether our actions are unskillful or skillful.

What does this mean?

An action is unskillful if it leads to suffering, for others, for ourselves. In using the term "suffering," we're referring to mental suffering. There are many expressions of mental suffering, including anxiety, anger, agitation, irritation, stress, depression, dissatisfaction, disharmony, desire, wanting, lust, confusion, uncertainty. The Buddha describes suffering as the distress we register when "being joined with what is displeasing, being separated from what is pleasing." This mental suffering encompasses a range of painful experience, from the most blatant forms, such as anguish and despair, to the most subtle forms of dis-ease.

Unskillful action is driven by unskillful intention. It's the quality of the intention that determines whether an action is unskillful or skillful. All unskillful intention derives from three mental factors:

1-Desire
2-Aversion
3-Delusion

Skillful action, on the other hand, leads to the end of suffering. It leads to happiness.

Skillful action is motivated by skillful intention; specifically, by love and compassion.

What is love? What is compassion? We may have different ideas. It's important, however, to know what the Buddha means when he uses these terms. In these pages, we'll talk at length about love and compassion. For now, I'll provide simple definitions.

Love, or lovingkindness, is a quality of the heart. When the heart is open, it radiates love. Love is expressed, in its essence, in the wish that we have for ourselves to be happy and the wish that we have for others, that they be happy.

Compassion is also a quality of the heart. It's the way the heart responds to suffering. It's the expression of our wish to be free from suffering and our wish for others, that they find freedom from suffering.

As dharma students we seek to abandon unskillful actions and develop skillful actions. We seek to act, more and more, from the heart, from the place of love, compassion. In the final analysis, this is what it's all about.

More love.

More compassion.

SELF-JUDGMENT

Skillful qualities manifest in skillful actions. Accordingly, as we develop skillful qualities, we're asked to pay close attention to our actions. We're asked to study our actions. In studying our actions, we're asked to discern whether they're leading us toward true happiness or suffering. In practicing this sort of discernment, we're engaging in what we might call "skillful judging." We're skillfully judging our actions.

We have to learn to skillfully judge our actions. If we fail to practice skillful judgment, we'll never learn to change our actions. We'll never learn to take actions that will move us toward a greater happiness in our lives.

There are certain misconceptions in dharma circles when it comes to the idea of "judging." It's important that we understand that there is skillful and unskillful judging. As dharma students, we have to learn to differentiate between these two kinds of judgment. We have to learn to abandon our tendencies to engage in unskillful judging and we have to develop the ability to skillfully judge our actions.

The ability to skillfully judge our actions is a mark of spiritual maturity.

When we practice skillful judging we judge our actions, not ourselves. We refrain from self-judgment. Self-judgment is unskillful; it's the primary way in which we participate in unskillful, unhealthy judging.

Practicing skillful judgment, we look at our actions clearly, objectively. We don't react emotionally. We don't register aversion. Typically when we engage in unskillful self-judgment, we look at our actions, at ourselves, with a negative eye. In practicing healthy judgment, we put aside this aversive quality.

As we look skillfully at our actions, we recognize whether they're unskillful or skillful, whether they're leading toward suffering or true happiness. We ask: Is this action causing me suffering? Is it causing others suffering?

It's all about suffering and finding the end to suffering. We study our actions in an effort to see whether they're causing suffering. We do this because we have the wish to be free from suffering. We study our actions, then, motivated by compassion for ourselves and others.

It may be our habit, of course, to engage in unskillful judgment when we consider our actions. It may be our habit to engage in self-judgment. It may be our habit to criticize ourselves, put ourselves down, berate ourselves. We tend to judge ourselves a lot. For many of us, self-judgment is the primary strategy we employ in examining our actions.

Sometimes self-judgment is blatant. We criticize ourselves vehemently, harshly. Sometimes self-judgment is subtle. It's a soft voice, a whisper in the back of the mind. This soft voice is so faintly etched into the fabric of our consciousness that we don't notice it. But it's there, constantly objecting, criticizing, condemning, offering derogatory analysis.

When we observe this self-judgment we realize that it doesn't emanate from a source of truth, a fountain of certainty. It isn't based in fact. What we see is that it arises from our conditioning, often from what we've heard others say. The voices of self-judgment are often the voices of parents, friends, teachers. We're simply replaying old tapes, old scratched beat-up cassettes.

As you make an effort to study your actions, you may find yourself sliding into habitual patterns of self-judgment. There will be times when you'll struggle in your efforts to develop skillful qualities, and in response you may criticize yourself. There will be times when you'll act unskillfully, and in turn you may reprimand yourself, chastise yourself. It's important to recognize when you're judging yourself and it's important to question your self-judgment. It's important to ask: Is it useful?

If you think about it, you've probably been engaging in self-judgment for years, but you've never bothered to question the strategy. You've never asked if it's useful. It's as if you purchased a vacuum cleaner but never checked to see if it was working, if it was picking up the dust and bits of debris. As you recognize self-judgment, you have to begin to question it.

The way you're deriding yourself, putting yourself down. Is it useful? Is it serving you? Is it in your best interests? Is there a more compassionate way that you might relate to your actions?

(As you begin to notice self-judgment, you may find yourself judging your judging. It's understandable; after all, it's the way you've learned to consider your actions. So be careful of the tendency to judge the judging.)

Self-judgment is a major obstacle to our progress. When you judge yourself you move further from the path. If you're in the habit of constantly engaging in self-judgment, you'll eventually find yourself a good distance from the road.

It's imperative, therefore, that you recognize self-judgment.

Recognize it and question it.

Is it useful?

REFLECTION

Included in the activities at the end of each chapter are various suggestions for reflection. In practicing reflection, we deepen our understanding of where we are, where we need to go.

When I was in eighth grade, my science teacher, Miss Krimper, responding to the halfhearted efforts the class was making, explained that, "Sometimes you have to look at yourself. You have to do some soul searching." I don't remember anything I studied in that class, but I remember that. That stuck with me. That was important, I figured. And it is. It's important to reflect.

Reflection is a skill. It involves taking a step back from the circumstances of our lives, the play of events. The Buddha likened it to going up in a tower and looking down at our lives. It's an activity most of us don't partake in. Reflection isn't a priority. We don't have time for it. We're too busy. We have too many important things to do. In the present-day culture, we're driven by a desire to fill every moment with content. Every crevice in the day must be filled. The mechanisms of the culture are designed to satisfy this purpose. During moments that might've previously been "free," devoid of content, we engage in functions on the laptop, or connect with somebody on the cell phone, or listen to music on a portable device. It's a dire scenario.

We need to take a step back every now and again, to reflect, to follow Miss Krimper's injunction, to consider what we're doing, where we're going, what's important.

As a dharma student you need to take time to step back, to pause. If you look, you shouldn't have difficulty finding some time every day to pause. There may be occasions when you're able to take lengthy pauses, when you're able to go for a walk in the park, something like that. But that's not necessary. Small pauses, a few moments here and there, dedicated to reflection, will yield beneficial results. Sometimes you can pause while involved in another activity. When you're riding the bus, for instance. Instead of scrutinizing your smart phone, you can sit quietly, reflect.

Reflection is a skill that most of us haven't ever been taught. We may equate reflection with thinking. But while some thinking is necessary, reflection involves more than "thinking about" something. It transcends ordinary thinking, the thinking we engage in throughout the day. In reflecting we get beyond this sort of thinking. We get "out of the head." This shift doesn't occur magically; it's accomplished in thoroughly pragmatic fashion, by putting our attention on the body.

Let's say you're going to reflect on your propensity to judge yourself. Stepping back from the movements of your life, you'd put your attention on your body. You'd do this by putting your mind on your breath. You'd feel your breath, somewhere in the middle part of your body, in the abdomen perhaps.

Then you'd ask a question. Some questions you might ask are:

Do I participate in self-judgment?

Is this a habit I engage in on a regular basis?

Is judging myself serving me, in my efforts to find happiness in my life?

Keeping your awareness in your body, you'd let the question reverberate. You'd let it echo, through the body. Refraining from answering, you'd simply let the question be there. You'd try to get a felt sense of the "answer."

You'd allow the "answer" to come from someplace other than the thinking realm. You'd allow knowledge to form.

It's a good idea to ask questions as a way of supporting our ability to reflect. We ask questions but don't try to answer. Of course, it can be tricky. We want answers. We want to know right away. In reflecting, however, we have to learn to wait. We have to learn to "be with" the questions.

As we ask the question, "Do I judge myself," we may automatically answer: "Yeah, of course I do." It's in our best interest, in such cases, to put aside the voices in the mind that are attempting to provide immediate answers.

Reflecting, we allow our innate wisdom to respond to the question.

So right now you might want to try it.

Put your mind on your breath, somewhere in the middle of your body.

Feel a few breaths.

Then ask a question.

"Do I judge myself?"

Ask the question, but don't think about it. Don't try to answer. Stay with your breath. Let the question move, slowly, through your body.

See if you can get a felt sense of the "answer." Don't think. Don't try to verbalize a response. See if you can access deeper structures of wisdom.

Allow understanding to form in whatever way it chooses.

As you learn to reflect in this manner you'll begin to acquire knowledge that transcends intellectual knowledge. You'll begin to know things in the place where we want to know things: in the heart.

Work with the reflections. Develop the skill. It's an important skill. It's a skill you'll need as you make your journey along the Buddha's path.

THE BUDDHA'S HAPPINESS

Skillful qualities, when developed, manifest in skillful actions, which lead to happiness.

Which brings us to the question: what is happiness?

As we move along the path, we find ourselves faced with choosing between two kinds of happiness: the happiness of the world and the Buddha's happiness. The happiness of the world is the happiness most people seek, the happiness that comes from acquiring sense pleasure, making money, gaining material possessions, attaining status, receiving praise. It's a happiness that the Buddha, as young Prince Siddhartha, knew quite well. As he said:

"Monks, I lived in refinement, utmost refinement, total refinement. My father even had lotus ponds made in our palace: one where red-lotuses bloomed, one where white lotuses bloomed, one where blue lotuses bloomed, all for my sake. I used no sandalwood that was not from Varanasi. My turban was from Varanasi, as were my tunic, my lower garments, & my outer cloak. A white sunshade was held over me day & night to protect me from cold, heat, dust, dirt, & dew.

"I had three palaces: one for the cold season, one for the hot season, one for the rainy season. During the four months of the rainy season I was entertained in the rainy-season palace by minstrels without a single man among them, and I did not once come down from the palace."
(AN 3.38)

Siddhartha wasn't convinced this kind of happiness was all it was cracked up to be. Despite the objections of his family, he began to cast his gaze beyond the life he was living; he began to wonder if there was a better way to live. He questioned the happiness of the world. He asked the questions that, as dharma students, we learn to ask: Where am I looking for happiness? Is there some other sort of happiness? Is there a greater happiness?

After making profound effort, after much trial and error, the Buddha discovered that there was indeed another happiness. It was a true happiness. It was reliable. It didn't rely on unreliable things. It wasn't dependent on the amount of money you had in the bank, the number of houses you owned, the notoriety you achieved in your career. It wasn't a happiness that depended on "getting things" or "being somebody."

The happiness the Buddha found is a happiness that depends on our actions. If our actions are skillful, we'll come to know this happiness.

The Buddha's teaching was aimed at showing people how to get to where they needed to go. He wasn't interested so much in talking about true happiness, but rather in explaining how we might get there. To this end, he taught skills. He taught the skills we need to learn, in order to know true happiness.

The Buddha didn't often describe true happiness. He realized that language couldn't accurately explain it. More importantly, he recognized that true happiness wasn't going to be found by talking about it or listening to others talk about it, but rather by doing something, taking action. For our purposes, we might think of this happiness as the happiness inside. The happiness of the heart.

The happiness of the world and the Buddha's happiness are very, very different. As we practice the dharma, we begin to realize that, in deciding where to look for happiness, we have two rather distinct choices.

As we move along the path, the fact of choice becomes apparent. The choices become clear.

Gradually, we comprehend the Buddha's happiness. Gradually, it becomes the happiness we seek.

CHAPTER ONE

GENEROSITY

PRECONCEIVED NOTIONS

As a young man I had a desire to follow a countercultural path. I grew up in the 60s, watching, mostly on television, the sweep of countercultural events that marked that period. Unfortunately, I wasn't old enough to participate. By the time I'd reached an age at which I might've been a participant, the 60s had ended, the era had faded, the landscape was deserted. I was thoroughly disappointed. However, I was still disposed to live in a way that was different from the way most people lived. I wasn't inclined to go along with the crowd, follow the herd. Eventually I found the Buddha's path. It was, I learned, a decidedly countercultural path.

In developing the skillful quality of generosity we're following a markedly countercultural course. What could be more countercultural in today's world dedicated to making money, acquiring possessions, receiving as much stimulation as possible from the instruments of technology, TV, internet, etc.?

The way of the world, clearly, is geared toward getting. The getting mind drives the culture. All of us are driven by it to some extent. If you examine your thinking, you shouldn't have difficulty detecting patterns of desire, the urge to get, whether it's sense pleasure, money, material things, status, praise.

The getting mind is embedded; it burns incessantly, like a basement furnace, firing our days and nights. It affects most of our actions. In fact, as you practice the dharma you may notice that you're influenced by the getting mind. You may notice that you're prone to think: "What can I get from the practice?"

Right now, as you're reading, you may be motivated by a desire to "get something" from this book.

Is this the way your mind is?

Can you see this?

The prevailing belief in the culture is that happiness comes from getting, from getting a better job, getting material things, getting married, getting a new place to live. All the forms of getting.

It's the message we've been receiving all our lives. It's what the world is telling us. It's the message we hear every day, everywhere we go. It's a loud message. Deafening. Happiness is in getting.

Can you see the tendency you have to listen to this message?

Can you see the tendency you have to believe that happiness is found in getting?

It may not be something you'd like to see in your mind, but the first movement in bringing about change involves seeing, clearly, truthfully, where you are. If you're able to acknowledge where you are, you can shift your course and head somewhere else. The Buddha's teachings rest on the premise that we can change. There wouldn't be much reason for following the path if it weren't leading to change. There wouldn't be any point in reading this book.

We change, the Buddha says, by changing our actions. We bring about affirmative change, we move toward happiness, by taking skillful actions.

So right now you might want to try shifting your course of action, the action you're taking in reading these words. You might want to shift from "what can I get from reading this?" to "what can I give to reading this?"

Try it.

Center yourself in your breath.

Ask yourself:

"What can I give to what I'm doing right now?"

You don't have to think about it. Inside, in your heart, you know what giving is all about.

Simply ask: "What can I give?"

As you make this shift, you may begin to realize that there's a lot you can give to the simple act of reading these sentences. You can give your full attention. Your care. Your heart. Your love.

You may notice that your experience changes as you move to "what can I give?" You may experience a diminishing of stress, anxiousness. You may feel a sense of ease. The act of reading may become more concentrated, more engaged.

As you move to "what can I give," you may begin to get a sense of the benefits in practicing generosity.

There are, in fact, many benefits.

Practicing generosity is life-changing. It's joyful. It's liberating. It leads us to a greater happiness.

The Buddha said:

"If beings knew, as I know, the results of giving & sharing, they would not eat without having given, nor would the stain of miserliness overcome their minds. Even if it were their last bite, their last mouthful, they would not eat without having shared, if there were someone to receive their gift. But because beings do not know, as I know, the results of giving & sharing, they eat without having given. The stain of miserliness overcomes their minds."

(Iti 26)

The first words of the passage are especially telling. "If beings knew." The truth, the Buddha realized, is that we don't know. We just don't know. We hear the Buddha talking about it. We hear dharma teachers extolling the benefits of practicing generosity. There's great joy in it, they declare. It's a path to happiness. We hear it, but we don't quite believe it. It can't be right, we think. It can't be true. Generosity, we may think, isn't that important. Practicing generosity isn't going to make a difference in my life. It isn't going to bring me happiness.

Do you harbor these kinds of preconceived notions?

Can you see the preconceived notions that you have about generosity?

It's important to recognize your preconceived notions and it's important to question them. You don't have to try to get rid of your preconceived notions. You don't have to try to alter them. Just begin to question them. Leave room for some other truth to emerge. Leave a bit of room, a crack wide enough for some new light to shine through.

Maybe it is true. Maybe the Buddha knew what he was talking about. Maybe there is an opportunity for transformation if I practice generosity. Maybe it will lead to a greater happiness.

As you shifted from "what can I get" to "what can I give," you may have started to get an inkling of your innate capacity to practice generosity. You may have begun to see that you've already got the ability.

As we've explained, the skillful qualities are qualities you have. Generosity is a quality you have. You can find it inside, within yourself. In fact, it's the only place you can find it.

It isn't something you can acquire. You can't get it from somebody. You can't get it by reading this book. You can't buy it at the mall. You can't purchase it online.

You already have it.

Of course, you may not believe it. You may not believe that you have the ability to practice generosity. There may be a voice in your mind that keeps insisting that you don't possess the quality of generosity. It's often our habit to listen to these negative voices. Certain voices become audible, loud, and we listen. "You don't have the ability to practice generosity." "You're not generous." As you develop the skillful qualities you have to be mindful, you have to watch out for these voices. You have to question them. You have to ask: Is this a voice I should listen to? Is this voice worthy of my attention? Is it useful to listen to this voice?

In any given day, many patterns of thinking invade the mind, all kinds of voices chatter and babble and cry and plead and groan. You're under no obligation, however, to listen to any of these voices.

Some voices may be insistent, but just because they're insistent doesn't mean you have to listen. As Thanissaro Bhikkhu suggests, you might want to think of the negative chatter in the mind as the voices of "crazy people." You wouldn't listen to a crazy person if he came up to you on the street and started talking to you. You wouldn't do what he told you to do. You wouldn't go where he told you to go. Basically, that's what we do, when we listen to certain voices in the mind.

When you hear voices that insist you don't have the capacity to develop generosity (or any of the skillful qualities), a good question to ask is: Is it true?

Is it true?

Is it true that I won't be able to develop generosity?

Is it true that I'm not a generous person?

It's important to put aside patterns of thinking that aren't serving us. It's important to make room for other understandings to present themselves.

As we go through life we tend to narrow our vision. We think that because we look at things a certain way, it's the only way to look at them. We're like somebody who never leaves the house and becomes convinced the view through the front window is the only available view of the world.

But it's not true.

"The universe," Thoreau said, "is wider than our view of it."

As dharma students, we're asked to take a wider view. As we develop skillful qualities, we open to the possibility that things may be different than we think. As you make an effort to develop generosity, you may very well find that you can do it. You may find, in fact, that you have a great capacity for generosity.

You may find that practicing generosity brings immeasurable joy. You may find that it's life-changing.

It's important that we question our preconceived notions about ourselves, about generosity, about all the skillful qualities. Our preconceived notions prevent us from moving ahead. They prevent us from changing. As long as they're lying there, in the road, we won't get very far. It's not enough to have the intention to develop generosity and the other skillful qualities; we have to be mindful of these roadblocks.

WAYS OF GIVING

Generosity, like all the skillful qualities, is a quality you have.

You don't have to get it.

You have it.

Your job is to cultivate it.

What does it mean to cultivate something?

Think about the way we cultivate a garden. We don't "create" the plants in a garden, the tomatoes, lettuce, string beans. That responsibility lies with some other force, call it nature. In cultivating a garden, we do what we need to do so that the garden flourishes. We take care of the plants. We water, fertilize, remove weeds, make sure the plants get enough light.

It's the same with cultivating skillful qualities. As human beings, we have a capacity to practice generosity; however, the garden of our generosity may be neglected. It may be inundated with gnarly weeds, overgrown foliage, all manner of unsightly debris. The plants may not be in very good shape. Cultivating generosity, we clear away all the scraggly weeds. We get rid of the debris. We nourish the soil. We take care of the plants.

We can cultivate the skillful quality of generosity by giving (1) material resources, (2) the resource of our time, (3) the gift of the dharma, and (4) the gift of fearlessness.

Our generosity is cultivated, the teachings indicate, when we give from the place of compassion, when we're motivated by the wish to help others.

In giving material resources, our generosity is authentic, a true expression of generosity, when we give in an effort to help others have their basic needs met. Specifically, the basic needs of food, clothing, shelter and medical needs. A gift doesn't necessarily qualify as generosity. If, for instance, you give somebody a bottle of whiskey, it almost certainly doesn't count as an act of generosity; the whiskey isn't going to help the other person meet his basic needs.

Since the time of the Buddha, householders have supported monastics by providing them with basic requisites: food, robes, shelter, medicine. The householder's generosity allows the monks to practice the dharma, to dedicate themselves completely to the Buddha's path. Monks benefit profoundly from this generosity, and householders benefit as well. The monks keep the Buddha's teachings healthy, strong; they keep the path open. Offering what they've learned, they teach householders the dharma. It's through this process of generosity that the Buddha's teachings have been able to stay alive and prosper for more than 2,500 years.

When we give skillfully we create a reciprocal relationship. As the Buddha says, generosity involves "mutual dependence." When motivated by compassion, generosity is beneficial to both the recipient of the gift and the giver. It supports both parties in their efforts to find true happiness.

As the Buddha explains:

"Monks, householders are very helpful to you, as they provide you with the requisites of robes, alms food, lodgings, and medicine. And you, monks, are very helpful to householders, as you teach them the Dhamma admirable in the beginning, admirable in the middle, and admirable in the end, as you expound the holy life both in its particulars and in its essence, entirely

complete, surpassingly pure. In this way the holy life is lived in mutual dependence, for the purpose of crossing over the flood, for making a right end to suffering and stress."
(Iti 107)

As you're reading this, many people are struggling, finding it difficult to meet their basic needs. Some are struggling terribly, in what we might call a blatant way. Others are faced with more subtle hardships. For most people there's a degree of suffering involved in the ongoing effort to make a living, put food on the table, pay bills, take care of family members, manage illness. There are many places where we might give material resources, in an effort to help others meet their most basic needs.

When we help others satisfy their basic needs, we provide them with an opportunity to turn their attention toward finding happiness in their lives. When others experience more happiness, the world becomes a more peaceful, more joyful place. In the process, we benefit.

When we give skillfully, motivated by compassion, we know a sublime joy. It's far greater than any joy we might experience when we indulge in sense pleasure, make a lot of money, buy something.

Of course, you'll have to come to see this for yourself.

Our time is another resource that we might give. We may think we're not going to be able to practice generosity because we don't have much money, because we don't have many material resources. But we still can practice generosity. We still have a lot to give. We can give the gift of our time.

We cultivate generosity when we give our time in response to another person's suffering, pain, difficulty. Practicing generosity we give our time out of compassion, in an effort to be of service, to help.

If you reflect, you'll surely recognize many ways you might give the resource of your time.

You shouldn't have to look far to find ways to be of service. You should be able to find opportunities to practice generosity, by giving your time, right where you are. It's a good idea, in fact, to "start where you are." You might practice generosity by helping an elderly neighbor. Or you might spend a few hours with a friend who's in the throes of a trying life-situation, going through a divorce, an illness, or the loss of a job. Your generosity might take the form of helping a sick parent. Or you might spend time with a brother or sister who's experiencing some kind of emotional upheaval. Or perhaps your partner is in need of your time, your support. Or perhaps you have a child who needs your time and attention. Growing up, by definition, includes struggle. Children need their parents' help in navigating the uncertain roads of life. Spending time with our children is one of the most significant ways that we can practice generosity.

There are myriad ways that you might offer service in your community. Reading to children in a local school. Coaching basketball. Volunteering at a hospital. The possibilities are just about endless.

You can volunteer in your dharma community. Practicing generosity in the service of passing on the dharma, making it possible for others to follow the path, is one of the most beneficial ways we can give.

Some of us may be involved in livelihoods in which we have an opportunity to help others. Certainly the helping professions, teacher, nurse, social worker, etc., offer an excellent means for practicing generosity. The Buddha was engaged in this sort of livelihood. He spent 45 years teaching the dharma. He lived a life of complete generosity. Many students, after practicing the dharma for a while, begin to think about forging a career path that's aligned with the teachings, that provides a way for them to help others. We should remember, however, that making a career change entails going through a process. In other words, it takes time. In my own case, I realized, after being a dharma student for about five years, that I wanted to find different work (I was a sales representative, working for a textbook company). But I wasn't in any position to hand in my resignation. I wasn't at all ready. It was another five years before I was able to make a definitive move. I certainly don't advocate quitting your job after reading this chapter. It's probably a much better idea if you begin to practice generosity right where you are, wherever you are.

Sometimes we like to make dramatic moves. But in dharma practice, small acts bring significant benefit. If you give the gift of your time in small, simple ways, you'll make great strides in cultivating the quality of generosity.

In relationships with others, one of the most wonderful gifts we can offer is the gift of the dharma. Unless you're a dharma teacher, this doesn't mean "teaching" the principles of the Buddha's path. Instead, it means simply being an example of somebody who's following the path, it means embodying the skillful qualities, as well as the qualities of concentration and insight. When our presence is an embodiment of the dharma, we have a powerful, profoundly beneficial affect on others.

Sometimes parents contact me and ask if I might be able to teach their young children how to meditate. Usually in these instances the parent is having difficulty with their kids. Invariably I suggest, gently, that the parents themselves might want to learn to meditate and develop skillful qualities; the notion being that if they cultivate their goodness, it will have the most favorable affect on their kids, it will be the best gift they can offer.

When family and friends are struggling with the pains and sufferings of life, another gift that we can offer is the gift of fearlessness. When we exemplify fearlessness, it helps the other greatly in their efforts to deal with their own fear. You might have an opportunity to offer this precious gift when you visit a friend who's ill, in the hospital; if you're calm, tranquil, if you embody non-fear in the face of your companion's illness, you'll be practicing a noble form of generosity, you'll be of great help to your friend.

As you cultivate generosity, as you seek to give to others, it's important to make an effort to be fully present, to give your full attention to the other.

I often meet with students to discuss their practice, help them end suffering, find happiness. After many years I've learned that one of the most important ways I can help people is by being completely, wholeheartedly present. Sometimes it doesn't matter so much what I say when I sit down with a student; what matters is that I'm fully awake, alert, present. My attention is one of the most valuable gifts that I have to give.

In giving our time, we have to pay heed to the quality of our attention. Are we present, alert, when we're with the other? Are we giving our full attention to the other? Is our attention fragmented?

Our attention becomes fragmented when, while interacting with another person, we drift into various patterns of thinking. You offer the gift of your time to a parent, a child, a friend, but your mind is somewhere else, somewhere other than where you are. You're thinking about the future, what you're going to do later on. Or you're thinking about the person you're trying to help, perhaps you're involved in an inner commentary, judging the person.

Our attention also becomes fragmented when, while giving our time, we choose to engage in another activity. This predicament has become increasingly prevalent in the technology-driven culture. You have a friend who's suffering. In an effort to practice generosity, you call your friend, but while you're talking to her, you're watching television. Your attention, in this case, is broken up. Part of it is with your friend, part is with the TV. There are countless versions of this scenario. You visit an ailing relative, but during your visit you're constantly pulled away by cell phone calls. You're having a conversation with your teenage daughter, but at the same time you're looking at the computer, checking email.

When we let our attention fragment, split off, the quality of our generosity is compromised. In fact, it may very well be that the interactions we have with another person when our attention is fragmented will have a detrimental effect on the relationship with the other. We experience a loss of empathy when our attention is siphoned off by technological forms such as the TV and cell phone. Our ability to connect is degraded. The other, picking up on our lack of empathy, registers a quality of separation, disconnection, dis-ease, rather than warmhearted fellow-feeling.

When we fragment our attention in this manner, we prevent ourselves from receiving the benefits of practicing generosity. We don't experience the extraordinary joy that comes from skillful giving. Instead, we suffer disconnection, dissociation.

As always, the Buddha asks that we go against the grain. In today's culture, seemingly devoted to fragmented attention and multi-tasking, we're asked, in practicing generosity, to give our full attention to the other.

SKILLFUL GIVING

Life, as Joseph Campbell says, is inherently meaningless. We give life meaning. We give life meaning through the actions we take.

Generosity is the first skillful action the Buddha teaches. In many ways, it sets the tone for the whole path.

As dharma students, we have to learn to give.

We have to learn the skill.

In cultivating generosity, we learn to practice skillful giving.

As we've explained, the quality of our intention determines whether our actions are unskillful or skillful.

As we cultivate generosity, we have to pay close attention to our intention; we have to recognize when our intention is corrupted by unskillful factors, by desire or aversion or delusion.

Sometimes giving is infected with desire, wanting. For example, you give, but your giving is influenced by a desire to get something in return from the person you're giving to. Maybe you want something the other person has, something they might be inclined to give you, a material object, a job. Or maybe you want to gain the other person's approval. Or maybe you want the other person to like you. When I was a sales rep, I gave gifts to clients, promotional items, etc., but that wasn't generosity. I wanted their business.

Sometimes giving is influenced by aversion. You give, but you really don't want to give. You give begrudgingly. You don't want to part with whatever you're giving, whether it's material resources or your time. Maybe your daughter needs help with her homework. You offer your assistance, but you feel a certain amount of anger; you don't want to spend time with her, you want to watch the ballgame. As you interact with your daughter, your action, the way you're speaking, is afflicted with anger. A subtle anger perhaps, but anger nonetheless.

Giving is frequently imbued with delusion. You give, but your giving is motivationless. You're just going through the motions. Your friend is in the hospital and you figure you should visit her. You go to the hospital, but you're not propelled by any sort of skillful intention. You give your time, but you go about it in an affectless manner. Your heart isn't in it.

The Buddha's path is a path of abandoning and cultivating. When we recognize an unskillful intention, we leave it to the side, abandon it, and we cultivate skillful intention.

Skillful giving is driven by skillful intention, by love, compassion. When we give in a skillful manner, we put our heart in it. Recognizing that the other is suffering in some manner, blatant or subtle, we give from the place of compassion. Skillful giving is motivated by the wish that we have for the other, that they be free from suffering.

It's important to understand that everybody can learn to develop skillful intention and, accordingly, skillful action. It's a skill. It's a skill everybody can learn. It doesn't require special talent. In order to master certain skills, like playing a musical instrument, it's necessary to possess exceptional talent. When I learned to play the guitar, I was able to get only so far. I took lessons, practiced diligently, but never became more than a fair-to-middling player. My brother, on the other hand, has musical ability, talent. Without much instruction, he became a rather expert guitarist. There are certain abilities that some people have and some people don't have. Everybody, however, has the ability to develop skillful intention/action. Everybody.

In order to develop the skill, you have to: (1) learn the method, and (2) make the effort.

The Buddha teaches skills. He gives specific instructions for developing skillful intention/action. He doesn't put forth philosophies and leave it up to the student to figure out what to do. He doesn't say, "Practice generosity," and leave it at that. He shows us how to do it. The Buddha knew that he couldn't expect students to develop skillful qualities on their own without being taught a well laid-out method for doing so. It's interesting to note that in delineating attributes a teacher must have, the Buddha indicated that a good teacher should be able to provide "step-by-step" instructions.

In the pivotal sutta, "Instructions to Rahula at Mango Stone," the Buddha lays out a design for developing skillful intention/action. Rahula was the Buddha's son and it's said the Buddha gave this teaching to Rahula when the boy was seven years old. This fact should come as good news to contemporary dharma students. If a seven year old could learn these skills, we can probably learn them as well.

Studying the "Rahula" sutta, we can break down the Buddha's instructions for developing skillful intention/action into five key steps:

1-Seeing what the mind is like.
2-Developing skillful intention.
3-Acting.
4-Seeing the benefits in skillful action.
5-Taking joy.

Let's look at each of the steps.
The first step is:

1-Seeing what the mind is like.

Before taking an action, the Buddha tells Rahula, you should see what your mind is like. What's your state of mind? What's the quality of your intention? Is it unskillful? Skillful?

In practicing generosity, before we act, we look at the mind. What's it like? What's the quality of the intention? Is the intention unskillful? Is it infused with desire? With aversion? With delusion?

If, before we act, we notice that our intention is unskillful, imbued with desire/aversion/delusion, we make an effort to abandon the unskillful intention. We try to put it to the side. In putting unskillful intention to the side, we don't attempt to eliminate it. That's not something we'll usually be able to do. Instead, we simply don't engage with the unskillful quality, the desire/aversion/delusion. We don't indulge in it.

If there's a big chocolate cake sitting on the table and you don't want to eat it, you don't have to throw it out; you can simply choose not to partake of it, not to feed on it. It's the same with unskillful intention; when you put an unskillful intention to the side, the desire/aversion/delusion is still there, but you don't feed on it.

In some cases, we might not be able to abandon an unskillful intention. We might not be able to prevent ourselves from feeding on it. If we're not able to put aside an unskillful intention, we should refrain from acting, from giving. We should back off. As the Buddha explains to Rahula:

"If, on reflection, you know that it would lead to self-affliction, to the affliction of others, or to both; it would be an unskillful bodily action with painful consequences, painful results, then any bodily action of that sort is absolutely unfit for you to do." (MN 61)

If we're able to put the unskillful intention to the side, or if there isn't any discernible unskillful intention in the mind, then we move to the next step:

2-Developing skillful intention.

There are two components to developing skillful intention: (1) asserting directed thought, and (2) connecting to a felt sense.

In asserting directed thought, we formulate a skillful intention. We fabricate thought, in a purposeful, constructive manner. For example, as you make your way to the supermarket to buy groceries for an elderly neighbor, you'd assert directed thought, you'd think: I'm going to go shopping for Mr. Smith out of compassion.

There are, you'll note, two aspects to this part of the process. In asserting directed thought, the practitioner fabricates an intention that includes (a) content and (b) the quality of the intention. In this example, the content comprises the gift of your time, the act of going to the store for your neighbor. The intention, however, must include more than "what" you're going to do; it must also include "how" you're going to do it, how you're going to give, the attitude with which you're going to give. Here, you're going shopping for Mr. Smith "out of compassion."

In asserting directed thought it's critically important to remind yourself of the quality of your intention.

As we've said, intention is skillful if it's motivated by the heart qualities of love and compassion. In setting intention, the practitioner asserts that he's going to take an action that's driven by love, compassion.

When I teach a dharma class, I always make sure to develop skillful intention. Before the class starts, I'll see what my mind is like. Then, asserting directed thought, I'll think something along the lines of: I'm going to teach this class out of compassion, in order to help the students find a way out of their suffering.

It's that simple.

It almost seems too simple, doesn't it? It doesn't seem possible that we might enact skillful action, skillful giving, by merely stating an intention, engendering a specific line of thinking.

The fact is, if we develop intention in this manner, if we assert directed thought, it will bring about extraordinary results. It will have a powerful effect. There have been many times when students have expressed astonishment in describing how implementing this step has affected the quality of their actions. A while back, a student in our group was struggling in her role as a parent. After we discussed this step in class, she made a concerted effort to assert directed thought when she interacted with her kids. After a week, she reported that taking this simple step had transformed her relationship with them. She was amazed. Many other students have related similar experiences.

When we fabricate skillful intention, we witness the power of our thoughts. The Buddha knew full well that our thoughts have tremendous power. Our thoughts, he realized, determine our happiness.

As the Buddha explains:

Phenomena are preceded by the heart (mind),
    ruled by the heart,
    made of the heart.
 If you speak or act
 with a corrupted heart,
 then suffering follows you —
 as the wheel of the cart,
    the track of the ox
    that pulls it.

Phenomena are preceded by the heart,
>   ruled by the heart,
>   made of the heart.
If you speak or act
with a calm, bright heart,
then happiness follows you,
like a shadow
>   that never leaves. (Dhp I)

(The reader should note that "heart" and "mind" are used interchangeably in translations of the Buddha's teachings.)

In asserting directed thought, there are a couple of things you can do to refine your skill.

When you fabricate an intention, don't just say the words; say the words with a degree of earnestness, sincerity. Say it like you mean it.

Be careful of the tendency to establish intention in a rote, mechanical fashion. State your intention wholeheartedly.

Also, when you assert directed thought, have a grasp of the meaning of what you're saying. What does it mean when you say, "Let me give out of compassion"? What is "compassion"? It helps if you have a working understanding of what the words signify. It helps if you understand the subtext.

The second component of developing skillful intention is "connecting to a felt sense." Upon asserting directed thought, we connect to a felt sense of the heart, a felt sense of love, compassion. This, we might say, is a more advanced step. Everybody, from the beginning, can assert directed thought, but for many practitioners the ability to connect to a felt sense will take time to develop. It will require cultivating a sensitivity to the heart; it's a skill that will evolve as we continue forward in dharma practice.

In connecting to a felt sense, we apprehend the actual feeling of love, compassion. We feel love and compassion. We place our attention in the area of the heart (not the physical heart, but what we might call the heart center, the place, usually somewhere in the middle of the chest, where we feel the heart qualities) and we touch into the feeling of love, compassion. Love and compassion are things we can feel. They're real things.

In the above example, as you head to the supermarket to shop for your neighbor, you'd assert directed thought and you'd connect to your heart, you'd feel the compassion that you have for your neighbor.

After developing skillful intention we move to the next step:

3-Acting.

Now, having set our intention, we act. From the place of love, compassion, we act.

While you're acting, the Buddha tells Rahula, you should be mindful, you should make sure you're acting skillfully.

While practicing generosity, we pay attention. We're mindful of our intention/action. Are we staying to our intention? Are we acting skillfully? Has our intention/action turned unskillful? Is our giving in any way leading to affliction?

There will be times when, after developing a skillful intention, we'll "lose" the intention. We'll put ourselves on a skillful path, a path of compassion, but at some point we'll veer off, we'll take a detour down a familiar, habitual path into desire or aversion or delusion. As Thanissaro Bhikkhu says, the road to hell is paved with unskillful intentions. The old adage is "the road to hell is paved with good intentions," but if we look we'll see that's not correct. What often happens is, we begin with a skillful intention, but at some point the intention fades, and, perhaps unwittingly, we adopt an unskillful intention. And, thusly, we end up on the road to hell.

We may also notice as we're taking action that the intention we originally thought skillful is, in fact, unskillful. We might have been unclear in establishing our intention. Our intention, which we thought was informed by the heart, may have been infected with delusion. As we act, we may realize that our intention isn't skillful and that, unbeknownst to us, we've put ourselves on the proverbial road to hell.

Skillful intentions will never lead us to hell. To the contrary. As Thanissaro Bhikkhu says, "The road to nirvana is paved with skillful intentions."

So, we have to keep paying attention.

As we're practicing generosity, we have to be vigilant. We have to watch our intention, we have to make sure that it's skillful, we have to notice if it's veered off, if it's turned unskillful. If our intention is on an unskillful track, we make an adjustment. We put aside the unskillful intention and set a skillful intention.

As you're shopping for your neighbor, walking down the aisle in the supermarket, you may notice that your intention has veered. It's turned aversive. You don't want to be doing what you're doing. Noticing the aversion, you'd put it to the side and you'd remind yourself of your skillful intention, to go shopping for Mr. Smith out of compassion.

The next step is:

4-Seeing the benefits in skillful action.

The practice of developing skillful action isn't finished after we've acted. As the Buddha explains, it's important after we've acted to look at the actions we've taken. After acting, we take time to reflect. If we've acted skillfully, we acknowledge our skillful actions. We recognize the benefits in our skillful actions.

After practicing generosity, we reflect on the benefits that derive from skillful giving. Reflecting, after bringing Mr. Smith his groceries, you might ask: What are the benefits in doing what I've done? What are the benefits that come from practicing generosity?

(We also learn, of course, to recognize when we've acted in an unskillful fashion. When we've acted unskillfully, we see the drawbacks.)

The next step is:

5-Taking joy.

After we've acted, recognizing the blessing of our skillful qualities, we take joy. We let ourselves experience the joy that emerges when we express our goodness.

To review, the five steps are:

1-Seeing what the mind is like.

2-Developing skillful intention.

3-Acting.

4-Seeing the benefits in skillful action.

5-Taking joy.

As we cultivate these steps over a period of time, they'll become integrated into our practice. We may not be able to proceed methodically through each step every time we take an action. Life moves too fast for that. But if we implement the steps whenever we can, we'll gradually turn toward them, include them, when we take action. We'll develop the skill.

In this book we'll refer quite often to the "Rahula" sutta. It's a teaching with which all serious dharma students will want to become familiar. It's included here in its entirety.

I have heard that on one occasion the Blessed One was staying near Rajagaha, at the Bamboo Grove, the Squirrels' Feeding Ground.

At that time Ven. Rahula was staying at the Mango Stone. Then the Blessed One, arising from his seclusion in the late afternoon, went to where Ven. Rahula was staying at the Mango Stone. Ven. Rahula saw him coming from afar and, on seeing him, set out a seat & water for washing the feet. The Blessed One sat down on the seat set out and, having sat down, washed his feet. Ven. Rahula, bowing down to the Blessed One, sat to one side.

Then the Blessed One, having left a little bit of water in the water dipper, said to Ven. Rahula, "Rahula, do you see this little bit of left-over water remaining in the water dipper?"

"Yes, sir."

"That's how little of a contemplative there is in anyone who feels no shame at telling a deliberate lie."

Having tossed away the little bit of left-over water, the Blessed One said to Ven. Rahula, "Rahula, do you see how this little bit of left-over water is tossed away?"

"Yes, sir."

"Rahula, whatever there is of a contemplative in anyone who feels no shame at telling a deliberate lie is tossed away just like that."

Having turned the water dipper upside down, the Blessed One said to Ven. Rahula, "Rahula, do you see how this water dipper is turned upside down?"

"Yes, sir."

"Rahula, whatever there is of a contemplative in anyone who feels no shame at telling a deliberate lie is turned upside down just like that."

Having turned the water dipper right-side up, the Blessed One said to Ven. Rahula, "Rahula, do you see how empty & hollow this water dipper is?"

"Yes, sir."

"Rahula, whatever there is of a contemplative in anyone who feels no shame at telling a deliberate lie is empty & hollow just like that.

"Rahula, it's like a royal elephant: immense, pedigreed, accustomed to battles, its tusks like chariot poles. Having gone into battle, it uses its forefeet & hindfeet, its forequarters & hindquarters, its head & ears & tusks & tail, but keeps protecting its trunk. The elephant trainer notices that and thinks, 'This royal elephant has not given up its life to the king.' But when the royal elephant... having gone into battle, uses its forefeet & hindfeet, its forequarters & hindquarters, its head & ears & tusks & tail & his trunk, the trainer notices that and thinks, 'This royal elephant has given up its life to the king. There is nothing it will not do.'

"In the same way, Rahula, when anyone feels no shame in telling a deliberate lie, there is no evil, I tell you, he will not do. Thus, Rahula, you should train yourself, 'I will not tell a deliberate lie even in jest.'

"What do you think, Rahula: What is a mirror for?"

"For reflection, sir."

"In the same way, Rahula, bodily actions, verbal actions, & mental actions are to be done with repeated reflection.

"Whenever you want to do a bodily action, you should reflect on it: 'This bodily action I want to do — would it lead to self-affliction, to the affliction of others, or to both? Would it be an unskillful bodily action, with painful consequences, painful results?' If, on reflection, you know that it would lead to self-affliction, to the affliction of others, or to both; it would be an unskillful bodily action with painful consequences, painful results, then any bodily action of that sort is absolutely unfit for you to do. But if on reflection you know that it would not cause affliction... it would be a skillful bodily action with pleasant consequences, pleasant results, then any bodily action of that sort is fit for you to do.

"While you are doing a bodily action, you should reflect on it: 'This bodily action I am doing — is it leading to self-affliction, to the affliction of others, or to both? Is it an unskillful bodily action, with painful consequences, painful results?' If, on reflection, you know that it is leading to self-affliction, to the affliction of others, or to both... you should give it up. But if on reflection you know that it is not... you may continue with it.

"Having done a bodily action, you should reflect on it: 'This bodily action I have done — did it lead to self-affliction, to the affliction of others, or to both? Was it an unskillful bodily action, with painful consequences, painful results?' If, on reflection, you know that it led to self-affliction, to the affliction of others, or to both; it was an unskillful bodily action with painful consequences, painful results, then you should confess it, reveal it, lay it open to the Teacher or to a knowledgeable companion in the holy life. Having confessed it... you should exercise restraint in the future. But if on reflection you know that it did not lead to affliction... it was a skillful bodily action with pleasant consequences, pleasant results, then you should stay mentally refreshed & joyful, training day & night in skillful mental qualities.

"Whenever you want to do a verbal action, you should reflect on it: 'This verbal action I want to do — would it lead to self-affliction, to the affliction of others, or to both? Would it be an unskillful verbal action, with painful consequences, painful results?' If, on reflection, you know that it would lead to self-affliction, to the affliction of others, or to both; it would be an unskillful verbal action with painful consequences, painful results, then any verbal action of that sort is absolutely unfit for you to do. But if on reflection you know that it would not cause affliction... it would be a skillful verbal action with pleasant consequences, pleasant results, then any verbal action of that sort is fit for you to do.

"While you are doing a verbal action, you should reflect on it: 'This verbal action I am doing — is it leading to self-affliction, to the affliction of others, or to both? Is it an unskillful verbal action, with painful consequences, painful results?' If, on reflection, you know that it is leading to self-affliction, to the affliction of others, or to both... you should give it up. But if on reflection you know that it is not... you may continue with it.

"Having done a verbal action, you should reflect on it: 'This verbal action I have done — did it lead to self-affliction, to the affliction of others, or to both? Was it an unskillful verbal action, with painful consequences, painful results?' If, on reflection, you know that it led to self-affliction, to the affliction of others, or to both; it was an unskillful verbal action with painful consequences, painful results, then you should confess it, reveal it, lay it open to the Teacher or to a knowledgeable companion in the holy life. Having confessed it... you should exercise restraint in the future. But if on reflection you know that it did not lead to affliction... it was a skillful verbal action with pleasant consequences, pleasant results, then you should stay mentally refreshed & joyful, training day & night in skillful mental qualities.

"Whenever you want to do a mental action, you should reflect on it: 'This mental action I want to do — would it lead to self-affliction, to the affliction of others, or to both? Would it be an unskillful mental action, with painful consequences, painful results?' If, on reflection, you know that it would lead to self-affliction, to the affliction of others, or to both; it would be an unskillful mental action with painful consequences, painful results, then any mental action of that sort is absolutely unfit for you to do. But if on reflection you know that it would not cause affliction... it would be a skillful mental action with pleasant consequences, pleasant results, then any mental action of that sort is fit for you to do.

"While you are doing a mental action, you should reflect on it: 'This mental action I am doing — is it leading to self-affliction, to the affliction of others, or to both? Is it an unskillful mental action, with painful consequences, painful results?' If, on reflection, you know that it is leading to self-affliction, to the affliction of others, or to both... you should give it up. But if on reflection you know that it is not... you may continue with it.

"Having done a mental action, you should reflect on it: 'This mental action I have done — did it lead to self-affliction, to the affliction of others, or to both? Was it an unskillful mental action, with painful consequences, painful results?' If, on reflection, you know that it led to self-affliction, to the affliction of others, or to both; it was an unskillful mental action with painful consequences, painful results, then you should feel distressed, ashamed, & disgusted with it. Feeling distressed, ashamed, & disgusted with it, you should exercise restraint in the future. But if on reflection you know that it did not lead to affliction... it was a skillful mental action with pleasant consequences, pleasant results, then you should stay mentally refreshed & joyful, training day & night in skillful mental qualities.

"Rahula, all those brahmans & contemplatives in the course of the past who purified their bodily actions, verbal actions, & mental actions, did it through repeated reflection on their bodily actions, verbal actions, & mental actions in just this way.

"All those brahmans & contemplatives in the course of the future who will purify their bodily actions, verbal actions, & mental actions, will do it through repeated reflection on their bodily actions, verbal actions, & mental actions in just this way.

"All those brahmans & contemplatives at present who purify their bodily actions, verbal actions, & mental actions, do it through repeated reflection on their bodily actions, verbal actions, & mental actions in just this way.

"Thus, Rahula, you should train yourself: 'I will purify my bodily actions through repeated reflection. I will purify my verbal actions through repeated reflection. I will purify my mental actions through repeated reflection.' That's how you should train yourself."

That is what the Blessed One said. Gratified, Ven. Rahula delighted in the Blessed One's words.

(MN 61)

AN EXAMPLE

Let's look at an example of how the process unfolds as we practice generosity, as we develop skillful giving in accordance with the Buddha's teachings.

You'll notice that in this example a parent is the recipient of our giving. Giving to our parents is one of the most important ways in which we might practice generosity. Granted, it's not always easy. For many practitioners, it might present a significant challenge. But we can learn to do it.

We may have elderly parents. Giving, offering service to somebody who's elderly is another way we might practice generosity. There's suffering inherent in old age. In helping an elderly person, we have an opportunity to respond to their suffering, to act in a compassionate manner.

In our culture we tend to shun the elderly. Aging, in many quarters, is considered offensive. As dharma students, however, we turn toward the elderly. We open our hearts to people suffering the vicissitudes of old age. Again, it's a path in which we go against the grain.

As you practice the five steps for developing skillful intention/action, your efforts might look something like this:

You set out to visit your mother. Your objective is to practice skillful giving, to give your mother the gift of your time, your attention.

She lives alone. She's in her late eighties. She suffers the physical challenges of old age, and she suffers mentally, she's often riddled with anxiety, fear, depression. Growing up, you didn't have a good relationship with her. You harbored a large amount of anger and resentment. You've worked through a lot of that painful emotional stuff, in dharma practice, therapy, etc., but you haven't worked through all of it. At times the habitual patterns of anger and resentment emerge and rise to the surface.

As you approach your mother's place, you check to see what your mind is like.

You notice a discordant voice in the mind. It's objecting. I don't want to do this. I don't want to have to deal with her.

Centered in your breath, you observe your aversion. You see it. But you don't engage with it. You don't feed on it.

You put the aversion to the side.

Keeping your attention on the breath, you feel the easeful sensations of the breathing.

Then you develop a skillful intention.

You assert directed thought. You tell yourself: I'm going to spend time with my mother out of compassion for her. I'm going to be of service.

You say the words wholeheartedly.

You have a sense of what it means to act out of compassion.

Then you connect to a felt sense of compassion. You put your attention on your heart. You feel compassion for your mother.

Then you knock on the door.

During the time you spend with your mother, you pay attention to your actions. You keep an eye on the quality of your intention. You check your mind. What's it like? What's your intention like? Are you staying with your skillful intention?

At some point you realize that your intention/action has turned unskillful. You've veered off into an aversive state. You're speaking to your mother in a slightly aversive manner. Observing the aversion, you put it to the side.

You re-set your skillful intention.

After leaving your mother's, you take a few moments to reflect. You acknowledge your skillful giving. You recognize the benefits that come from practicing generosity. You notice that you feel good. You feel easeful. You feel good about yourself.

Recognizing the blessing of your generosity, you take joy.

RESISTANCE TO GIVING

As you cultivate generosity, you'll meet resistance. You'll hit obstacles. Actually it's a good sign. It indicates you're making an attempt to move forward. I'm skeptical when students proclaim they're not experiencing resistance. It usually means either they're not aware of their resistance or they're not making much effort to move along the path.

You may have the idea that the exemplary dharma student travels a smooth, resistance-free road, but that's not the case. Everybody experiences resistance. The difference between skilled and unskilled practitioners is that skilled practitioners meet resistance in a skillful manner, while unskilled practitioners, you guessed it, meet resistance unskillfully. The skilled dharma student, confronted with resistance, isn't fazed; the unskilled person is thrown, knocked off balance.

The level of skill with which we handle resistance is, in fact, a good measure of the progress we're making in our practice.

When we meet resistance, we might consider it a problem. We might think we need to get rid of it. We might become discouraged by it. But as dharma practice matures we perceive resistance differently. We take a wider view. We understand that the places of resistance are places where we learn. We realize that if we pay attention to resistance, bring interest to it, it will provide an opening, a door we might pass through in our efforts to get further along the road. We learn to view resistance as a doorway.

As you cultivate generosity, you might notice that you have an aversion to giving. You don't want to give. You don't want to part with your material resources, the resource of your time. This is perhaps the most obvious way in which resistance manifests.

You might notice that you're afraid to give. You're afraid you'll be giving up something that you need, something you can't afford to give.

You might notice, as you seek to practice skillful giving, that you're hindered by desire, greediness. You want to hold on to the resource you're thinking about giving, if it's a material resource or the resource of time.

You might notice, in cultivating generosity, that you're afflicted with both desire and aversion. They're often closely related, two sides of the same coin of resistance. You want to hold on to something and you don't want to give it up.

As dharma students we have to learn to work skillfully with resistance. It's an important part of the process of developing skillful qualities. First and foremost, our objective in working with resistance is to notice it. We have to be mindful. Like a lifeguard sitting on his perch scanning the beach, we have to be on the lookout for resistance. We have to notice it when it appears. Recognizing resistance, we locate the place in the body where it manifests. We feel the resistance. It may take shape as a contraction, a tightness, a dis-ease in the body.

Mindful of resistance, we establish a skillful relationship to it. What this means is we take the role of the observer. Stepping back from the resistance, refraining from feeding on it, we simply observe it.

In taking the position of the observer, we create a subject-object relationship to resistance. We move from "I don't want to give" to "there's aversion." This is a critical shift. In engineering this shift, it helps to make a mental note: "There's aversion." Or simply: "Aversion." Or: "Resistance." The note fortifies the subject-object dichotomy. It helps us separate from the resistance. It helps us form a non-attached relationship to it.

When we're no longer involved in it, feeding on it, resistance begins to lose its power.

From a distance, we observe the resistance. We don't try to eliminate it. We don't fight it. We accept that it's there. We allow it to be there. Observing the resistance, we're like somebody on one side of a room observing somebody on the other side of the room. We don't tell the resistance to leave the room. By the same token, we don't go over and embrace it. We just watch it.

Resistance arises for a reason. It arises, we might say, because it needs to arise, it needs to present itself, come to the surface. It needs to move. If we interfere with it, or push it away we create more difficulty. So, without getting enmeshed with it, we learn to let it be. Resistance, as we've said, is part of the process; we have to let the process unfold.

If we set up a skillful relationship to resistance, we gain insight into it. In cultivating insight, we don't think about the resistance. Really, we don't have to do anything, except observe the resistance. We observe, and let our innate wisdom understand it.

Observing, feeling resistance in the body, we gain knowledge: we understand that resistance is just part of our experience. It's just part of what's happening within the confines of our human structure. It's just another phenomenon coming and going.

Observing, we realize that we're under no obligation to become involved with the resistance. We don't have to latch onto it. Observing, we might ask: Is the resistance useful? Is it useful to latch onto it? Is it necessary to latch onto it? What would it be like if I simply let it be?

Observing resistance, feeling dis-ease in the body, we cultivate compassion for ourselves. Resistance is a product of suffering; the skillful response to suffering is compassion.

From the place of compassion, we move forward. We develop skillful qualities.

When we struggle to cultivate generosity and the other skillful qualities, it helps to remember the role resistance plays in the process. It helps to remember that resistance is a necessary part of the process. It doesn't mean something is wrong. On the contrary, the fact that resistance is occurring is an indication that we're right where we're supposed to be.

The Buddha himself experienced resistance as he set out to practice generosity. After awakening, the Buddha hung out for a while, enjoying the awakened state. He wondered if this was how he might spend his life, soaking up the bliss. But he quickly realized that he had to take action. His heart was wide open; he didn't have any choice but to express his love, his compassion. He had to help others. He had to teach the dharma.

But after deciding to teach, the Buddha began to have second thoughts. He began to experience resistance. It's going to be difficult, he thought. I'm not going to be able to do it.

As he put it:

"And if I were to teach the Dhamma and if others would not understand me, that would be tiresome for me, troublesome for me."
(SN 6.1)

Eventually the Buddha recognized his resistance.

He re-set his intention, to teach the dharma, out of compassion, so that others might find an end to suffering, so they might know a greater happiness. And for the next 45 years he did just that.

When you experience resistance, remember that you're in good company. Even the Buddha experienced it.

THE DEVELOPMENT OF GENEROSITY

Over time, we develop our ability to practice skillful giving. It takes time. It takes time to develop skillful qualities.

The development of generosity often looks something like this:

A friend visits your home. He spills coffee on his shirt. You tell him you'll give him one of your shirts. You go into the bedroom, open the dresser drawer. Your favorite shirts, the ones you wear most frequently, lie at the top of a stack of shirts. You dig past these shirts, then past the shirts in the middle of the stack, shirts you hardly wear at all. At the bottom of the drawer there are a few bedraggled shirts. You remove one of these shirts. It's in pretty bad shape. You haven't worn it in about ten years. But still, you don't feel like parting with it. You really don't want to give it to your friend.

In the beginning, it's often like this. Giving is strained, tentative. Gradually, though, we're able to practice generosity in a more openhearted manner.

Maybe a year later, the same friend stops by your place. He spills cranberry juice on his shirt. You go into the bedroom, open the dresser. You unearth another old tattered shirt. You give it to your friend. This time, however, you don't feel any resistance. You don't feel averse to giving.

Sometime after that, your friend visits, and, once again, spills something on his shirt. This time you take a shirt from the middle of the drawer.

Maybe a year later, your friend comes over. He spills coffee on his shirt. You open the dresser drawer and, without the slightest hesitation, remove your best shirt. You give it to your friend. You're glad to be able to give. You feel joy.

It's like that. It's a process. A gradual process. Generosity evolves like seasons. In the depth of February, we yearn for spring to arrive. In March, when winter refuses to relinquish its grasp, we ache for warm days. But spring will arrive when it arrives. We have to respect the natural process. It's the same with generosity, with all the skillful qualities. We have to respect the natural process.

In cultivating generosity, we seek to give with an open heart. Giving is skillful when we give with an open heart, with compassion. But the fact is, the heart opens slowly. We'd like, perhaps, to open the heart the way we open an automatic garage door, by pressing a button, but that's not how it works. The heart opens slowly, incrementally. What else should we expect? If the heart has been stuck in a somewhat closed position for a good while, it's not reasonable to expect it will open up all the way, right away.

It's important to understand what you're able to give. That's the key. What are you able to give skillfully, with an open heart, with compassion? You may have ideas about what you should give, or what you'd like to give, but the truth may be that you're not ready to give these sorts of gifts. And that's okay. You have to respect where you are.

When you begin to practice generosity, you may think you should take bold action. You should work in a soup kitchen. You should donate your life savings to a worthy cause. But you'll be much better served if you "keep it simple."

A good rule of thumb as you set out to develop generosity is to "start at home." Help a family member. Help your parents. Help your partner. Help your kids. Help a friend.

Another good rule of thumb is "start small." There are many small ways that you might practice skillful giving. Making a phone call to a friend who's going through a divorce. Bringing a pot of soup to a sick neighbor. You don't have to work in a soup kitchen; bringing some chicken soup to somebody who's ailing is almost certainly a more reasonable way to begin.

When I teach courses on skillful giving, I suggest the students perform one act of generosity every day. It can be something small. It probably should be something small. The development of generosity begins by taking small steps. We build on these small steps. Day after day, year after year, the small acts of generosity gradually add up. The heart gradually opens; our capacity to give skillfully grows, deepens.

If performing one act of generosity every day is too difficult, I tell students, execute a small act of generosity every few days. Or every week. Or every two weeks. Do what you're able to do. Give what you're able to give.

It's important to know your limits, to be clear about what you're able to give. It's okay to stretch yourself slightly; if you have a clear idea what your limits are, where the edges are, you might try, on occasion, to move a fraction or so beyond the edges. But you have to be careful. There isn't any good sense in trying to give if your heart isn't open.

As a teacher I have to be mindful of the quality of my generosity. I have to discern whether I'm teaching with an open heart. I have only so much to give. If I overextend myself, if I try to do too much, teach too many classes, I'm not going to be able to offer the teachings heartfully, with compassion. As a result, I have to be careful not to over-schedule. I have to see clearly what I'm able to give.

We have to remember that our purpose in cultivating generosity is to practice skillful giving.

A few years ago a member of our group, a woman in her forties, was stricken with liver cancer. After bravely fighting the illness, she began to fail. During her final months, group members visited her on a regular basis. One student who'd been especially generous in giving her time told me that one day, while she was with the dying woman, she began to feel agitated, fearful. We talked about it. It seemed clear that on that day she'd reached her limit. She hadn't had anything left to give. We talked about being careful about trying to give too much. We agreed that she probably should have backed off.

Backing off when we're not able to give skillfully is good practice. It's an act of compassion for the giver and the recipient of the gift.

You may be apt to judge yourself when you back off. You may be apt to judge yourself when you give in a "small" way. You might condemn yourself, tell yourself you should give more. You might decide you're not very generous. As always, it's important to watch out for self-judgment. Recognize it and question it.

In cultivating generosity, you have to let the process unfold. As you move forward skillfully, generosity will blossom like flowers in the spring. Giving will be joyful.

PRACTICE SUGGESTIONS

REFLECTION:

Where am I in terms of the skillful quality of generosity?

REFLECTION:

In what ways might I practice skillful giving? How might I give material resources? How might I give the gift of my time?

PRACTICE:

Develop generosity. When there is an opportunity, practice skillful giving. Follow the five steps for developing skillful intention/action. As you begin your practice of developing skillful giving, try to keep it simple. Observe the basic rules of thumb: (1) start at home and (2) start small.

PRACTICE:

Develop generosity by giving the gift of your time. Make sure in giving your time that you give your full attention.

PRACTICE:

During the period of one week, perform an act of generosity every day. It can be a small act of generosity. In giving, follow the five steps for developing skillful intention/action.

PRACTICE:

Be mindful of your resistance to practicing generosity. In being mindful of resistance, practice taking the role of the observer.

PRACTICE:

At some point during sitting meditation pause and ask: What can I give to the meditation? See what it's like when you bring an attitude of generosity to the meditation.

REFLECTION:

What benefits do I derive when I practice generosity?

REFLECTION:

When I practice generosity, is it a joyful experience?

PRACTICE:

At the beginning of sitting meditation practice, take a few moments to reflect on the blessing of your generosity. Recollect your generosity in a specific way, bringing to mind an example of your skillful giving. Recognizing your generosity, take joy.

CHAPTER TWO

ETHICAL CONDUCT & RENUNCIATION

FIVE PRECEPTS

In some ways dharma practice is a subtraction practice. We subtract certain things and what's left, we find, is what we're looking for. The same way as when we clear debris from a neglected lot we discover, right there, a lovely garden, or at least the potential for a lovely garden.

In cultivating ethical conduct, we subtract certain actions that cause harm to others and to ourselves. We refrain from taking these harmful actions.

The Pali word we translate as ethical conduct is "sila." Sila is also sometimes translated as virtue or morality. Terms like ethical conduct, virtue, morality, oftentimes provoke a negative reaction. We might associate the terms with a kind of Puritanism. We might ascribe a prim, pious, holier-than-thou quality to the words. We might think that developing ethical conduct is a repressive practice. All told, we may have preconceived notions about ethical conduct. As we've said, it's important to recognize our preconceived notions. It's important to question them. Are they useful? Are they serving us, in our efforts to move along the Buddha's path? Can we put aside our limited ideas? Can we allow ourselves to take a wider view? Can we open to the possibility that there may be value in developing ethical conduct?

The Buddha gave specific parameters for developing ethical conduct. For householders, he delineated five precepts. The precepts identify five modes of harmful action that we should attempt to subtract.

The five precepts are:

1-To refrain from taking the life of any living creature.

2-To refrain from stealing.

3-To refrain from engaging in illicit sexual conduct.

4-To refrain from harmful speech.

5-To refrain from consuming intoxicants that cause heedlessness.

Four of the precepts offer guidelines for refraining from harmful physical action. These include the precepts pertaining to killing, stealing, illicit sexual conduct and consuming intoxicants. We may not find it difficult to hold to some of these precepts. It may not be that hard, for instance, to follow the precepts on killing and stealing. However, sometimes students struggle to follow certain precepts related to physical action. The precepts on illicit sexual conduct and consuming intoxicants, in particular, pose a challenge for some dharma students.

In adhering to the precept concerning illicit sexual conduct, we refrain from engaging in sexual conduct that causes harm. Primarily, this entails committing adultery. It should also include having sex with somebody other than your partner when you're involved in a committed relationship as well as having sex with somebody who is in a commited relationship even when you are single.

Following the precept on intoxicants, we refrain from consuming any amount of alcohol and/or drugs that causes us to take action that brings about harm to others or ourselves.

Most of us will want to closely monitor our relationship to the precept pertaining to verbal action. Following this precept, we refrain from harmful speech.

The Buddha had clear insight into the ways we cause harm with our speech. He delineated four kinds of harmful speech:

1-False Speech (all forms of lying, blatant and subtle)

2-Abusive Speech (harsh, abrasive, loud, angry, aggressive, violent speech)

3-Divisive Speech (speaking in ways that create rifts between people; setting people apart from and against each other)

4-Idle Speech (frivolous speech, including gossip; speech that isn't useful and doesn't contribute anything worthwhile)

In subtracting harmful speech, we strive to refrain from engaging in each of these four modes of speech. It isn't always easy, of course. We may have a well-established habit of taking these kinds of harmful verbal actions. But if we make a commitment to cultivating ethical conduct, we'll find in time that we're able to follow this precept.

As Thanissaro Bhikkhu explains, the five precepts provide "clear-cut" guidelines for developing ethical conduct. The instructions are explicit, precise. We refrain from killing, stealing, illicit sex, harmful speech, consuming intoxicants. Following the precepts is meant to be a straightforward practice. Sometimes, as Thanissaro Bhikkhu notes, there's a tendency to complicate the precepts, to add to the instructions, to expand, elaborate, extrapolate. For instance, some teachers, embellishing the precept on stealing, include the way we plunder the environment. Or the way we "take" another person's time. We have to understand, however, that the five precepts denote a baseline. They indicate five harmful actions we should refrain from. There are many other ways that we might act unskillfully. As we develop skillful qualities, as we continue forward, we'll want to put effort into abandoning all the different forms of unskillful action. But we begin here, with these five harmful actions. These five actions, the Buddha posits, are the most pernicious, most damaging. If we don't subtract these actions, it will be difficult or impossible for us to move toward true happiness in our lives. If, on the other hand, we refrain from taking these five harmful actions we'll put ourselves in a good position to move along the Buddha's path.

In cultivating ethical conduct, it's important to keep it simple. If we keep it simple, it's a do-able practice. As Thanissaro Bhikkhu says, it's "practical." Again, it's not always easy. Most of us labor, at times, in our efforts to stay to the precepts. But it's something we can do. If we add to the precepts, broaden the scope of the precepts, they will, undoubtedly, become too difficult to follow. We'll be setting ourselves up for frustration, disappointment, self-doubt.

The fact is, if we follow the five precepts as they are we'll reap extraordinary benefits. If we refrain from taking these five baseline actions, we'll make significant headway in our journey toward true happiness. As it is, it's a powerful practice. It's a transforming practice. Think about what the world would be like if everybody followed the five precepts. Think about what the world would be like if everybody followed just one of the precepts. Think about what it would be like if everybody followed just the first percept, if everybody refrained from killing. It would be a vastly different world.

It's to our advantage to attend to the five precepts in the manner the Buddha suggested. After all, the Buddha was a pretty good teacher. Like any good teacher, he knew where to begin. The guidelines for developing ethical conduct offer a clear road out of the wilderness of unskillfulness. If we follow this well-marked road we'll begin to know the sublime fruits of dharma practice.

DEEPENING INTENTION

If you practice the dharma wholeheartedly, your practice will flourish. If you follow the precepts wholeheartedly, with compassion, your ethical conduct will develop in profound and joyful ways. It's important to pay attention to how you're attending to the precepts; it's important to see to it that you're following the precepts in a skillful, heartful manner.

In this spirit, it may help to reflect:

What's my mind like as I set out to develop ethical conduct?

Is my heart in it?

What's the quality of my intention? Is it skillful? Is it infused with compassion?

At times, as you attempt to stay to the precepts, you might notice that you're afflicted by unskillful mental qualities. The weather in your mind may not be bright and clear.

You might notice a quality of delusion. The mind may be overcast, riddled with clouds. You're following the precepts, but you're not quite sure why you're doing it. You're just going through the motions.

You might find that the mind is stained with aversion. The weather in the mind may be turbulent, stormy.

Perhaps you simply don't want to follow the precepts.

Perhaps you feel as though you're being forced to follow the precepts. You feel like you're being told what to do. You don't like it.

You may recognize, as you consider the notion of "refraining," that you're experiencing resistance. You're reacting negatively. Your reaction may be similar to the kind of reactions you had when you were a kid, when your parents told you to do something you didn't want to do. The voice in your mind may in fact be similar to the voice of a protesting child.

Your aversion may be fueled by the perception that the precepts represent a form of punishment. You've been bad. Now you're going to have to pay the price.

Often students indicate that they associate ethical conduct with forms of harsh discipline imposed by parents, teachers, religious structures. Looking at the precepts, they register sharp aversion. Students who've had unfortunate experiences in the past, who've been subjected to traumatic forms of discipline and abusive rules, may be inclined to ignore the practice of ethical conduct. And, unfortunately, some teachers, recognizing that students have this sort of history, choose to de-emphasize the Buddha's teachings on ethical conduct. But downplaying this element of dharma practice is never a good idea. As dharma students, we need to learn to work skillfully with our resistances. Just because we've been hurt in the past isn't good enough reason to avoid developing skills that will lead us to happiness in our lives. Dharma teachers who don't teach ethical conduct because they're afraid of re-wounding students are doing students a marked disservice.

As you seek to cultivate ethical conduct, you might be plagued by doubt. It's another kind of inclement weather, like thick fog. You might, perhaps, be apt to think that ethical conduct isn't "that important." You might think it isn't a big part of the Buddha's teachings. It isn't a crucial aspect of the path. It isn't relevant.

Our capacity to practice ethical conduct is effected significantly by the attitude we bring to the practice. In order to develop ethical conduct our resolve must be skillful, informed by the heart. Our intention must be skillful. As we follow the precepts, it's essential that we pay attention to the weather in the mind. It's essential that we're mindful of the quality of our intention. As dharma students, developing ethical conduct, we're asked to notice when the mind is influenced by delusion, aversion, doubt. We're asked to observe these unskillful qualities calmly, in a non-attached manner, like somebody standing at a window watching the early morning rain. We're asked to see the drawbacks in these agitated states, in following the precepts motivated by these states. We're asked to put the unskillful qualities to the side and, in turn, to foster skillful resolve, skillful intention.

The serious dharma student resolves to put wholehearted effort into following the five precepts. He keeps this resolve in mind. He reminds himself on a regular basis that he's going to follow the precepts out of compassion for himself. The dharma student cultivates an attitude of compassion as he follows the five precepts. Compassion for himself. He stays connected to his heart.

At Theravada Buddhist monasteries, lay men and women chant the five precepts. At Downtown Meditation Community, we chant the precepts at the beginning of most classes. Many DMC members chant the precepts every morning. Chanting is effective in part because it connects us to the lineage of householders who've been following the precepts for thousands of years. This connection is empowering. It helps to open our hearts.

Whether or not we chant, it's a good idea to take time every day to reflect on our intention to develop ethical conduct, to follow the five precepts. It's a good idea to affirm our resolve.

In establishing resolve, the dharma student sets an intention to follow the precepts out of compassion for himself.

If you like, you can try it now.

Put your mind on your breath.

Establish your resolve.

Assert your intention to follow the five precepts.

"I'm going to make an effort to observe the five precepts, out of compassion, so that I might come to the end of suffering."

Tune in to your heart, to a felt sense of compassion, compassion for yourself.

Following the precepts, deepening our intention, we cultivate intention imbued, more and more, with compassion. We're connected, more and more, to the heart, to the quality of compassion. We possess the sublime attitude of compassion.

We develop ethical conduct because we suffer, because we want to come to the end of our suffering. This is the reason, plain and simple. We follow the precepts, subtract harmful actions, because it's going to help us come to the end of our suffering.

As we cultivate ethical conduct, we come to know, in the heart, that following the precepts is an act of compassion for ourselves. We realize that, in subtracting these five harmful actions, we're taking good care of ourselves.

Moving along the path, our intention strengthens, deepens. Connected to the heart, to the quality of compassion, the wish we have to be free from suffering, we develop ethical conduct.

PURIFYING ACTION

As we make an effort to follow the precepts there will be times when, for lack of a gentler way of putting it, we'll fail. We'll take actions that will cause harm to others and to ourselves. We'll be forced to confront an unavoidable fact: we aren't perfect.

When we fail, when we make mistakes, we may judge ourselves, condemn ourselves.

For whatever reason, we think we should be perfect.

It's important to learn to relate skillfully to our imperfections. As we travel the Buddha's road we have to learn to accept that we have a long way to go. We have to realize that we've been cultivating unskillful habits for most of our lives and that it's going to take time to change our habits and purify our actions. Recognizing our patterns of unskillfulness, the karma we've produced over the span of many years, we have to learn to have compassion for ourselves. We have to learn to replace self-judgment with compassion.

As we develop ethical conduct, we'll hit obstacles. There will be times when we'll fail to follow the precepts. There will be times when we won't be able to find the motivation to follow the precepts. There will be times when we'll lack the willingness. At times we may make a determined effort to stay to the precepts but may fall short of our objectives, slip into so-called old behavior. We may vow, for instance, to refrain from speaking divisively about a co-worker but find ourselves doing it, perpetuating a longtime habit of divisive speech.

When we're not able to follow the precepts, we can try to change our behavior. We can try to effect change by putting forth effort. But sheer effort will take us only so far. We might believe that we'll be able to change our ways, transform habitual patterns, if we try hard enough, exert exceptional effort. But what's almost always required when we struggle to practice ethical conduct is to develop wisdom. Ultimately we purify our actions by developing wisdom.

Developing wisdom may seem like a complicated endeavor; however, it's actually rather simple. We develop wisdom by seeing the drawbacks in the unskillful and the benefits in the skillful.

In the final set of instructions the Buddha gives Rahula, he tells the boy how to look at his actions after he's acted in an unskillful manner. The Buddha recognizes there will be times when we'll fail. He knows we'll make mistakes. He knows we're not perfect. His teaching is humane, designed for fallible human beings.

When you act unskillfully, the Buddha says, acknowledge it. Then make it a learning experience.

(It should be noted that the Buddha tells Rahula that after taking an unskillful physical or verbal action he should talk to somebody about it. Talk to a teacher or a wise friend. This is an integral facet of the learning process.)

Learn from your mistakes, the Buddha says. Develop wisdom. See the drawbacks in your unskillful actions. See that your unskillful actions have brought about suffering, affliction, for others, for yourself.

We always have to remember that in scrutinizing our unskillful actions we're not judging ourselves. We're not criticizing ourselves. We're not despairing. We're not engendering an emotional response. Instead, we're looking at our actions calmly, evenly. We're looking objectively. We're simply seeing that our actions have caused suffering.

This is how we develop wisdom: by seeing the drawbacks, by seeing that unskillful actions lead to suffering, by seeing that these actions aren't serving us.

We develop wisdom, the Buddha emphasizes, by seeing for ourselves. We don't develop wisdom, the sort of wisdom that will lead to changes in our actions, by listening to what somebody says, but rather by seeing for ourselves that there are drawbacks in acting unskillfully and benefits in acting skillfully. Teachers guide us, show us where to look. But we have to look for ourselves.

It's not enough for somebody else, the Buddha, the teacher, or whomever, to tell us there are drawbacks in not following the precepts. We have to see it for ourselves.

In the early years of my practice, I was unwilling to subtract gossip. Gossip is an aspect of idle speech, the fourth category of harmful speech. While not as damaging as other forms of harmful speech, gossip brings about suffering. It leads us away from the path. I'd heard that, but I guess I wasn't convinced. I guess I didn't think it was important to refrain from gossip. At any rate, I wasn't willing to give it up. However, I was willing to pay attention to what happened when I gossiped. I didn't stop gossiping, but I made an effort, when I gossiped, to look at the results. When I engaged in gossip, I asked: What are the consequences of doing this? Are there drawbacks in it?

I watched closely. What I saw, again and again, was that when I gossiped I experienced dis-ease.

I felt this dis-ease in my body.

As time went on, it became more and more apparent. When I gossiped, I suffered. I caused myself harm.

I kept watching. Gradually, I lost interest in gossip. I became disenchanted with it. And gradually, I stopped gossiping. I stopped because I'd developed wisdom. I'd seen the drawbacks.

In seeing the drawbacks in unskillful actions, we're not partaking in an intellectual process. We're not thinking about the drawbacks. Instead, we're allowing ourselves to experience the actual results of our actions. We're seeing what it's like when we act unskillfully. To put it bluntly, we're feeling the pain.

Thinking about suffering is very different from experiencing it, knowing it firsthand. In seeing the drawbacks of our unskillful actions, we're dealing with reality. As the Buddha puts it, we're seeing "according to reality."

The most effective way to comprehend the drawbacks in acting unskillfully is to consider the body. This is a key aspect of the skill: to be able to ascertain the consequences of our actions, to recognize our suffering, by being mindful of the body.

As dharma students we learn, after acting unskillfully, to pay attention to the body. After we lie, after we speak divisively, after we gossip, we bring our awareness to the body. We notice what's happening in the body. After acting out on some form of unskillful behavior, we may notice dis-ease in the body. We many notice dissonance, discord, contraction, tightness, tension, agitation.

The dis-ease we detect in the body is a manifestation of mental dis-ease, mental suffering. As dharma students, we learn to develop sensitivity to painful mental qualities as they're articulated bodily. The Buddha realized more than 2,500 years ago what contemporary scientific research is beginning to demonstrate, that mental qualities are expressed throughout the landscape of the body. As we develop the ability to discern dis-ease, suffering, as it's being expressed in the body, we strengthen our capacity to develop wisdom, to understand the drawbacks of acting unskillfully.

It's by developing a wisdom that transcends intellectual wisdom, what we might call felt wisdom, or embodied wisdom, that we effect change.

In cultivating ethical conduct we're asked to notice how our meditation is affected when we don't stay to the precepts. If we speak falsely, if we speak harshly, we'll experience dis-ease, agitation, and when the mind is afflicted in this fashion, meditation is problematic. If we're involved in illicit sexual conduct, if we're having an affair with somebody who's married, the mind, needless to say, will be greatly agitated. If we're taking intoxicants and thus harming others and ourselves, we'll experience much agitation. It's difficult to practice meditation, to still the mind, when we're subject to these highly agitated states.

In order to cultivate a bona fide meditation practice, in order to foster strong concentration, the concentration we'll need to move along the path, it's imperative that we become developed in generosity and ethical conduct and the other skillful qualities. This is a foundational principle in the Buddha's teachings. Students who put a lot of effort into breath meditation but struggle to follow the five precepts get only so far, and not that far, in terms of their ability to cultivate concentration. This is something I've seen numerous times from my perspective as a dharma teacher. Conversely, I've seen students well-developed in ethical conduct make remarkable progress in breath meditation practice. It's always been clear to me that these students are able to build strong concentration in large part because they adhere to the precepts.

Sometimes students face significant challenges when it comes to following the five precepts. They may, for instance, be battling an addiction to alcohol or drugs. In these situations, I tell students that they've got to stop the behavior. I suggest, accordingly, that they seek help from other sources, go to a therapist, join a 12-step program, etc.

More frequently, students indicate they're confronted with less threatening quandaries with regard to the precepts. They may, for example, have a habit of drinking a couple glasses of wine with dinner. Or they may be on the verge of telling a "small lie." Or they may have a tendency to engage in gossip. They're not sure if they should refrain from these actions. Usually, in these instances, I don't tell students that they shouldn't do what they're doing or what they're intending to do. I don't tell them pointblank that they should eliminate the behavior. They're usually not ready to make that sort of change. More often than not, I tell students that they've got to see for themselves if there are drawbacks to these actions. If you take the actions, if you drink the wine, if you tell the lie, pay attention. Pay attention to the consequences. What's it like when you do it? What are the results? Are there drawbacks? Do your actions bring about suffering? How does it affect your meditation practice?

I don't necessarily ask students to refrain; I ask them, instead, to pay attention, to develop wisdom.

We owe it to ourselves to do that. We owe it to ourselves to study our actions. Through this kind of self-examination, we purify our actions.

RENUNCIATION

Developing renunciation is also a subtraction practice. In developing renunciation, we subtract sense pleasure. We don't attempt to subtract all sense pleasure; instead, we diminish our consumption of sense pleasure. This approach, not denying ourselves sense pleasure, but at the same time not over-indulging, is largely what's meant by the "middle path."

We acquire sense pleasure when we take in pleasant experience through the sense doors. In the Buddha's teachings, there are six sense doors: the eyes, ears, nose, mouth, the body, and the mind. Through these portals we receive sense experience; through the eyes we receive visual forms, though the ears we receive sounds, and so on. We receive mental experiences (thoughts, emotions) through the sense door of the mind.

In our culture, we put much emphasis on the acquisition of sense pleasure. It's a primary means through which we seek happiness. To a large degree we gauge our happiness by the amount of sense pleasure we receive. We put significant time and energy into gaining sense pleasure and making money so that we can gain sense pleasure. We're driven by a forceful desire to acquire sense pleasure. The machines of the culture, the economy, are geared to aiding us in fulfilling this desire; they offer an increasing, and increasingly potent, supply of sense pleasures.

As dharma students cultivating renunciation, we're asked to reflect on our relationship to sense pleasure. We're asked to ask questions that most people never think to ask. How much effort do we put into acquiring sense pleasure? Do we over-indulge in certain sense pleasures? To what degree do we measure our happiness by the sense pleasure we receive? Would we benefit by practicing renunciation?

Given that we look for happiness in sense pleasure, we might resist when it's suggested that we practice renunciation. We might rebel against the idea. We might scoff at the notion of renunciation, calling the Buddha's path "repressive." We might complain that we're being asked to submit to a form of "deprivation." Reacting aversely, we might insist that we're "not saints" or that we're "not monks." Dredging up themes promulgated in the sixties, we might extol the virtues of sense pleasure. As dharma students our task, as ever, is to notice resistance when it arises. Notice it and question it. Is it useful? Is it true that renunciation is a bummer? Is there a possibility that developing renunciation, on some level, might lead to greater happiness?

It's suggested that as you begin to cultivate renunciation, you don't attempt to relinquish too much; it's suggested you gradually subtract sense pleasure. For most of your life you've put a good deal of effort into acquiring sense pleasure. You've looked for happiness in sense pleasure. You've relied on sense pleasure. Now you're shifting your priorities. You're bringing about change. In seeking to change the habits of a lifetime, it's important to move forward in a wise, compassionate manner, which means taking gradual steps.

You've put a good amount of weight on sense pleasure. Now begin to shift the scales. Slowly decrease the weight you put on sense pleasure. Slowly put more weight on renunciation.

For instance, if television is a sense pleasure in which you over-indulge, begin to watch a little less TV. Cut back slightly. Moderate your consumption. Your impulse, as you set out to practice renunciation, might be to take a big action. Having concluded that television is a problematic sense pleasure, you might decide that you need to get rid of your TV. Eliminate the offending machine. You might fantasize about trashing the set, lugging it behind your apartment building, tossing it, ceremoniously, in the dumpster. Generally, though, the most useful course isn't quite that dramatic. Instead of getting rid of the TV, you might vow to watch less frequently. If you normally watch three hours of television every day, you might vow to watch just two hours. Or you might commit yourself to refraining from watching TV after 10PM. Or you might decide that one day every week you'll keep the TV turned off.

As you practice renunciation, your intention must be skillful, motivated by compassion. If you make a big move, like disposing of the TV, your intention may at first be skillful. But you may find somewhere along the line that it's changed. You may find that the attitude with which you're practicing renunciation has shifted, turned unskillful. You began on the road to nirvana but you've veered off onto the road to hell. After several television-less weeks, you feel resentful. Practicing renunciation has become an ordeal, a drag. You're doing it, but you're not happy about it.

If we discern, when practicing renunciation, that our intention is imbued with unskillful mental qualities, we can try to put the unskillful qualities to the side. We can try to develop skillful intention. However, this may not be possible. We may not be able to abandon the unskillful mental qualities. If our intention has been corrupted by aversion, we may not be able to put aside the aversion. It may be too strong. This often happens when we relinquish more than we're ready to relinquish. If we give up too much, we might not be able to practice renunciation skillfully. This is completely understandable. Throughout our lives we've never made an effort to practice renunciation. It's not realistic to expect that we'll suddenly be able to relinquish a large amount of sense pleasure in skillful fashion. It's going to take time to develop the skill.

It's going to take time.

As we move along the path, our ability to practice renunciation skillfully will be determined by the degree to which we've comprehended the benefits of renunciation and the drawbacks to over-indulging in sense pleasure. It will depend on the wisdom we've gained, little by slowly.

We're better off, then, if we gradually cultivate renunciation. If we try too hard to subtract sense pleasure, the heart will close up. We'll find ourselves trudging through painful territories, besieged with anger and resentment. We'll be turned off to the idea of renunciation. Often when we exceed our limits we experience a backlash. Recoiling, rebelling against the practice of renunciation, we grasp desperately after sense pleasure, we indulge in an out-of-control way.

So the rule is go slow. We all know the story of the tortoise and the hare. In dharma practice, the tortoise pretty much always wins the race.

UPOSATHA

The Buddha encouraged householders to dedicate certain days, known as Uposatha days, to deepening commitment to dharma practice. Uposatha days occur four times each month, roughly a week apart, in conjunction with the lunar calendar (full moon, half moon, etc.). On Uposatha days householders practice meditation, listen to the dharma and observe the eight precepts.

The eight precepts include guidelines for ethical conduct and for practicing renunciation.

The eight precepts:

1-To refrain from taking the life of any living creature.

2-To refrain from stealing.

3-To refrain from sexual activity.

4-To refrain from harmful speech.

5-To refrain from consuming intoxicants that cause heedlessness.

6-To refrain from eating outside the time (12pm).

7-To refrain from dancing, singing, music, going to see entertainments, wearing garlands, using perfumes, and beautifying the body with cosmetics.

8-To refrain from lying on a high or luxurious sleeping place.

In our dharma community many students observe the eight precepts on Uposatha days. It's a good way, students find, to cultivate renunciation.

On Uposatha days students practice renunciation together. It's one reason why it's an effective practice. Practicing renunciation is often difficult. We often experience resistance. But if we share the practice with each other, support each other, it's not quite as difficult.

The fact is, it's nearly impossible to maintain a strong dharma practice without support. It's especially difficult to practice renunciation without the support of teachers and dharma friends. Most students find that when they observe the eight precepts together, they're more able to stay with the practice. They're more able to practice skillfully, with an open heart. They find, in fact, that it's joyful when they do it with others. It's joyful to go through it together.

Whether or not you follow the eight precepts on Uposatha days, the precepts can serve as a template for practicing renunciation. In delineating the eight precepts, the Buddha specifies sense pleasures that, when we over-indulge, become problematic. The sense pleasures he includes are those you might think about subtracting, to some extent, as you cultivate renunciation.

You'll note that the precepts regarding killing, stealing and taking intoxicants are identical to their counterparts in the five precepts. These precepts relate to practicing ethical conduct.

The precept pertaining to sexual conduct, you'll note, is different. On Uposatha days, observing the eight precepts, we refrain from all sexual activity. The precept speaks to the strong effect that sex can have on our dharma practice and our lives. As dharma students we seek to establish a skillful relationship to sex. This doesn't mean we don't enjoy sex. It means that we refrain from sexual activity when it's unhealthy, unskillful, when it leads to suffering. Sex, as we all know, is an extremely powerful force. If we engage in sexual activity in an unskillful manner, the results, invariably, will be disruptive, damaging, painful. Think about people whose lives have fallen into disarray, whose careers have been destroyed, because they weren't able to restrain their desire for this potent sense pleasure. We hear about it all the time. We've seen the President of the United States put his presidency in jeopardy because he wasn't able to subtract certain sexual activities.

If you're frequently knocked off-balance by your desire for sex, if your sexual conduct is unskillful, if it causes suffering for yourself or for others, it will be important to practice renunciation in this area.

(It's important to remember that if we're engaging in harmful, self-destructive behavior with regard to any of the sense pleasures, we may very well need to seek professional help, the support of a twelve-step program, etc. Dharma practice doesn't provide all the answers to all of our problems. More severe difficulties surrounding food, sex and sleep are often symptoms of deeper psychological issues, including unresolved trauma; in such instances it's essential to elicit the help of a skilled professional.)

The sixth, seventh and eighth precepts pertain to the practice of renunciation with regard to food, entertainment and sleep. These are sense pleasures we might want to think about subtracting, to some degree.

Food is a sense pleasure that many people partake of in an unskillful manner. Some dharma students, in considering how to practice renunciation, will want to look closely at their relationship to food.

Reflecting on how we might practice renunciation in terms of food, the key question is: How much do we need? This is the key question when it comes to many sense pleasures. How much do we need? We need to eat. We need food to sustain us, to provide the strength and energy we need to meet our daily tasks and practice the dharma. But how much do we need?

In cultivating renunciation, we ascertain what we need in order to nourish ourselves, maintain our health, and, in turn, we subtract what we don't need. Of course, we probably won't ever want to subtract everything we don't need. For most of us, there's nothing wrong with a nice piece of apple pie with a scoop of ice cream every now and then. As we practice renunciation, we don't deprive ourselves. We don't reject all sense pleasure. We don't put ourselves in a painful, resentful position. We moderate our intake.

Monks in the Theravada tradition live simply, relying on basic requisites, eating food put in their bowls by householders, never eating after twelve noon, wearing plain robes, living in modest structures. As householders navigating the modern world, we have different needs. We need suits and ties, dresses and skirts. We need cars. We need the internet. We need, probably, to go to the movies every once in awhile. We need music. We need sex, physical contact. We need to go to a baseball game every now and then. As householders, we've chosen to live a life in which we consume certain sense pleasures, in which we acquire more than the basic requisites, in which we possess a certain amount of stuff. But how much do we need? Again, that's the question.

How much stuff do we need? Do we need as much stuff as we've got? Most of us have a lot of stuff. How much of it do we need? How much clothing? Do we need so many pairs of shoes? Do we need three leather jackets?

In classes, when we discuss our habits with regard to acquiring sense pleasure, students often talk about the manner in which they shop, the tendency they have to spend a lot of time looking at stuff they might possibly buy, the tendency they have to buy lots of stuff. Nowadays the opportunities to shop have increased exponentially, thanks to the phenomenon of online shopping. We can sit in front of a computer, touch a few keys, click a few icons, and, in moments, buy a terrific amount of stuff. But how much do we need?

With regard to sleep, the question is the same: How much do we need? In observing the eight precepts, we "refrain from lying on a high and luxurious sleeping place." In monasteries monks, nuns and lay people sleep on the floor, perhaps in a sleeping bag or on a mat. Sleeping on the floor, we're less likely to succumb to the sense pleasure that derives from sleep; we're less likely to stay in bed.

How does this translate to the day-to-day experience of a householder? As somebody who tends to over-indulge in sleep, this is a subject of which I have much firsthand knowledge. Again, it's about developing a skillful relationship to the sense pleasure. In cultivating renunciation with regard to sleep, we make sure to get enough sleep, but not too much. Sleep, for many, is a potent sense pleasure. Staying in bed buried beneath the sheets and blankets, lingering in a warm cocoon. It's another means of getting lost in sense pleasure. It's another means of drowning ourselves.

Over-sleeping, we squander large pieces of time, time that might be well spent, attending to meaningful areas of our lives, practicing the dharma. Too much sleep dulls the mind. It's difficult, in fact, to practice meditation if we spend too much time under the covers, embedded in a world of slumber.

Lastly, we come to the precept regarding "entertainments." Most of us shouldn't have any problem identifying areas, with regard to entertainment forms, where we might benefit from reducing the amount of sense pleasure we receive.

On Uposatha days, practitioners refrain from partaking in all forms of entertainment. As the precept stipulates, they "refrain from dancing, singing, music, going to see entertainments." More than 2,500 years ago, long before the advent of cable TV, the Buddha realized it was important to practice renunciation of the sense pleasures we acquire through entertainment sources. We can only imagine what he'd think if he were around today. In recent years, of course, there's been an explosion of entertainment modalities. The "entertainments" provide constantly flowing, forever overflowing fountains of sense pleasure. As a culture, we indulge hungrily. We spend tremendous amounts of time feeding on the visual images, sounds, ideas, opinions, stories that these entertainment forms offer. We spend countless hours watching television, viewing sporting events, listening to music, surfing the internet, etc. We're mesmerized by the non-stop outpouring of information supplied by the internet, cable TV, the so-called 24 hour news cycle. We're fixed, as though surgically attached, to the laptop, cell phone, smart phone, portable listening device. In the last thirty years there's been a staggering expansion of vehicles that provide entertainment and information. When I graduated college in 1977, you played records on a turntable. If you wanted to see a movie, you had to go to the theater. Since then, numerous entertainment-based technologies have been introduced, the VCR, DVD, CD player, portable listening device, personal computer, laptop, tablet computer, internet, email, cell phone, smart phone (note: since I began writing this book, I've had to add items to this list).

When I was a kid living in the suburbs of New York City, there were seven TV channels. Now many households own a cable TV set up that boasts as many as 150 channels. When I was growing up, if you were watching television and wanted to change the channel, you had to get off the couch, go to the TV, switch the dial; now all you have to do is push a button on the remote control. There are more opportunities to acquire sense pleasure from entertainment sources and we're able to receive these sense pleasures much more quickly, in many cases almost instantly. Sense experience arrives with startling velocity. High-speed internet connections allow us to absorb new images in seconds. Everything is available, in a moment, with a click.

More and faster. In our culture, these are the qualities deemed most critical.

All the moments of our lives, it seems, are clogged with experience. The sense doors are jammed, like the doors to the Lexington Avenue subway during the height of rush hour. In New York City, citizens are often seen walking along the sidewalk completely wired, talking on a cell phone, earplugs stuffed in their ears. Gone are the days of a reflective stroll along the city boulevards.

Every day the desire grows. The desire for more sense pleasure, more rapid access to sense pleasure. It just keeps growing. That's how desire operates. We want more and we want it faster.

As the Buddha put it:

Not even if it rained gold coins
would we have our fill
of sensual pleasures.
(Dhp. 186)

All things considered, it's necessary that dharma students, seeking true happiness, develop the quality of renunciation. We have to learn to skill-fully subtract sense pleasure. If we consistently over-indulge in sense plea-sure we're not going to be able to move ahead along the Buddha's path. It's a challenging task, developing renunciation in today's world. But we can learn the skill.

As we travel along the path, we'll gradually reduce our intake of various sense pleasures, including food, entertainment and sleep. Gradually, we'll make added effort to practice renunciation. We'll make this effort because we've come to understand the drawbacks of sense pleasure and the benefits in practicing renunciation.

SEEING THE DRAWBACKS OF FEEDING ON SENSE PLEASURE

What's it like when you feed on a sense pleasure, whether it's actual food, like ice cream, or some other "food source" such as television or email?

Are there drawbacks?

If we look while we're feeding on sense pleasure, we may notice agitation, dis-ease, suffering. However, if we don't make an effort to look we may not notice anything. The dis-ease may be subtle. So we have to pay attention. In cultivating renunciation, we're asked to put wholehearted effort into studying the drawbacks of feeding on pleasure. We're asked to develop sensitivity to the drawbacks.

There's suffering inherent in looking for happiness in sense pleasure. As dharma students, we have to see that. We have to understand that.

We have to remember, in developing renunciation, that the main problem is not sense pleasure itself, but rather the way in which we feed on it, pursue it, look for happiness in it.

In studying the drawbacks of feeding on sense pleasure, it's important to recognize the dis-ease that manifests in the short term and long term. Often, when indulging in sense pleasure, we're blinded by the initial rush of pleasure. It's all we notice; we don't notice any pain. But if we keep looking, we may begin to notice dis-ease, suffering.

As you take that first taste of chocolate ice cream you might feel elation, a blast of pleasant feeling. But what's the quality of your mind after you've taken several spoonfuls of ice cream and there's not much left? Is there disappointment? Is there anxiousness, in recognition of the fact that your source of pleasure is almost depleted? What's your mind like after you've taken the last spoonful? Is there desire for another bowl of ice cream? What does this desire feel like? What's your mind like a few hours later, when you pass the refrigerator, knowing that the container of ice cream lies, waiting, inside? As you study the long term effects of grasping after sense pleasure, you may notice chronic patterns of dis-ease, suffering.

During the course of any day there are countless opportunities to see the drawbacks in sense pleasure. However, you don't want to attempt to "see the drawbacks" every time you engage in a sense pleasure. You have to pick your spots. As the Buddha puts it, you have to find "openings."

Let's say, once again, that you have a habit of watching a lot of TV. Let's say you want to moderate your TV intake, but you're not able to do it. You've tried, but you always end up grabbing the remote and flicking on the set. The bottom line is, you're not ready to practice renunciation. That's okay. You can't force yourself to subtract sense pleasure. What you can do, however, is develop wisdom. You can begin to recognize the drawbacks in feeding on the sense pleasure of television.

How might you "see the drawbacks"?

Let's say one evening you turn on the television. You watch several programs. But at some point, you pause and ask: "Are there drawbacks in doing this?" You bring your awareness to your body, in an effort to notice any dis-ease, any signs of suffering. You stay with this investigation for about ten seconds, keeping your awareness in the body, allowing yourself to understand, on a felt level, the consequences of indulging in the sense pleasure of television. After about ten seconds, you let go of the investigation, and re-focus your attention on the program you're watching.

You could also make an effort to recognize the drawbacks of your TV-watching after you've turned off the set.

However you practice, you shouldn't try to "see the drawbacks" for more than ten seconds; if you spend any more time than that you'll start to dwell in the dis-ease. You'll start thinking, analyzing your television habit. You'll probably end up judging yourself.

It's important, of course, not to judge yourself, condemn yourself for watching so much TV. You want to examine the drawbacks in a calm, non-attached manner, like a scientist.

If you're not able to "see the drawbacks" objectively, you shouldn't attempt this sort of examination; you don't have sufficient concentration, equanimity.

As we study our actions, we notice all kinds of drawbacks in looking for happiness in sense pleasure.

When immersed in sense pleasure, we lose our connection to the present moment. We submerge ourselves. We enter another world, a dream world. We're no longer awake. We're no longer in touch with our aliveness. When we spend our days and nights grasping after sense pleasure, we're cut off from what it is to be truly alive.

When indulging in sense pleasure, we're not able to pay attention to our actions. We're not able to discern whether our actions are unskillful or skillful.

Let's say you're sitting at the computer, scouring the internet, going from website to website. Your partner enters the room. She asks you to do something that, to put it bluntly, you don't want to do. Anger arises. You've been staring at the computer for a couple of hours and your sense doors are clogged. You don't notice your anger. Because you don't notice it, you act on it. You act out. You speak harshly to your partner.

The ability to be mindful of our actions, to discern whether they're unskillful or skillful, is called heedfulness. Too much activity at the sense doors is an obstacle to heedfulness. This is a basic law, important to remember.

One of the most common ways we over-involve ourselves with sense experience is by multi-tasking. In the present-day culture we place much value on multi-tasking. It's considered a vital skill. Because of the proliferation of new technologies, there are ever-increasing possibilities for multi-tasking. There's an extensive stock of permutations. Talking on the cell phone and walking down the street. Listening to music and walking. Talking on the phone and answering email. Studying the laptop and listening to music on a portable device. Watching TV and eating. Watching TV and talking on the phone. Watching TV and eating and talking on the phone. And so on.

As dharma students we learn to see for ourselves what's in our best interests. The cultural message may be that there's great value in multi-tasking, but that doesn't mean there is great value in it. As dharma students we don't allow ourselves to be slaves to the cultural dogma. We make our own decisions about what's good for us, based on what we've seen for ourselves. We learn by seeing for ourselves what we have to do to find happiness, to have a better life.

We learn.

The Buddha's teachings would suggest that when we multi-task it's not possible to be fully present. It's not possible to put our full attention on a task, to have a focused relationship with what we're doing. When we multi-task, we're never quite with our experience. We're never quite awake.

See if this is true.

See for yourself.

In a previous chapter we talked about how we fragment our attention when interacting with others. If while walking down the street, you're talking to somebody on a cell phone, you can't be fully present, fully engaged with your experience, either experience, the experience of walking or the conversation you're having, trying to have, with the person on the other end of the line. As we've said, when attention is fragmented our ability to connect to the other deteriorates, our ability to empathize degrades. Instead of making a connection with the other, perhaps our original intention, we manufacture disconnection. In our culture, our interaction with others, because it's so often engineered through technological means, is becoming increasingly affectless. We're becoming an affectless society.

The teachings indicate that if we put a lot of energy into pursuing sense pleasure, it's going to be difficult to practice meditation, to develop concentration. Again, it's up to you to see if it's true. What's your breath meditation practice like when you're indulging in lots of sense pleasure?

It's our habit to look for happiness in sense pleasure. And sense pleasure does offer a certain kind of happiness. But it's a limited happiness. That's because it's impermanent. The core drawback of sense pleasure is that it's impermanent. It arises, changes, passes. It doesn't last. None of it. The chocolate ice cream. The ecstasy of sex. The excitement you feel when your team plays in the Super Bowl. The drama on the silver screen. It's all impermanent. When you look for happiness in impermanent things, you set yourself up for disappointment, pain, suffering.

You know how it is. You garner a certain sense pleasure. You watch a DVD. The movie ends, the pleasure passes. In order to regain the happiness that's just dissolved, you've got to acquire more sense pleasure, and, thusly, you make an effort to acquire it. And you acquire it. And it passes. And so on and so on. It's a painful cycle. It's painful, having to constantly replenish your food source, your source of happiness.

When we look for happiness in sense pleasure, the pain is ongoing. We're like kids building sandcastles; we build an elaborate castle, the waves crash, ruin the castle, and we build another castle, and the waves ruin it. It's like that.

There's an unsatisfactoriness inherent in sense pleasure. Because it doesn't last. Because if we look for happiness in it, we'll suffer.

As dharma students, we learn to see what kind of mind we develop when we indulge, again and again, in sense pleasure. When we continually feed on sense pleasure, we tend to manifest rather unskillful mental qualities: impatience, irritability, frustration, dissatisfaction, dependency. As always, we should pay close attention and see this for ourselves.

If we're committed to finding happiness in sense pleasure, we're going to have to put a substantial portion of our time into acquiring it. Which means that we're not going to have time to look for another kind of happiness. Preoccupied with finding happiness in sense pleasure, we block ourselves off from looking for happiness elsewhere.

There is another kind of happiness. A happiness that, in fact, is not impermanent. It's a reliable happiness. A greater happiness. But if we spend all our time seeking a happiness that's impermanent, if we dedicate ourselves to that exhaustive pursuit, we'll be prevented from looking for a greater happiness. And that, indeed, is a drawback.

MAKING A TRADE

According to the Buddha, practicing renunciation involves making a trade. A skillful trade. As the Buddha puts it:

If, by forsaking
a limited ease,
he would see
an abundance of ease,
the enlightened man
would forsake
the limited ease
for the sake
of the abundant.
(Dhp 290)

Yes, we're giving something up. But we're exchanging it for something else, something better. We're exchanging a "limited ease" for an "abundance of ease." We're trading a lesser happiness for a greater happiness. As Thanissaro Bhikkhu puts it, we're trading "candy for gold."

When we consider relinquishing sense pleasure, we might be afraid that we'll be left with nothing, remanded to a cold empty zone, deposited in a void. But this isn't what the Buddha indicates. The Buddha doesn't leave us high and dry.

It's important to understand that in practicing renunciation we're making a skillful trade. This is right view. This is the right way to think about it.

Practicing renunciation, we trade the treacherous road of sense pleasure for the Buddha's road. We trade the temporary happiness of sense pleasure for the happiness we come to know when we follow the path. Sometimes this entails replacing the time we spend chasing after sense pleasure with formal practice, sitting meditation, retreats, and the like. As householders, however, we have only so much time to put into formal "eyes closed" practice. It's essential, therefore, that we practice renunciation, make a skillful trade, within the context of our everyday lives. As we go through our days and nights, we have to find ways to moderate our acquisition of sense pleasure, and, in turn, trade sense pleasure for the cultivation of skillful qualities, concentration, insight.

In practicing renunciation, we make an effort to put less time into pursuing sense pleasure and more time into developing generosity, ethical conduct and the other skillful qualities. This is a good trade. We trade the limited happiness that comes from sense pleasure for the happiness, the joy, that we know when we develop skillful qualities.

Very importantly, in cultivating renunciation, in making a trade, we seek to replace external sense pleasure (the pint of mint chocolate chip ice cream, the channel surfing) with internal pleasure. Specifically, the pleasure we develop by practicing breath meditation. In following the Buddha's own example, we transition away from external sense pleasure. In making this transition, we don't deny ourselves pleasure, but rather replace unskillful sense pleasure with a more skillful form of pleasure.

Subscribing to the Buddha's instructions, we learn to cultivate the breath. We learn to cultivate an easeful, pleasurable breath. We learn to cultivate a pleasant abiding, within, in the body.

As we move further along the path, it's crucial that we learn to trade external sense pleasure for the pleasure developed when we practice mindfulness of breathing. A pivotal moment in the Buddha's own journey occurred when he realized that the path must include the development of wholesome inner pleasure. After spending the first part of his life in luxurious surroundings, indulging in every type of sense pleasure, the Buddha, Prince Siddhartha at that point, began to understand that the acquisition of sense pleasure wasn't going to lead to a true happiness. He decided, to his family's dismay, that he was going to pursue a spiritual path. Some of the spiritual masters in his day, in Northern India, taught ascetic practices, believing that happiness could be found only by depriving yourself of all forms of pleasure. The Buddha diligently followed these teachers. But after practicing ascetic disciplines for six years, he saw clearly that the absolute denial of pleasure wasn't the answer, wasn't going to provide a way to happiness. Finally he realized that in moving away from a life of indulgence, a skillful trade had to be made. The path to happiness, he saw, had to include the cultivation of wholesome pleasure. There was nothing wrong, he concluded, with the pleasure of a concentrated mind.

"I thought: 'I recall once, when my father the Sakyan was working, and I was sitting in the cool shade of a rose-apple tree, then — quite withdrawn from sensuality, withdrawn from unskillful mental qualities — I entered & remained in the first jhana: rapture & pleasure born from withdrawal, accompanied by directed thought & evaluation. Could that be the path to Awakening?' Then, following on that memory, came the realization: 'That is the path to Awakening.' I thought: 'So why am I afraid of that pleasure that has nothing to do with sensuality, nothing to do with unskillful mental qualities?' I thought: 'I am no longer afraid of that pleasure that has nothing to do with sensuality, nothing to do with unskillful mental qualities" (MN 36)

The moment when the Buddha decided that the path must include wholesome pleasure is the moment, we might say, when Buddhism became Buddhism. The cultivation of wholesome pleasure is integral to the path.

As Theravada Buddhist practice has emerged in the west, primarily in the form of Insight Meditation, there's been a tendency to de-emphasize the cultivation of internal pleasure. In fact, it's not taught. In fact, there's a bias against it. The prevailing notion held by some teachers is that the cultivation of internal pleasure shouldn't be taught because students will become "attached" to the pleasant states, they'll strive for the pleasant states, and, consequently, disregard important facets of the path. This, however, represents a striking misunderstanding of the Buddha's teachings. The fact is, it's okay to strive after healthy inner pleasure. It's not a problem. The problem is striving after unhealthy external sense pleasure. The problem is looking for happiness in external pleasure, in filet mignon, in a new smart phone, in television, in internet porn.

In providing a means for cultivating internal pleasure, through breath meditation, the Buddha offers a way to shift away from looking for happiness in external pleasure. The Buddha knew from his own experience that we couldn't be expected to give up all pleasure in one fell swoop. He knew that we had to gradually transition from sense pleasure. And he gave us a way to do it.

The pleasure we cultivate through breath meditation is skillful, healthy, wholesome. It's wholesome because it's pleasure that isn't dependent on external sources. We're not creating dependency. We're not taking anything from anybody or anything outside ourselves. We're not hurting anybody.

We're not hurting ourselves. To the contrary, we're moving toward a greater happiness. It's wholesome pleasure, in the end, because it enables us to follow the path, alleviate suffering, find true happiness.

The pleasure we cultivate through concentration practice doesn't cloud the mind; to the contrary, it leads to greater clarity.

In his instructions for mindfulness of breathing, the Buddha delineates basic steps for developing concentration. The Buddha's concentration is a specific kind of concentration known as jhana. In developing jhana, we cultivate one-pointedness, the ability to focus. But there's more to it than that. We also cultivate physical ease (sometimes known as "rapture" or "refreshment"). And we cultivate mental ease, pleasure. Developing jhana, we cultivate an easeful, pleasurable breath, and then we cultivate these qualities, ease and pleasure, throughout the body. Having a "full body awareness" and practicing "full body breathing" is central to the practice. As Thanissaro Bhikkhu explains, the term "jhana" is related to "jhayati," a word used to describe a small steady flame, like the flame from a kerosene lamp that can clearly illuminate an entire room. Developing jhana, we begin by focusing on the breath at one point. We cultivate an easeful, pleasurable breath. A small steady flame. As we keep our mind on the breath, the light of the flame gradually spreads to the entire body. We let the pleasant breath quality pervade the body. The body fills with ease, pleasure.

In his description of the first level of jhana, the Buddha explicates, in no uncertain terms, the pleasant quality that arises when we practice mindfulness of breathing:

> "There is the case where a monk — quite secluded from sensuality, secluded from unskillful qualities — enters and remains in the first jhana: rapture and pleasure born of seclusion, accompanied

by directed thought and evaluation. He permeates and pervades, suffuses and fills this very body with the rapture and pleasure born of seclusion. There is nothing of his entire body unpervaded by rapture and pleasure born of seclusion.

"Just as if a skilled bathman or bathman's apprentice would pour bath powder into a brass basin and knead it together, sprinkling it again and again with water, so that his ball of bath powder — saturated, moisture-laden, permeated within and without — would nevertheless not drip; even so, the monk permeates, suffuses and fills this very body with the rapture and pleasure born of seclusion. There is nothing of his entire body unpervaded by rapture and pleasure born of seclusion..." (AN 5.28)

At DMC, students follow the Buddha's approach for practicing breath meditation, for developing jhana. They foster the "seclusion" the Buddha speaks about by practicing renunciation, moderating the degree to which they feed on sense pleasure. And they foster seclusion by practicing meditation, having a daily breath meditation practice. Even within the context of New York City, they've demonstrated it is possible to find seclusion.

In meditation, the students learn to cultivate an easeful, pleasurable breath, and to allow this breath quality to unfold, spread through the body. They learn to cultivate wholesome inner pleasure.

It's altogether possible for householders, laden with jobs, relationships, myriad responsibilities, to develop the factors of jhana. I know it can be done, because I've seen the students in our community doing it. By learning the skill and making the effort, they're able to develop inner ease, pleasure. They're able to establish a pleasant abiding.

As they develop the skill, students learn to connect to internal ease, pleasure, when they're "off the cushion," in the throes of their daily lives, at work, interacting with others, in the supermarket, on the subway, on the bus, etc. It's extremely important to be able to maintain inner ease, pleasure, by being mindful of the breath, during all parts of the day. It's during the course of the day that we'll confront the many different forms of sense pleasure. But if we're able to maintain a degree of inner pleasure, we'll be less likely to chase after external sense pleasure. That students are able to cultivate the qualities of ease, well-being, pleasure, in the midst of their daily affairs, while living in New York City, shouldn't be ignored. As the song goes, if you can do it in New York, you can do it anywhere. And you can.

It's possible to make a skillful trade, to exchange sense pleasure for wholesome internal pleasure. Not only is it possible, it's necessary. The Buddha himself said that when he was a Bodhisatta, striving for awakening, he wasn't able to resist the temptation of external sense pleasure until he learned to develop a pleasant abiding within.

"I myself, before my Awakening, when I was still an unawakened bodhisatta, saw as it actually was with right discernment that sensuality is of much stress, much despair, & greater drawbacks, but as long as I had not attained a rapture & pleasure apart from sensuality, apart from unskillful mental qualities, or something more peaceful than that, I did not claim that I could not be tempted by sensuality. But when I saw as it actually was with right discernment that sensuality is of much stress, much despair, & greater drawbacks, and I had attained a rapture & pleasure apart from sensuality, apart from unskillful mental qualities, or something more peaceful than that, that

was when I claimed that I could not be tempted by sensuality."
(MN 14)

Clearly, this is something we've got to learn. We've got to learn to cultivate a wholesome inner pleasure. If we're able to develop inner pleasure, we'll be less inclined to look for happiness in external pleasure. We'll be well on our way to developing the skillful quality of renunciation.

THE BENEFITS OF RENUNCIATION

A key step in developing skillful qualities is "seeing the benefits" in these qualities. It's one of the primary ways we cultivate the garden; the perception of the benefits in the skillful qualities is like sunlight that nourishes plants and flowers.

It's important, given our preconceived notions, that we put a thorough effort into seeing the benefits of renunciation. Most of us, as matter of habit, don't feel enthusiastic about practicing renunciation. It's not something we're apt to get excited about. We're not apt to jump out of bed in the morning, pull the curtains, and exclaim, "What a great day to practice renunciation!" When it comes to renunciation, we're usually not chomping at the bit.

Even the Buddha, as a Bodhisatta, suffered a degree of reluctance when faced with the prospect of developing renunciation. As he put it, his heart didn't "leap up" when he thought about practicing renunciation. It wasn't until he was able to see the benefits in renunciation, and the drawbacks in sensual pleasure, that he became more enthusiastic.

"So it is, Ananda. So it is. Even I myself, before my Awakening, when I was still an unawakened Bodhisatta, thought: 'Renunciation is good. Seclusion is good.' But my heart didn't leap up at renunciation, didn't grow confident, steadfast, or firm, seeing it as peace. The thought occurred to me: 'What is the cause, what is the reason, why my heart doesn't leap up at renunciation, doesn't grow confident, steadfast, or firm, seeing it as peace?' Then the thought occurred to me: 'I haven't seen the drawback of sensual pleasures; I haven't pursued [that theme]. I haven't understood the reward of renunciation; I haven't familiarized myself with it. That's why my heart doesn't leap up at renunciation, doesn't grow confident, steadfast, or firm, seeing it as peace.'

"Then the thought occurred to me: 'If, having seen the drawback of sensual pleasures, I were to pursue that theme; and if, having understood the reward of renunciation, I were to familiarize myself with it, there's the possibility that my heart would leap up at renunciation, grow confident, steadfast, & firm, seeing it as peace.'

"So at a later time, having seen the drawback of sensual pleasures, I pursued that theme; having understood the reward of renunciation, I familiarized myself with it. My heart leaped up at renunciation, grew confident, steadfast, & firm, seeing it as peace."

(AN 9.41)

The Buddha, you'll note, made it a practice to see the benefits of renunciation. He sought to "familiarize" himself with the benefits. He "pursued that theme." He engaged in an active process. He didn't take a passive approach. He didn't wait around for an awareness of the benefits of renunciation to suddenly materialize, like a bird landing on a windowsill. He purposefully looked to see the benefits. In seeing the benefits in skillful qualities, it's imperative that we take a proactive approach.

Actively looking isn't an endeavor we regularly partake in. We often choose a more passive stance. Think about how we acquire most of our information. By pressing a button on the remote control. By clicking icons on computer screens. As dharma students, however, we're asked to take decisive action. We're asked, in seeing the benefits of renunciation, to follow the Buddha's lead, to make wholehearted purposeful effort.

We're asked to look.

If we look, we'll perceive many benefits in developing renunciation.

When we subtract sense pleasure, large portions of time become available to us. This is a notable benefit of renunciation. We're able to put to good use all the time we'd spent pursuing sense pleasure. We're able to put more time into dharma practice, into developing skillful qualities, concentration, insight. We're able to put more energy into doing what we need to do, to end suffering, find true happiness.

Even if we relinquish small amounts of sense pleasure, we'll begin to have more time.

Time is so precious. Practicing renunciation, we make the most of the time we have in this life.

Practicing renunciation, we develop tranquility, calmness. The mind, less involved in grasping after sense pleasure, settles down. We become less agitated.

The emergence of the unagitated state, in the wake of practicing renunciation, is exemplified in the story of Venerable Bhaddiya, a monk who'd previously been a king. It seems that some monks overheard Bhaddiya uttering, "What bliss! What bliss!" The monks were suspicious. They figured Bhaddiya, who was supposed to be meditating, was recalling the past, thinking about his days as a king, his bygone life, all the luxuries and sense pleasures he'd known. The Buddha asked Bhaddiya about it. Why did he keep repeating, "What bliss! What bliss!"? It was because he was happy, Bhaddiya explained. He was happy because he was no longer living a life of acquisition and indulgence. He was happy because he no longer had to be concerned with the burdens that came from trying to maintain that sort of life. Now, as a monk, he was blissfully free from the agitation that came, necessarily, from keeping his kingdom afloat.

As Venerable Bhaddiya puts it:

"Before, when I was a householder, maintaining the bliss of kingship, I had guards posted within and without the royal apartments, within and without the city, within and without the countryside. But even though I was thus guarded, thus protected, I dwelled in fear — agitated, distrustful, and afraid. But now, on going alone to a forest, to the foot of a tree, or to an empty dwelling, I dwell without fear, unagitated, confident, and unafraid — unconcerned, unruffled, my wants satisfied, with my mind like a wild deer. This is the meaning I have in mind that I repeatedly exclaim, 'What bliss! What bliss!'" (Ud 2.10)

When we cultivate renunciation, we put ourselves in position to train the mind. Another key benefit. Less engrossed in acquiring sense pleasure, less agitated, we're more able to practice breath meditation. We're able to develop concentration. Strong concentration.

As we've said, too much activity at the sense doors is an obstacle to heedfulness. Conversely, when we reduce the traffic at the sense doors, we see more clearly. We're able to practice heedfulness. This is a critical benefit of practicing renunciation. Normally our sense doors are clogged, and, consequently, we're not able to pay attention to our actions. It's like you're in a room crowded, crammed, with people. There are so many people that you can't tell who's there. You can't see what everybody is doing. If there's somebody you're looking for, you're going to have a hard time finding that person. When we practice renunciation, it's as if the room clears out. A bunch of people leave. There are still a few people scattered about, but not too many. You can see who's there. If there's somebody you're looking for, you're not going to have any problem finding the person. When we subtract sense pleasure, we can see what's going on. We can see clearly. We can observe our actions. We're able to discern whether our actions are unskillful or skillful.

There are, indeed, many benefits in practicing renunciation. As always, though, we have to see the benefits for ourselves.

It's important to grasp what we mean by "seeing the benefits." In seeing the benefits in renunciation and the other skillful qualities, we're not merely thinking about the benefits, we're not merely engaging in an intellectual or analytical exercise. We're looking directly at the benefits. As the Buddha explains, we're cultivating "direct knowledge." There's a world of difference between thinking about a sunrise and experiencing a sunrise.

In seeing the benefits in the skillful qualities, we take time to look at the benefits. We avoid the tendency to merely acknowledge the benefits, then turn away, move on to the next thing. We sit with the truth of what we see. We take some time to let understanding formulate, on a felt level, in the body. We let our awareness of the benefits sink in, seep into the body, like water after a rainfall seeping into the ground. We acquire felt wisdom.

When we "see the benefits" with the body, with the heart, we deepen our capacity to develop the skillful qualities.

SELF-ESTEEM

As we develop skillful qualities, we come to recognize our goodness. We feel better about ourselves. We build self-esteem.

As we practice skillful giving, we recognize our capacity for generosity, compassion, helping others.

As we follow the five precepts, we let go of negative perceptions that we have about ourselves; we no longer think of ourselves as somebody who causes harm, suffering.

When we practice renunciation, we feel good about ourselves, realizing we've got the ability to put aside sense pleasure, realizing we don't need sense pleasure to be happy.

When we pin our hopes for happiness on sense pleasure, we're dependent. When dependent, we're in a position of weakness. We don't feel good about ourselves. We don't feel we're good enough on our own.

As we lessen our dependency on sense pleasure, we gain confidence, faith in ourselves.

As we relinquish certain sense pleasures, we come to understand that we don't need these sense pleasures. We see that we've got everything we need, inside us. We've got a capacity for goodness. We've got inner worth.

Most of my life, I've suffered from low self-esteem. I think it's fair to say that most people are afflicted, to some extent, with low self-esteem. It's a pervasive cultural characteristic. We live in a culture, of course, where people depend on external factors, sense pleasures and the like, for their happiness. Low self-esteem is a widespread malady. And it's a significant malady. Because self-esteem is necessary. In order to find true happiness, we have to have self-esteem. In order to move ahead in dharma practice and in life we have to have self-esteem.

As you're reading, you might be wondering why we're talking about self-esteem. You might be asking: Isn't the Buddha's doctrine aimed at dismantling the self? As dharma students, shouldn't we be concerned with deconstructing the self, rather than building it up? It's important to understand that the Buddha is all for building self-esteem. "Healthy ego development," as Thanissaro Bhikkhu puts it, is a critical element of the path.

Self-esteem, in and of itself, is a beneficial quality. We feel at-ease, uplifted, knowing we're capable of acting skillfully, knowing we have a certain goodness. We feel strong.

Girded by self-esteem, we're able to function effectively in the world. We're able to attend to the different aspects of our lives. In order to navigate the terrain of everyday life, work, relationship, we need self-esteem, self-confidence.

If you're going to practice the dharma, take on the challenges of a spiritual journey, you're going to need an appreciable amount of self-esteem. If you're going to deconstruct the self, you're going to need a strong self, you're going to need strength, fortitude, self-esteem. As noted in the psychological arena, before you can transcend the ego, you've got to have a strong ego. It's not a job for those lacking self-esteem.

Twelve-step programs provide a good picture of the role of self-esteem in undertaking personal and spiritual transformation. Anyone who enters a program such as Alcoholics Anonymous, is invariably suffering a loss of self-esteem. It's a primary symptom of addiction. After years of dependency on alcohol and/or drugs, after engaging in all manner of unskillful actions, the alcoholic usually isn't feeling too good about himself. He isn't a paragon of self-esteem. In joining AA and undergoing the process of recovery, one of the first things the alcoholic is encouraged to do is practice generosity. Ample opportunities are provided for him to perform service. Making coffee at AA meetings. Setting up chairs. Putting away chairs. Speaking at meetings. Right from the start, the alcoholic is urged to help other recovering alcoholics. If he's been sober five days, he's told, he can reach out to an alcoholic who's been sober four days. Practicing generosity, the alcoholic builds self-esteem. After years of engaging in derelict behavior, he begins to take skillful actions, to help others. For the first time in a long time he starts to feel good about himself.

After helping others, offering service, and allowing himself to be held in the embrace of a group of other recovering people, the alcoholic gets to the point where he's ready to take on the hard work of recovery; he's now strong enough, inside, to practice the twelve steps, begin the process of self-exploration, make a "searching and fearless moral inventory," reintegrate into society as a sober person.

As a dharma student, travelling the road to true happiness, it's imperative that you build self-esteem. The Buddha asks that you attend to some difficult tasks. He asks that you engage in the most daunting confrontation you'll ever engage in: the confrontation with yourself. He asks that you open to the truth of your suffering. The Buddha's way isn't for the faint of heart. It's a demanding journey. You're going to need to be well-equipped. You're going to need self-esteem.

As you develop the skillful qualities, you'll build the self-esteem you're going to need to make the journey of self-exploration. You'll build the self-esteem you're going to need to head in a countercultural direction.

It's one of the most important benefits of developing skillful qualities.

PRACTICE SUGGESTIONS

REFLECTION:

Where am I with regard to the five precepts? Do I follow the precepts? Which precepts must I make more effort to follow?

REFLECTION:

What is the quality of my intention to follow the five precepts? Do I approach the practice of ethical conduct with a skillful attitude?

REFLECTION:

What is my resistance to developing ethical conduct?

PRACTICE:

Establish a resolve to follow the five precepts. Assert directed thought, reminding yourself that you're going to develop ethical conduct out of compassion for yourself. Connect to a felt sense of compassion.

PRACTICE:

To the best of your ability, follow the five precepts. See what your mind is like as you keep to the precepts. Recognize when your intention is unskillful.

PRACTICE:

Choose one precept that you need to develop. Make an effort to follow this precept. When you aren't able to follow the precept, see the drawbacks.

PRACTICE:

Choose one of the four areas of harmful speech where you might improve. Make an effort to refrain from this form of harmful speech.

PRACTICE:

Being mindful of your speech, notice your humor. Is the way that you attempt to be humorous skillful? Or is it abusive? Divisive?

PRACTICE:

As you make an effort to develop ethical conduct, be mindful of resistance. When resistance arises, observe it, question it.

PRACTICE:

When you're not able to adhere to the guidelines for ethical conduct, see the drawbacks. Acknowledge the drawbacks in a calm, objective manner, recognizing that your unskillful actions bring about suffering for yourself and for others.

REFLECTION:

Where am I in regard to developing renunciation? How do I tend to over-indulge in sense pleasure? How might I practice renunciation?

REFLECTION:

What is my relationship to entertainment and technology? Is it skillful? Do I tend to become over-involved with entertainment forms?

PRACTICE:

Practice renunciation. Choose a specific sense pleasure (watching television, surfing the internet, etc.). Make a reasonable plan for practicing renunciation of this sense pleasure. As you make an effort to subtract the sense pleasure, use the five-step process for developing skillful intention/action. Make sure to enact a skillful trade, exchanging the road of sense pleasure for the path of dharma practice.

REFLECTION:

What are the drawbacks when I indulge in sense pleasure?

PRACTICE:

Be mindful of the drawbacks in indulging in sense pleasure.

REFLECTION:

Where am I in my breath meditation practice? Do I understand that by cultivating the factors of jhana I can bring about a skillful trade, exchanging external sense pleasure for wholesome internal pleasure?

PRACTICE:

Select one way that you frequently multi-task. For the period of one week, refrain from multi-tasking in this fashion. For instance, if it's your habit to watch television while you're eating dinner, refrain from watching TV and "just eat." See the benefits in renouncing this form of multi-tasking.

PRACTICE:

One day, preferably on an Uposatha day, follow the eight precepts. During the day, deepen your dharma practice. Attempt to connect with others for support.

REFLECTION:

What are the benefits when I practice renunciation?

PRACTICE:

Recognize the benefits in practicing renunciation. Recognize the benefits of practicing generosity and ethical conduct as well. In seeing the benefits in developing skillful qualities, take some time to reflect; bringing your awareness into your body, connect to a felt sense of your understanding of the benefits.

PRACTICE:

Notice how the development of skillful qualities leads to self-esteem.

CHAPTER THREE

TRUTHFULNESS

REFRAINING FROM FALSE SPEECH

The Thai meditation teacher, Ajaan Fuang, liked to say, "If you can't have any control over your mouth, how can you expect to have any control over your mind?"

The fact is, you can meditate with the ardency of a Zen monk, you can go on myriad retreats, but if you don't learn to practice skillful speech, you're not going to get very far along the Buddha's path.

It's crucial as you move along the path to grasp the importance of skillful speech, to understand the importance of refraining from false speech, to understand the importance of truthfulness. In cultivating truthfulness, you're asked to examine the ways in which you engage in false speech, the ways you lie. Over the years you may have constructed a barrier between yourself and the truth. You may have built up an immunity to the truth. But as a dharma student developing skillful qualities, you have to engender a willingness to tear down these barriers and practice truthfulness.

Most of us lie in some way, shape or form. We lie to family, friends. We lie in work contexts (in my job as a salesman, lying seemed part of the process, a required function in conducting business). From what I've heard, even statesmen and politicians lie. It would seem that, on a certain level, lying is accepted behavior. It would seem that it's not considered such a big deal. But is it a big deal? Is lying a problem? These are questions we need to ask. These are important reflections. Are there drawbacks in lying? Does it cause harm? Does it lead us further from the road to happiness?

In cultivating truthfulness, we're asked to be mindful of our speech. We're asked to recognize the ways in which we engage in both blatant and subtle forms of false speech. It might not be hard to discern blatant lies (then again, it might be). You tell your partner you're going to the gym when you're heading to a rendezvous with the person with whom you're having an affair. You tell your boss that you've completed a task when in fact you haven't. You include untrue information on your resume.

For many of us, the main issue isn't blatant false speech, but rather the more subtle kinds of lying. There are many subtle forms of false speech. There are the so-called white lies. You tell a friend you can't go to dinner with him because you're not feeling well, when the truth is, you just don't want to spend time with him. You tell somebody you didn't return her phone call because you never received the call, when in fact you did.

There are the ways we lie by exaggerating. You tell somebody that you've been meditating for six years, when it's been only four. You tell your friend that you've been waiting for her for twenty minutes, but it's been just five minutes. You tell a business associate that you called her office three times, when you called just once.

There are the occasions when we tell purposeless lies. There's absolutely no reason to lie, but you lie anyway. You say you went to the movies on Tuesday, but actually you went on Wednesday. You say that you took the bus, when you took the train.

There are times when our attempts to be humorous lead us to speak falsely. We may be telling a story about another person and, in an effort to be funny, we may exaggerate the truth. Or we may tell a story about ourselves and stretch the truth. We may not think of humor as a vehicle for false speech, but when we pay attention we see that it often is; we see that lying in the service of "joking" is detrimental, it results in a loss of integrity.

There are many different ways that we might speak falsely.

(Note: it's false speech only when we lie intentionally; if we unintentionally give false information it's not considered a breach of a precept.)

As dharma students striving to act skillfully, we make a commitment to truthfulness. Or at least we begin to make a commitment. We begin to move in the direction of truthfulness. For many of us, it's a significant move. Many of us have had a lifelong inclination to shirk the truth, avoid the truth. In cultivating an earnest motivation to practice truthfulness, we're taking a major step forward in our efforts to find happiness in our lives.

In practicing truthfulness, we make sincere effort to notice the different ways that we engage in false speech; we make an effort to see the drawbacks in our unskillfulness.

When I discuss the subject of false speech, there's always somebody who asks: "Isn't it okay to lie sometimes? Aren't some white lies okay?" In response, I explain that I can't answer that question. I explain that it's up to the student to see for himself. What I know, what the Buddha knew, will take him only so far. He has to find the answer for himself, not by thinking about it, not by ruminating on the ethical vagaries, but by looking at his actions. He has to study the consequences of his actions. He has to see for himself if there are drawbacks when he speaks falsely. He has to see if his lying causes suffering. In particular, if it causes him suffering.

(Sometimes, students ask: "Isn't it better to lie rather than to tell the truth and hurt somebody's feelings?" It's important to remember that the Buddha, most certainly, doesn't advocate telling somebody the truth if doing so would cause harm; he says, clearly, that we should speak the truth, but that our words, in addition to being truthful, should be useful, beneficial, an expression of love and compassion. If speaking the truth would be harmful, then the dharma practitioner, rather than lying, should simply refrain from speaking. Brutal honesty is never skillful.)

If you pay attention to the results when telling a lie, even a subtle lie, you may notice an assortment of painful consequences, unfortunate results. You may notice agitation in your mind. You may notice that you're afflicted with painful mental states, such as remorse or shame or worry. Bringing awareness to your body, you may detect contraction, disease. In short, you may see that you're suffering.

As you examine the consequences of your false speech, you may notice that you feel a loss of integrity, self-esteem. You don't feel good about yourself. You might've been motivated to lie by the idea that it would strengthen your position, but now you feel a certain weakness.

Before speaking falsely, you might've thought that lying would improve your connection with the person you were going to lie to, but after lying you may feel a diminishment of connection, you may feel separation.

It's important to remember that the results of your actions may not be immediately apparent. Initially, speaking falsely might not seem problematic. But if you watch, you may see that over time painful consequences manifest, sprout up like weeds in an abandoned lot. The pain grows, elongates, twists, interweaves. Eventually you're strangled by feelings of disease. The results of unskillful actions may prove more damaging than, at first, they might've seemed. This is part of the law of karma. Actions have short term and long term results. In practicing truthfulness, you're asked to perceive the long term results of speaking falsely. The harmful outcomes of your lying may be long-lasting. You may feel repercussions days, weeks, years afterwards. You can probably think of an example of when you told a small lie, recalled it years later, and felt definitive pain. Perhaps in high school you told a friend you got an A on your English paper, when, in truth, you got a C. A small lie, but for the next thirty years every now and then the thought of that lie has entered your mind and you've experienced a pang, a dissonant vibration. It shows the enduring power of false speech. Even small lies have far-reaching effects.

Another facet of the law of karma suggests that small actions may yield big results. A small act of lovingkindness may lead to deep happiness. And a small lie, in the long run, may bring about notably damaging results. You tell your friend a subtle lie, it causes a fissure in your friendship, the fissure gradually lengthens, widens, like a crack in the foundation of a building, and the friendship eventually disintegrates.

The law of karma also indicates that certain actions may bring unexpected results. You lie in an interview for a job, and, consequently, you get the job. You become entrenched in the job and stay with it for years, decades. But you're not cut out for the work. As the years go on, you get further and further away from fulfilling your deepest wishes for yourself in terms of your life's work.

The dharma student, practicing truthfulness, looks closely, recognizes the drawbacks in lying, the different shapes the drawbacks take.

Before she speaks, the dharma student reminds herself that her actions will have consequences, short and long term. When she's thinking about lying, she remembers what she's learned, what she's seen, what she knows from her own experience, about the drawbacks in lying.

When you're not truthful in speaking with others, you impair your capacity to be truthful with yourself, about yourself. This is a profoundly damaging consequence of false speech. If you lie to others, you'll lie to yourself. When you lie to others, you condition an atmosphere of deception in your mind. As your lies add up, the atmosphere gets thicker and thicker, like thick heavy pea soup fog. Your ability to see the truth becomes severely hindered. As a result, when you act unskillfully you'll be likely to deceive yourself. You'll tell yourself that your actions won't lead to suffering. Or you'll tell yourself that it's okay to act the way you've acted. Or that what you did wasn't that bad, wasn't unskillful. Or you'll simply ignore your actions, pretend nothing happened.

When the quality of truthfulness isn't well developed, we lack the ability to be honest with ourselves.

In the "Instructions to Rahula," the Buddha begins his teaching by talking to Rahula about the importance of truthfulness. He takes a dipper filled with a small amount of water, shows Rahula the few drops of water, says:

"Rahula, do you see this little bit of left-over water remaining
in the water dipper?"
"Yes, sir."
"That's how little of a contemplative there is in anyone who
feels no shame at telling a deliberate lie."

The Buddha's message is clear: if we don't develop the quality of truthfulness, we're not going to be able to develop the path, we're not going to get far along the road to true happiness. We'll remain mired in unskillfulness.

The Buddha goes on to say:

"In the same way, Rahula, when anyone feels no shame in telling a deliberate lie, there is no evil, I tell you, he will not do. Thus, Rahula, you should train yourself, 'I will not tell a deliberate lie even in jest.'"

It's said that the Buddha, before he became the Buddha, developed the skillful qualities, but, like all of us, wasn't perfect, wasn't always successful. At times he failed in his efforts. With one exception. There was one skillful quality that he practiced unfailingly: truthfulness. What the story implies is, in seeking the happiness the Buddha found there are going to be times when you'll struggle, when you'll make mistakes, but if you can be truthful about it, you'll be okay, you'll progress along the path. The Buddha, as a Bodhisatta, made mistakes. But he was truthful about it. As you strive to develop generosity, ethical conduct, renunciation, and the other skillful qualities, there are going to be times when you'll slip up, fail. But it's only a problem if you're not truthful about it. When you're truthful, you give yourself an opportunity to grow. It's how you grow. You grow by making mistakes, being truthful about your mistakes, acknowledging that your unskillful actions lead to suffering, and, in turn, changing, purifying your actions, out of compassion for yourself. It's important to learn to be truthful with yourself about your actions, all your actions, physical, verbal, mental. The Buddha's path, like any authentic spiritual path, requires rigorous honesty. Nobody, of course, likes to look at their unskillfulness, their mistakes, their faults, their failures. But it's necessary. It's necessary to develop the skill of truthfulness.

Again, we're not talking about judging ourselves. In looking truthfully at our unskillful actions, we relinquish self-judgment; instead of judging ourselves, we recognize that our actions have brought about suffering. We examine our actions objectively, the way a grocer inventories his stock: he counts the cans of peas on his shelves, but doesn't comment, editorialize, criticize ("These are the worst peas I've ever seen!"). As dharma students, we take inventory: we identify whether our actions are unskillful or skillful, whether they're leading to suffering or the end of suffering.

It's not about self-judgment; self-judgment is action informed by aversion. It's about compassion. Looking truthfully at our actions is an act of compassion.

We develop the skillful quality of truthfulness out of compassion for ourselves. Because we have a wish to come to the end of suffering.

As always, it's a process. As we move further along the path, we gradually make more effort to be truthful. We develop a desire to practice truthfulness. The spirit that Thoreau describes in *Walden* begins to resonate:

"Rather than love, than money, than fame, give me truth."

TRUE TO YOUR WORD

Thanissaro Bhikkhu describes a form of truthfulness considered very important in Asian Buddhist countries such as Thailand: being true to your word. Being true to your word, simply enough, means that when you say you're going to do something, you do it. You stick to your word.

As Thanissaro Bhikkhu explains:

> "If you say you're going to do something, you do it. If you say you're going to give up something, you give it up. You keep your promises—both the ones you make to yourself and the ones you make to others. In other words, truthfulness is not just a quality of your words. It's a quality of your character."

You might believe that, in the grand scheme of things, being true to your word isn't all that important. You might not think it's a theme that requires much attention.

But it's important.

If you don't think it's important, you're not going to make an effort to look to see if, in fact, you're not being true to your word. But if you look, you might see that you have a greater tendency than you thought for not sticking to your word.

The ways in which we engage in this form of unskillfulness may be blatant and subtle.

Some blatant examples:

You make an appointment with a business partner and don't show up for the meeting.

You tell your kid you're going to take him to a baseball game and don't follow through.

You tell your partner you're going to pay the electric bill, but you spend all your money at the mall and can't pay the bill.

Perhaps these are harsh examples. Perhaps you don't generally act in these sorts of blatantly unskillful ways. There may, however, be subtle ways that you don't stick to your word. There may be times, for instance, when you say to a friend, "I'll give you a call," but then you don't bother to call. Or you tell your partner that you'll take out the trash but then neglect to do so. Sometimes students indicate that they're going to attend a class, but they don't show up.

Often in these situations you make an offhand remark. "I'll give you a call." Maybe you're not sure that you'll actually make the call. You're just saying it. It seems like the thing to say. But you should be careful about what you say. You shouldn't say, "I'll give you a call," unless you're pretty sure that you're going to stay to your word.

We make these offhand remarks because we don't realize that there will be harmful consequences if we don't keep to our word. In cultivating truthfulness, we're asked to study the results of our actions, to notice the drawbacks in not being true to our word. If we scrutinize the results when not true to our word, we may notice that we're beset by some form of suffering. If we look at the body we may notice agitation, dis-ease. Several years ago I was an instructor in an Insight Meditation correspondence course. Students completed exercises pertaining to different meditation themes, and after writing about their experiences, sent me their work. I responded, guided them, offered suggestions. After doing this for a while, I began to feel a decided agitation. The reason was, I wasn't sticking to my word. In the introductory letter I'd sent the students, I had indicated that I'd respond to their work in 7 – 10 days, but I wasn't doing that. In some cases it was two or three weeks before I sent off a return letter. As I continued to send my responses later than I'd said I would, my agitation increased. I felt a self-loathing. I didn't feel good about myself. Finally, realizing I wasn't being true to my word, I made a vow to respond to every student in 7 – 10 days. I stuck to that vow, and my agitation dissolved.

When we don't stick to our word, we suffer a loss of self-esteem. We perceive ourselves as untrue, lacking trustworthiness. We perceive ourselves as somebody with questionable integrity.

When we aren't true to our word, others view us with a negative eye. They consider us somebody who isn't trustworthy, who can't be depended upon.

If we haven't been true to our word, if we haven't followed through in the manner we've promised, others may remember that days, weeks, even years later. Somewhere along the line they may decide they can't rely on us.

When we're not true to our word, we attract unreliable people. It makes sense. People with a good deal of integrity don't want to spend time with people of doubtful integrity. Monopoly players don't hang out with Scrabble players; they hang out with other Monopoly players. When we're in the habit of being untruthful, we find ourselves, more and more, in the company of other people who have a hard time sticking to their word.

In relationship, truth is essential. In an atmosphere marred by a lack of truthfulness, relationships fracture. At times it might seem easier to tell somebody, your partner, your kid, that you're going to do something, even though you know you're not going to do it. In these instances, you must be heedful. You have to pay attention to what you're doing. You have to remember that the consequences of your actions may prove more detrimental than you might think.

The "easiest" route isn't always the most beneficial, the most compassionate. In any case, dharma practice isn't about taking the easy way out; it's about doing what's necessary so that you might find a greater happiness in your life.

The good news is, if there are drawbacks in not being true to your word, there are benefits in cultivating this form of truthfulness.

Instead of being plagued by agitation, you experience tranquility, ease.

You perceive yourself as somebody with integrity.

You build self-esteem.

As you develop in truthfulness, you attract people with similar qualities. An important benefit. As the Buddha explained, community with wise and skillful beings is the most critical external factor that supports our efforts to find happiness.

As you develop the ability to stay to your word when you make promises to others, you'll develop your ability to stay to your word when you make promises to yourself. As you cultivate truthfulness you'll find, more and more, that you're able to stick to the vows you make to yourself, in terms of your dharma practice, in terms of the facets of your life, work, relationship, and so on. In the past, you may have found it difficult to keep to your word when you made promises to yourself. There may have been times when you vowed to put more effort into meditation practice, but failed to stay to that vow. You may have promised yourself to spend more time pursuing your creative interests, but didn't keep that promise. It may not be easy to be true to your word when it comes to the promises you make to yourself. If it's been difficult in the past to be true to your word, it may represent a significant challenge. But you can learn to do it. You can change.

If you begin to make a wholehearted effort to keep to your word when you make promises to others, you'll begin to move gradually toward being able to be true to your word when you make promises to the person with whom you have the greatest struggle: yourself. When you tell yourself that you're going to put more effort into practicing the dharma, you'll keep to your word. When you make a vow to yourself to spend more time with your kids, you'll hold to that vow.

For most of us, not staying to our word is a habit. It's a habit, undoubtedly, that we've learned by watching others. Perhaps our parents didn't stick to their word. Or our teachers, co-workers, friends.

It's a habit, however, that we can change. We can learn to be true to our word. We can learn to develop truthfulness.

It's a skill.

It requires that you practice heedfulness. The framework, as ever, is provided in the Rahula sutta. Before you act, you ask: Is this action going to be skillful? Before you tell somebody that you're going to do something, you ask: Is this what I should say? Am I going to be able to follow through on this promise? Will there be drawbacks if I don't?

Before you "blow off" your friend, you ask: Am I being true to my word? If you tell your friend you're going to help her paint her apartment, but then find yourself thinking about backing out, you ask: Am I being true? Am I doing what I said I'd do? Will there be consequences if I don't stick to my word?

It's a skill.

If you develop the skill of being true to your word, it will make a great difference in your dharma practice and your life.

It's important.

TRUE TO THE PRACTICE

What does it mean to be true to the practice? Think about a personal relationship. If you're in a committed relationship, you're true to your partner. You're there for your partner. No matter the situation, whether things are going well or not so well, you're there. You're true.

As dharma students we resolve to keep to the path, to make every effort to find a greater happiness, a happiness that transcends the happiness that comes from subscribing to the "ways of the world." There will be times, however, when we'll veer off the path, when we'll decide to go along with the ways of the world, when we'll decide to look for happiness in sense pleasure, gain, status, praise. In veering off, in following the world's "dharma," we're not being true to the practice. Of course, it's a process. Typically we stay on the path for awhile, then veer off, then eventually get back on the path. After practicing the dharma for a while, we're able to stay on the path for longer stretches. When we veer off, we don't go as far from the path. We return more quickly. More and more, we're true to the practice.

When we're true to the practice, we practice. We show up for the practice.

When we're true to the practice, we put effort into developing skillful qualities, concentration, insight. We put in the work. Some people don't like that word: work. They take a negative view of the concept, the whole idea of work. Some people think dharma practice shouldn't be work. But the unalterable fact is, the practice requires work. Often hard work.

It's a practice that asks that you do something. It's why the word "practice" is a good word for it. "Practice" implies that you've got to do something. It's all about doing. It's important to understand this. Certainly there's an inclination amongst those interested in the Buddha's path to bypass the work, the day-to-day practice, and instead to try to establish a foothold in the dharma by reading books, listening to dharma talks, etc. There's an abundant supply of dharma books, and in recent times there's been a profusion of dharma talks made available through internet technology. The danger of this proliferation of books and talks is that prospective students will choose a passive approach, believing they can be genuine dharma students by sitting on the couch, reading books, listening to downloaded talks. For some time I've resisted writing a dharma book, afraid I'd be contributing to this sort of misguided approach. One of the things I'd like to make clear in this book is that true happiness won't be found by reading these words. You've got to do something. You've got to practice. Skillful qualities are only developed by engaging in an active process. The Buddha frequently emphasized the active, hands-on nature of the practice. His message is especially important today, in our technology-driven culture where there's an ever-increasing tendency to sit back and passively receive information, push a button, click an icon.

The practice requires that you practice. If you're not practicing, if you're not doing the work, you're not being true to the practice.

We study the dharma, go to classes, and read books so that we might learn about the skills the Buddha taught, so that we might learn about the methods for developing skillful qualities, concentration, insight. We study the teachings, in other words, to learn how to practice. But we have to practice.

In the west, at this juncture, we're in the fortunate position of having unprecedented access to the Buddha's teachings. When I began my practice there were hardly any viable English language translations of the Pali Canon, the collection of the Buddha's suttas (the teachings he gave as he traveled Northern India). Today we have an opportunity to learn from clear, readable translations of the Canon. Today we're able to study these teachings, put them to use. The question is: Are we putting them to use?

Following the Buddha's instructions, developing the skills he taught, is an important way that we can be true to the practice. As dharma students interested in finding a greater happiness, we should give serious thought to how we're implementing the Buddha's teachings. Are we following the Buddha's instructions? Are we giving short shrift to the Buddha's methodologies? Are we picking and choosing what we like? Are we doing our own thing, devising our own dharma?

There isn't any question that leaders in dharma communities should learn to adapt the Buddha's teachings to the conditions of modern life. Creativity is essential. Improvisation is essential. Much of the instruction I provide is geared to teaching students to develop dharma practice as householders living in New York City amidst the complexities of urban life. As I see it, in offering these teachings it's my responsibility to stay true to the practice, to maintain the direction the Buddha gave us. From my experience, it's entirely possible to make the teachings relevant and still be true to the practice.

We have to pay attention to what the Buddha taught. Teaching the dharma in the west, in today's world, is a work in progress, an unfolding process. But it's important, as we engage in this process, that we don't lose sight of the heart of the teachings. In an attempt to make the dharma more accessible there's sometimes a tendency to allow integral elements of the Buddha's message to filter away. There's a tendency to disregard critical aspects of the path, to throw out the proverbial baby with the bathwater.

The Insight Meditation style that's evolved over the last few decades has placed its emphasis on silent meditation practice. For many students, the occasional retreat and a daily meditation period of perhaps 30 minutes comprises their dharma practice. But, clearly, this emphasis on "closed eyes" practice isn't consonant with what the Buddha taught. Retreats are helpful. Daily sitting meditation is important. But there's a lot more to dharma practice. The focus on "closed eyes" practice is limited. For one thing, it leaves a substantial quantity of time, most of the day, when the practitioner isn't practicing, isn't following the path. Dharma practice is meant to be a way of life; it isn't meant to be a discreet event, a compartment in a life. It's critical that we learn to practice the dharma in the "open eyes" posture. Contemporary students attempting to be true to the practice have to learn to make every moment a moment when they're on the path. They have to learn to align their lives with the dharma. They have to learn to live the dharma.

As we develop qualities such as generosity and ethical conduct, we learn to live the dharma. However, developing skillful qualities isn't emphasized in most western dharma settings.

Breath meditation, the Buddha's central method for developing concentration, is generally taught in a watered-down form. The instructions for cultivating jhana generally aren't given. But the fact remains that students must to learn to cultivate the factors of jhana if they wish to deepen their practice and truly understand suffering, find freedom from it, and know a greater happiness in their lives. It's what the Buddha taught. And he had good reasons for teaching it.

As serious dharma practitioners, we should reflect on the direction we're taking. We should ask: Am I following the path the Buddha laid out? Am I being true to what the Buddha taught?

In being true to the practice, you commit yourself to the practice. You commit yourself to ending your suffering and finding true happiness. You forge a commitment to yourself. In thinking about what it means to make a commitment, we might once again consider the analogy of a personal relationship. If you have a commitment to your kid, you show up for him, you're there for him. Moreover, you're there in a wholehearted manner. If you show up for your kid, but you're consumed with resentment, you're not being true in the deepest sense. If you take your kid to the ballgame as promised, but all the while you're wishing you were somewhere else, you're not being true inside, in the heart. When you're true to the practice, you practice wholeheartedly. You're motivated by the heart, by love, compassion. Your heart is in it.

It's important every now and again to take a hard look at your practice, to look at what you're doing, how you're doing it. Are you being true to the practice? Are you showing up? Is your practice wholehearted? Is your heart in it?

As you move forward wholeheartedly your commitment will grow. As you come to know the benefits of dharma practice, your commitment will grow. As you learn to take joy in the practice, your commitment will grow. It's a process. Commitment grows little by slowly, over time.

One of the ways I mark my progress as a dharma student is by the growth of my commitment. As the years have gone on, I've seen my commitment strengthen, become increasingly wholehearted. More and more, my heart is in it.

As we move further along the path, the commitment in the heart strengthens. We become more true to the practice.

PRACTICE SUGGESTIONS

REFLECTION:

Do I engage in false speech?

REFLECTION:

How do I lie?

REFLECTION:

Do I understand the drawbacks in false speech?

PRACTICE:

Resolve to practice truthfulness, to refrain from false speech, including blatant and subtle lying. Notice the benefits. If you engage in false speech, notice the drawbacks.

REFLECTION:

How does lying influence my ability to be truthful with myself? Do I understand the correlation?

REFLECTION:

Am I truthful with myself about myself, about my actions, physical, verbal, mental?

REFLECTION:

Am I true to my word?

PRACTICE:

Make a vow to be true to your word. Pay particular attention to the subtle ways in which you say something but do not follow through. Notice the benefits in sticking to your word. If you're not true to your word, notice the drawbacks.

REFLECTION:

Where am I in terms of being true to the practice?

REFLECTION:

Do I practice? Or is my relationship to the dharma focused on dharma study, reading books, listening to talks, etc.?

REFLECTION:

Am I following the Buddha's instructions? Am I being true to the teachings?

REFLECTION:

To what extent do I practice the dharma in the "open eyes" posture? Do I tend to emphasize formal "closed eyes" practice? Do I under-stand that dharma practice is not meant to be a compartment in a life, but rather a way of life?

REFLECTION:

Is my relationship to my practice wholehearted? Is my heart in it?

PRACTICE:

Take a broad view of your dharma practice. Establish a "vision" for your practice. What is your purpose in following the path? Write it down. Delineate a "game plan" for practice in both the "closed" and "open" eyes postures. Be specific; write down ways that you'll seek to cultivate skillful qualities, concentration, insight.

REFLECTION:

What is my commitment to dharma practice?

CHAPTER FOUR

EFFORT & DETERMINATION

SKILLFUL EFFORT

Some dharma teachers may be reluctant to encourage students to make strong effort. The Buddha, however, wasn't at all shy about urging his disciples to put strong effort into their practice. The Buddha stressed the criticalness of making effort. In doing so, he often explained to his followers that he was exhorting them because he had compassion for them, because he wanted them to find an end to suffering.

It takes strong effort to practice the dharma. It takes strong effort to follow the Buddha's path. It isn't a path for the lazy or halfhearted. It isn't a path for anybody looking for an easy way out.

Like any meaningful undertaking dharma practice requires great effort. Think about anybody who's achieved a high level of proficiency in a particular area. Chances are, they've made exceptional effort. Very little in life is accomplished without a degree of perspiration, a good amount of effort. I recently watched an interview with a renowned guitar player. I'm always interested in listening to people who've attained virtuosity in their chosen field. In the interview the guitarist indicated that as he cultivated his skill he practiced eight hours every day. When we watch somebody display great expertise, it all may seem rather effortless; but the truth is, it takes a lot of practice, a lot of effort to reach that seemingly effortless state.

As dharma students we're asked to make strong effort. But we're asked to make a certain kind of effort: skillful effort. Our effort must be skillful.

During the course of our lives, most of us have probably had a rather unskillful relationship to the subject of effort. In making effort, in whatever context, we've probably cultivated bad habits. We've probably caused ourselves suffering. Most of us, of course, were never shown how to make skillful effort. It wasn't a subject that was taught in school. The people who served as models for us, parents, teachers, bosses, probably showed us how to make unskillful effort. In all likelihood we've learned ways of making effort that aren't useful in terms of finding true happiness in our lives.

You might want to take a few moments right now to reflect on the relationship you've had during your life to the quality of effort.

Put your attention on your breath. Have a sense of your body.

Reflect.

"What kind of relationship do I have to effort?"

"What have I learned in my life when it comes to effort?"

"Do I tend to make effort in an unskillful fashion?"

Allow the reflection to reside in the body. Let understanding form.

Many of us don't take a positive view of the subject of effort. This may be why dharma teachers don't like to talk too much about this particular skillful quality, why they don't urge students to make strong effort. Because students may have an historically problematic relationship to effort, because they may have a tendency to push themselves too hard, because they may have a tendency to be hard on themselves, because their habitual ways of making effort may be stress-producing, because they may have been pressed, treated unkindly by parents, teachers, etc., the inclination, for some teachers, may be to bypass the subject. But when teachers don't encourage students to make strong effort, they aren't doing students any favors. To meet the needs of students who have a difficult relationship to the subject of effort, the solution isn't to ignore the subject. The solution is to teach students to make skillful effort.

As dharma practitioners we make effort in the service of abandoning the unskillful and developing the skillful.

As the Buddha explains:

"And what, monks, is right effort? (**i**) There is the case where a monk generates desire, endeavors, activates persistence, upholds & exerts his intent for the sake of the non-arising of evil, unskillful qualities that have not yet arisen. (**ii**) He generates desire, endeavors, activates persistence, upholds & exerts his intent for the sake of the abandonment of evil, unskillful qualities that have arisen. (**iii**) He generates desire, endeavors, activates persistence, upholds & exerts his intent for the sake of the arising of skillful qualities that have not yet arisen. (**iv**) He generates desire, endeavors, activates persistence, upholds & exerts his intent for the maintenance, non-confusion, increase, plenitude, development, & culmination of skillful qualities that have arisen: This, monks, is called right effort."
(SN 45.8)

In developing skillful effort we pay attention to: (1) the quantity of our effort and (2) the quality of our effort.

It's important to be mindful of the quantity of our effort. In practicing the dharma we have to make sure we're putting in the right amount of effort. Effort must be balanced. To this end we're asked, in developing skillful effort, to discern whether we're making too little effort or too much effort.

In observing the quantity of our effort, we examine the effort we're making on what we might call the "macro" and "micro" levels.

In examining our effort on the macro level, we step back and take a broad view of our practice. Assessing the quantity of your effort on the macro level, you may discern that you're not making enough effort. You may discern that you're not putting enough time into developing skillful qualities. You may discern that you're not putting enough effort into developing a specific skillful quality.

You may recognize that you need to make greater effort to practice breath meditation. You've been meditating perhaps four or five day a week. It's not enough, you realize. In order to develop sufficient concentration you're going to need to meditate every day.

You may perceive that you need to meditate for longer periods. You usually sit for about twenty minutes, but if you're going to move forward, you realize, you're going to need to meditate for at least thirty minutes every day.

You may conclude that you're not putting enough effort into practicing natural mediation. You're not keeping the breath in mind during the course of the day. You're not attempting to maintain present moment awareness. (We'll talk more about natural meditation in a later chapter.)

Conversely, you may discern that you're making too much effort.

You may discern that you're putting too much time into "closed eyes" practice. You've been sitting twice a day, for long stretches. You've been going on lots of retreats. You've been overdoing it, you realize. As a result, you've been neglecting other parts of your life. You haven't been taking much-needed actions with regard to your work life. You haven't been attending to important relationships. All the meditation, you see, isn't supporting your efforts to end suffering. You need to cut back, reduce the amount of time you're spending on the proverbial cushion.

When we observe our effort on the micro level, we observe the effort we're making from moment to moment, as we're practicing the dharma. Scrutinizing your effort while meditating, you may discern that you're not applying sufficient effort. You're chasing after thoughts, going off on tangents, and you're not making much, if any, effort to bring your attention back to the breath. Recognizing that your effort is slack, you increase it. You turn it up.

We increase effort largely by inclining to the quality of effort. We assert the intention to make more effort. We tell ourselves: More effort. We have an innate ability for making effort. We have the skillful quality of effort. It may not be well-developed, but we have it. By inclining to this quality, shining the light of our awareness on it, we're able to connect to our capacity for making effort.

You can try it right now.

Have the intention to increase the effort you're putting into reading these words.

"More effort."

Incline toward the skillful quality of effort.

As you're reading, apply increased effort.

Examining your effort on the micro level, you may notice, while practicing breath meditation, that you're making too much effort. You may notice that you're trying too hard. Gritting your teeth, dripping sweat, you're pushing like a jogger with a twisted ankle trying to run up a hill. This sort of over-efforting creates tension, dis-ease. It prevents you, in fact, from developing concentration.

Sometimes I notice, while I'm working with the phase of breath meditation known as "evaluation," that I'm trying too hard. In practicing "evaluation" we cultivate an easeful breath. Perhaps needless to say, my over-trying undermines my ability to cultivate a comfortable, easeful abiding. Aware that I'm pushing, I'll turn down my effort, soften it. Inclining my mind to the faculty of effort, I'll assert an intention to make less effort.

In the sutta, "About Sona," the Buddha explains how to cultivate skillful effort. Sona was a monk with a propensity for making an inordinate amount of effort. It seems he was putting so much effort into walking meditation that his feet were bleeding. Clearly, the way Sona was going about things wasn't working. And he was getting discouraged. In fact, he was considering giving up the monk's life.

When effort is unskillful, we often find dharma practice unpleasant, and, consequently, we often build up an aversion to the practice. The aversion frequently leads to doubt. We doubt our ability to practice. We doubt the practice itself. Many practitioners get caught in this syndrome. It's something to watch for. If your effort is unskillful, chances are you'll fall into this trap. You'll begin to dislike the practice. You'll begin to register doubt.

Luckily for Sona, the Buddha was clued in to his dilemma. He taught Sona to develop skillful effort:

"Now what do you think, Sona. Before, when you were a house-dweller, were you skilled at playing the vina?"

"Yes, lord."

"And what do you think: when the strings of your vina were too taut, was your vina in tune & playable?"

"No, lord."

"And what do you think: when the strings of your vina were too loose, was your vina in tune & playable?"

"No, lord."

"And what do you think: when the strings of your vina were neither too taut nor too loose, but tuned to be right on pitch, was your vina in tune & playable?"

"Yes, lord."

"In the same way, Sona, over-aroused persistence leads to restlessness, overly slack persistence leads to laziness. Thus you should determine the right pitch for your persistence."

(AN 6.55)

If effort isn't balanced, the Buddha says, we'll produce an untoward result, in the same way that a stringed instrument such as a vina (lute or guitar), if not tuned properly, will produce a dissonant sound. If the strings of a guitar are too tight or too loose, the effect will be unpleasant. It doesn't matter if the musician is profoundly talented; if Eric Clapton is playing a guitar that's out of tune, he isn't going to generate a pleasing sound. In dharma practice, if our effort isn't "in tune" we'll get similarly unpleasant results.

Like a musician who learns to detect when his guitar is out of tune, the dharma student learns to discern the "pitch" of his effort. When he notices he's making insufficient effort, he turns the effort up. He tightens the strings. When he's making too much effort, he turns it down, loosens the strings.

As dharma students cultivating skillful effort we learn to distinguish the "right" amount of effort. Not too little. Not too much. Just right. In tune. When we find the right pitch, our practice flourishes.

There have probably been times during your life, when you were involved in certain endeavors, when you didn't mind making a lot of effort. You didn't hesitate to make effort. In all likelihood your strong exertion was in the service of doing something you wanted to do, something you enjoyed. This was my experience when I played soccer in high school and college. The sport required much effort. Practices were often grueling, but I didn't mind. To the contrary, I loved every minute of it. I loved the practices. I loved everything about the game. Putting effort into it wasn't a problem; it was a joy.

In traversing the Buddha's path, we have to learn to develop this same kind of heartful effort. We have to learn to practice heartfully. We have to learn to put our heart into the practice.

The heart quality that motivates dharma practice is compassion; we practice out of compassion for ourselves, so that we might end our suffering.

In making effort, the quality of our effort must be skillful, driven by skillful intention, by compassion.

You may not have a heartful relationship to dharma practice; you may not be in the habit of making effort that's informed by the heart, by compassion. But that's okay; you can learn to put your heart into your practice.

It's all about intention. If your intention is skillful, imbued with compassion, the quality of your effort will be skillful.

And you can develop skillful intention.

As you practice the dharma, it's important to pay close attention to the quality of your intention. Is your intention unskillful? Is it driven by unskillful mental factors, by desire, aversion, delusion? Or is it driven by love, compassion?

As you take a broad view, as you scrutinize your practice on the macro level, you may discern that the quality of your effort is unskillful.

You may discern that your effort is informed by unskillful desire. As a dharma student you must have a desire to follow the path. Without the desire to practice and achieve a true happiness, we won't get very far. The Buddha emphasized the importance of cultivating "skillful desire." But desire sometimes turns unskillful. You may, for instance, have a desire to get further along the path than, at the moment, you're ready to get. You may have a desire to achieve things that, at this point in your development, you're not ready to achieve. If you get caught in this kind of desire, your forward movement will in fact be hampered.

You may notice, in looking at your dharma practice on the macro level, that you have an aversive relationship to your practice. You're at odds with the practice.

You may discern that your intention is imbued with delusion. You're moving along the path like somebody moving through a thick fog. You're not quite sure where you're going.

In being mindful of your effort on the micro level (while practicing) you might see that your effort is corrupted by unskillful factors.

You might see that you're compelled by an excessive desire to obtain results. You're spending more time thinking about what you want from the practice rather than actually practicing. You're pushing too hard. You're getting frustrated when you don't achieve certain results. We might think of unskillful desire as "wanting what we don't have." While practicing breath meditation you might not be experiencing the jhana factors, ease, pleasure, and you may begin to crave these states, your mind may be afflicted with a painful wanting. "Wanting results" is one of the primary manifestations of unskillful effort. This sort of wanting will only hinder your ability to cultivate concentration.

When desire becomes unskillful we often find ourselves trying to manufacture results, instead of putting our effort into developing the causes that will lead to results. In practice, this is where the effort is put: in developing the causes.

As you sit down to meditate, you may notice that you're riddled with aversion. You don't want to be doing what you're doing. Like a kid who doesn't want to play the piano, you're practicing, but you're not happy about it.

You might notice, while practicing at home, that you keep checking the clock, longing for the meditation to be finished. This is usually a sign that there's aversion in your mind, that your intention has turned unskillful.

There may be times when you're consumed with dread. During my early years of practice, I was frequently stricken with dread when I approached the meditation cushion.

You may discern, when meditating, that your intention is marred by delusion. You're not in touch with any clear-cut intention. As you take your seat on the cushion or chair, you're like somebody who's been getting on the same commuter train every day for the past twenty years. You're going through the motions.

As dharma students developing skillful effort, we seek to purify our intention. We recognize when our intention is unskillful, infused with desire, aversion, delusion. In recognizing our intention, we assume the role of the observer. We step back from the unskillful mental quality, observe it. We get some distance from it. We stop feeding it. The unskillful quality, in turn, begins to lose its power.

Abandoning unskillful intention, we develop skillful intention.

As we've said, we develop skillful intention by: (1) asserting directed thought and (2) connecting to a felt sense.

Taking the broad view, considering our practice on the macro level, we establish a skillful resolve. We resolve to follow the path out of compassion for ourselves, so that we might come to the end of suffering.

On the micro level, we develop a skillful intention whenever we make an effort to cultivate skillful qualities, concentration, insight.

When we sit down to meditate, we see what the mind is like. Then we set a skillful intention. We assert that we're going to practice mindfulness of breathing, and we're going to practice out of compassion for ourselves. We connect to a felt sense of the heart, the feeling of compassion.

It's important to set a skillful intention at the beginning of every period of formal meditation. In teaching mindfulness of breathing, I always emphasize the importance of setting intention. If we remember to set a heartful intention every time we practice breath meditation, it will make a significant difference. It will put us on the right track. It will put us on the path.

After my morning meditation and before attending to the day's affairs, I'll set an intention to practice natural meditation as the day goes on. Asserting directed thought, I'll say something along the lines of: I'm going make an effort to keep the breath in mind throughout the day. I'm going to practice natural meditation out of compassion for myself. I'll put my attention on my heart center and apprehend a felt sense of compassion.

During the day I'll check my intention, I'll look to see if I'm staying to it, if I'm making a wholehearted effort to keep the breath in mind. If I see that I've lost the thread, I'll re-set my intention.

In order to move forward toward a greater happiness, we have to learn to make skillful effort. It's such an important element of the path. When effort is unskillful, our ability to move forward is greatly diminished. Think about Sona. Plagued by his out-of-tune effort, he came close to forsaking the dharma.

In many ways, it's the skillfulness of our effort that determines our ability to go on. When effort is skillful, we keep going.

Sona, in fact, became fully enlightened, an arahant, not long after he learned to adjust his effort. And although we might not become arahants, we'll certainly come to know the fruits of the path if we learn to make skillful effort.

TAKING JOY

As we've said, the five key steps in the process for developing skillful action include:

1-Seeing what the mind is like.
2-Developing skillful intention.
3-Acting.
4-Seeing the benefits in skillful action.
5-Taking joy.

Taking joy is integral. It's necessary, the same way that water is necessary for plants to live and grow. Joy enables the skillful qualities to grow.

The fact is, the Buddha and his companions were not a grim bunch. They made great effort, but they were joyful. They didn't gripe, didn't complain, as they journeyed along the path. They took joy in their effort. Their hearts were filled with joy.

As a dharma student, you're asked to follow the example set by the Buddha and his cohorts. You're asked to cultivate joy. You're asked to practice joyfully.

Joy is a quality of the heart. It's the quality that responds to goodness, our own goodness, the goodness in life. It's an everpresent quality, part of the way things are, the dharma, the truth. It's a quality that exists within us, always. It's there, in the heart. But we're often not connected to it. In practicing the dharma, we learn to connect to joy. We learn to take joy.

It's a skill. Taking joy is a skill.

As dharma students, we're proactive. We don't hang out waiting for things to happen. We don't wait around for joy to suddenly appear. Maybe, if we're lucky, joy will arise. Maybe one day our ship will come in. No. We act. We actively cultivate joy.

There are three basic steps for cultivating joy:

1-Recognizing the blessing of our goodness (skillful qualities).
2-Connecting to gratitude.
3-Connecting to joy.

In the Rahula sutta, the Buddha instructs young Rahula in taking joy in his skillfulness. After you've acted skillfully, he tells Rahula, recognize it, take note of your goodness, take joy in it.

> "(Having done a bodily action) if on reflection you know that it did not lead to affliction... it was a skillful bodily action with pleasant consequences, pleasant results, then you should stay mentally refreshed & joyful, training day & night in skillful mental qualities."

In the "Mahanama Sutta" the Buddha encourages Mahanama, a householder, to recollect his skillful qualities and take joy in them. In the following passage, the Buddha speaks to Mahanama about recollecting his generosity:

"Furthermore, there is the case where you recollect your own generosity: 'It is a gain, a great gain for me, that — among people overcome with the stain of possessiveness — I live at home, my awareness cleansed of the stain of possessiveness, freely generous, openhanded, delighting in being magnanimous, responsive to requests, delighting in the distribution of alms.' At any time when a disciple of the noble ones is recollecting generosity, his mind is not overcome with passion, not overcome with aversion, not overcome with delusion. His mind heads straight, based on generosity. And when the mind is headed straight, the disciple of the noble ones gains a sense of the goal, gains a sense of the Dhamma, gains joy connected with the Dhamma. In one who is joyful, rapture arises. In one who is rapturous, the body grows calm. One whose body is calmed experiences ease. In one at ease, the mind becomes concentrated.

"Of one who does this, Mahanama, it is said: 'Among those who are out of tune, the disciple of the noble ones dwells in tune; among those who are malicious, he dwells without malice; having attained the stream of Dhamma, he develops the recollection of generosity.'
(AN 11.12)

In cultivating the skillful qualities we recollect our goodness. We think about our good qualities, the ways we've acted skillfully. It may not be the sort of stuff that you normally think about. It's something, however, that you've got to learn to think about.

You're asked, in taking joy in your skillful effort, to reflect on the effort you've made to abandon the unskillful and develop the skillful. You're asked to reflect on the effort you've made to practice breath meditation. And the effort you've made to stay with the breath during daily life.

There might be voices in your mind that object. As you acknowledge your effort, there might be voices that contend you're not making very good effort. The voices may insist that you're not doing enough, that you're not doing it right, and so on. It's important to notice these voices, these tendencies to criticize yourself, sabotage yourself. It's important to see these voices for what they are, just voices in the mind, just thoughts.

It's sometimes helpful to think of these voices as Mara. Mara, in Buddhist tradition, is the personification of unskillfulness, desire, aversion, delusion. Hearing one of these voices, you might identify it as Mara babbling on, trying to cause trouble, trying to throw you off the path. In a firm tone, you might tell Mara: "Thanks for sharing. But I'm not going to put any stock in what you're saying."

As you reflect on your skillful qualities, recognize that it's a blessing to have these qualities. This is a crucial perception. It's a blessing. It's a blessing that you're able to act skillfully, that you're able to express your goodness. It's a blessing that, as a human being, you have the ability to develop these good qualities.

As you reflect, let your awareness reside in your body. Allow the perception of your skillful qualities to infiltrate your body. "Sit" for a moment with the understanding that these qualities are a blessing. See if you can move beyond merely thinking about the blessing of your good qualities. Move beyond the level of "verbal" or "intellectual" thought. Recognize the truth, the truth of your blessings, in your body.

Reflecting on your blessings, begin to connect to a feeling of gratitude. When we recognize that we're blessed, we feel gratitude. Gratitude is a mental state, an emotion. In fact, it's one of the most useful emotions. As you connect to the quality of gratitude, keep your attention on your body and see if you can connect to a felt sense of gratitude. Feel gratitude.

Then incline your awareness toward your heart, toward the quality of joy.

Gratitude gives rise to joy. Appreciative joy. The joy that emerges in the heart as we appreciate our goodness.

Joy is there. It's always there, in the heart.

As you shift your awareness toward the heart, try to distinguish the quality of joy. You may experience joy as a brightness in the heart area. A light. It's hard to describe. It's something you'll have to come to know for yourself. The way I experience it may be different than the way you'll experience it. In any case, you'll have to discover how it arises for you. It takes practice. That's basically it. You've got to practice.

It is perhaps a subtle art, connecting to the heart. But if you practice, you'll develop the ability to connect. You'll learn to know the brightness in the heart, the quality of joy.

In the beginning, as you attempt to connect, you may notice just a hint of joy. Maybe just a faint bit of light. And that's okay. In fact, it's more than okay. It's just what you need. It's all you need. Often times, in trying to connect to the heart, we make the mistake of looking for a big experience, a grand spectacle of light, an explosion of light, something like that. It's how we are. We like big things. But it's not what we're looking for; we're looking for some brightness, some light, a bit of light, a small subtle bit of light.

There are various times when you might cultivate joy.

Really, you can do it just about any time.

The most obvious time to take joy, keeping to the Buddha's instructions to Rahula, is right after you've acted skillfully. After practicing generosity, after making skillful effort, after taking any skillful action, you might take time to reflect, to recognize the blessing of your goodness.

At different times during the day you might also pause and reflect on the blessing of your skillful qualities. It's a good habit to develop. It's particularly helpful to cultivate joy when you're feeling downhearted, when there's darkness in the mind.

You might reflect on your skillful qualities at the outset of a period of formal meditation. This is an ideal time to take joy. If you make it a habit to "brighten the mind" before practicing sitting and walking meditation, it will have a remarkably beneficial effect on your ability to develop concentration.

It's important as you strive to abandon the unskillful and develop the skillful that you recognize the blessing of your effort. We tend to look for joy in the results, but as dharma students we learn to take joy in the effort we're making. When teaching beginners I encourage students, right off the bat, to take joy in their effort. Beginning students usually have a difficult time practicing breath meditation. They often become discouraged. They doubt their ability to meditate. After a while they may give up. For this reason, I teach new students to reflect on the blessing of their effort at the conclusion of every period of sitting meditation. The meditation might not have gone the way you wanted, I tell them. You might not have been able to pay attention to more than a couple of breaths. But you put in the effort. You developed the quality of effort. Instead of judging yourself, acknowledge your effort, the fact that you've made an effort to meditate, the fact that you're making an effort to do what you've got to do, to end your suffering and find a better life. Acknowledge the blessing of your effort, I tell them. Feel gratitude. Take joy.

Every meditation, I explain, is an opportunity to develop your practice. If you're not able to cultivate much concentration, you can still develop the skillful quality of effort.

When new students learn to take joy in their effort, they're less apt to become discouraged and give up. When things don't go according to plan (they often don't), when things are difficult (they often are), they recognize that they're developing important qualities, and, in turn, they stay with the practice, they go on.

Taking a few moments at the end of a sitting to reflect on the blessing of our effort is, of course, a good practice for all dharma students, regardless of how long we've been on the path.

There are always students who protest when I suggest they acknowledge their skillful qualities, their goodness. It's wrong, they say, to recognize their generosity, ethical conduct, truthfulness, effort. It's selfish. It's immodest. It indicates a lack of humility. They believe they shouldn't draw attention to themselves in this manner.

If you harbor these kinds of preconceived notions, it might be helpful to look at what the Buddha said. He said it was alright to recognize your goodness, and, in recognition, to take joy. He said that this was exactly what you should do. In the above sutta, he gives Mahanama explicit instructions: to recollect his skillful qualities. He says that the practitioner who engages in this recollection is "in tune" with the dharma.

> "Of one who does this, Mahanama, it is said: 'Among those who are out of tune, the disciple of the noble ones dwells in tune; among those who are malicious, he dwells without malice; having attained the stream of Dhamma, he develops the recollection of generosity.'

The truth is, it's alright to admit to your goodness. It's alright. More than that, it's essential.

It's essential that you learn to take joy.

We all need joy. It's a crucial element in our emotional, psychological, and spiritual health. Most of us could probably use a little more joy in our lives. Actually, most of us could probably use a lot more joy.

If you're going to continue forward along the Buddha's path, you're going to have to learn to take joy, to practice joyfully, to be a joyful dharma student.

In many ways, we're a cynical, skeptical lot. Standing in the thick shadows of the machineries of modern life, we tend to downplay things like joy. But as a dharma student it's essential that you to learn to take joy.

DETERMINATION:
TRAVELING THE LONG ROAD

The skillful quality of determination is characterized by the effort we make to practice the dharma over a period of time. Developing determination, we make ongoing, persistent effort. In breath meditation. During retreats. During the course of our days as we maintain mindfulness of the breath. During the long journey, the span of days, weeks, months, years, as we seek to abandon the unskillful and cultivate the skillful. We keep going. We stay with it.

Determination is an elemental skillful quality because dharma practice, by its nature, requires that we make effort over the long haul. Dharma practice is a gradual undertaking. It's a process that unfolds, usually pretty slowly, over time. As one teacher puts it, as we follow the path we experience a "gradual awakening." The Buddha compared the way the path unfolds, the way we evolve, the way our skills develop, to the way the ocean floor slopes: gradually, gradually, gradually.

> Just as the ocean has a gradual shelf, a gradual slope, a gradual inclination, with a sudden drop-off only after a long stretch, in the same way this Doctrine and Discipline has a gradual

training, a gradual performance, a gradual progression, with a penetration to gnosis only after a long stretch.
(Ud 5.5)

Generally speaking, we make slow progress. This is important to understand and to accept. If we expect to get on a fast track, we'll be setting ourselves up for struggle; we'll get bogged down by disappointment and frustration and self-doubt, and we'll inhibit our capacity to move forward. In the end, we won't get very far at all. The fact is, it's going to take a while to change the habits of a lifetime. Most of us are lugging heavy parcels of karma, all the consequences of our past actions, our tendencies for acting unskillfully, our deeply grooved patterns. It's going to take time. It's going to take time to develop skillfulness, train the mind, end suffering, find true happiness. It's a long road. Understanding this, we develop determination.

Cultivating the skillful quality of determination, we keep going, day after day, week after week, year after year. Realizing it's going to take an ongoing effort, we keep making effort. We keep at it. Skillfully. Joyfully.

It's a long road. And there will be times, undoubtedly many times, when you'll veer off the road. You'll veer off while practicing breath meditation. You'll lose purchase on the breath, veer off into daydreams, fantasies, planning, reminiscing. You'll be in your apartment in Brooklyn, meditating, but in your mind you'll be lying on a beach somewhere in Spain. In the middle of July, you'll be sitting on your meditation cushion, deeply involved in planning for Thanksgiving dinner.

As the months and years go on, there will be times when you'll lose the path. There will be times when you'll be detoured by the affairs of your householder's life, your work, your relationships. There will be times when you'll be sidetracked by your desire to follow the ways of the world, to seek after sense pleasure, gain, status, praise. There will be times when you'll stagger down the painful roads of depression, despair, grief, stress, anger, resentment, desire. There will be times when you'll find it difficult to put effort into developing skillful qualities (there will be times, almost certainly, when you'll put a concerted effort into developing unskillful qualities). There will be times when you'll have a hard time getting to the proverbial cushion, when you'll struggle to maintain your meditation practice. There will be times when you'll lose interest in the path. There will be times when you'll lose faith.

All of this is normal.

The fact is, everybody veers. The dharma student who has developed determination isn't somebody who doesn't veer; rather, he's someone who veers but then gets back on the path. This is how we cultivate determination: we veer but then, realizing we've veered, we make an effort to get back to the path.

We cultivate determination by making the effort, again and again, to regain the path.

As we practice breath meditation, we develop the quality of determination. The mind wanders incessantly. But we keep coming back, returning our attention to the breath. Again and again, we return.

In practicing the dharma over the course of weeks, months, years, we do the same thing. We keep coming back. When we veer off, we return to the path. We keep returning.

We cultivate determination by being mindful, by paying attention to what we're doing, where we're going. We notice when we've veered off. We're truthful about it.

Acknowledging that we've turned down a side road, we might take some time to reflect, to ask some simple but pointed questions.

What am I doing?

Where am I?

Where am I going?

Is this the most useful course to be taking?

Am I acting out of love and compassion for myself in following this road?

What's my most heartfelt wish for myself?

How can I most skillfully, most happily, take care of myself?

What's my intention for practicing the dharma?

The questions guide us. When we veer off the path, they re-orient us. They help us recognize, or re-recognize, where we want to go and why we want to go there. We ask the questions, but don't answer. Instead, we let the questions resound, move in gentle waves through the body. We foster embodied knowing, felt wisdom. When we live in the questions, as the poet Rilke advises, we begin to know, in the heart, what we've got to do.

After veering off the Buddha's road, we should reflect on our purpose, our intention for practicing the dharma. This is a crucial step in regaining the road. We should remind ourselves of why we practice. We should remind ourselves that we follow the path out of compassion for ourselves.

The bottom line is we make an effort to follow the path, we stay with it, day after day, year after year, because we suffer, because we want to come to the end of suffering. As we strive to regain the road we should remember that there's suffering in our lives and that we have a wish to find freedom from it. We should, in returning, connect to the heart, to the quality of compassion. Compassion for ourselves. Compassion is the heart's response to suffering. Compassion drives us, motivates us to practice the dharma in an effort to end our suffering. Compassion informs our journey toward true happiness. It empowers our intention.

Re-finding the path, you should establish clear intention: to practice the dharma out of compassion for yourself. If you don't develop skillful intention, you'll return, in all likelihood, influenced by an unskillful mental factor. You'll return, perhaps begrudgingly, like a kid who's been apprehended by the truant officer. You'll come back weighed down by self-judgment. You'll be stricken with regret or guilt or shame. You'll be afflicted with self-doubt.

After you've veered off the path, you might judge yourself. Self-judgment, it's critical to remember, is a major obstacle to moving forward in dharma practice. If you allow yourself to wander into self-judgment, it will be more difficult for you to get back on the path. As you make a determined effort to return to the path, you have to watch out for self-judgment. You have to make it a point to put aside thinking imbued with this kind of unskillful judgment. You have to replace self-judgment with compassion for yourself. In light of the fact that you've drifted from the road, you should have compassion for yourself. Compassion is the appropriate response.

As we travel the long road we'll find ourselves again and again confronted with the choice of following the Buddha's path or the world's path, the path of sense pleasure, gain, status, praise. We might face that choice every morning, as we consider whether to meditate or switch on the TV and watch the news. As we continue forward in dharma practice we acquire a deeper understanding of our choices. We begin to understand that the choice of which road to follow isn't much of a choice at all.

Gradually, we come to see with greater clarity that the Buddha's path offers the more beneficial option. Gradually, we veer less. We gain conviction in the path.

The path is often difficult, but as we move forward we realize that we don't have much choice but to follow it. What else are we going to do? Are we going to turn around and head back to where we were? Are we going to go back to the sort of life we had before? Gradually, we realize that it's a no-brainer. We know what we've got to do. And we do it. We keep at it. We keep going.

COMPLACENCY

As a teacher, I've been blessed to have students who've demonstrated great determination. They've stayed with it. They've kept practicing year after year.

I've been fortunate, as guiding teacher of DMC, to be able to work with a good number of students for many years. In the process I've come to see that the challenges faced by veteran practitioners take distinct shapes. After practicing eight, nine, ten years, students are often subject to complacency.

As a dharma student making effort over the long haul, you have to take stock on a regular basis. You have to practice circumspection. Circumspection is the capacity to self-monitor, to be mindful of the state of your practice, where it is, what direction its going in. It's a key skill, essential to the development of determination.

As you get further down the road, you have to watch for complacency. You have to check to see if you're resting on your laurels.

You have to learn to ask:

Where am I in my practice?

Am I continuing to move forward?

Is my practice stagnant?

Am I complacent?

Am I continuing to grow?

What do I need to do in order to grow?

In practicing the dharma, you have to keep moving forward. You can't stand still. You have to keep moving. You have to keep growing, always. If you don't continue to grow, your practice will deteriorate, wither.

As dharma students cultivating determination, we notice when we're standing still and, in turn, we ascertain what we have to do to get ourselves moving forward. This is a key aspect of the skill of developing determination: seeing what we need to do, what adjustments we need to make, so that we might get further down the road. Working with a teacher in deciding a course of action is always advised. It's often hard to see exactly where we have to go; a wise being, such as a teacher, can provide the needed guidance.

If your dharma practice has become stagnant, flat, you may need to take some time to re-establish your resolve; you may need to review your intention, remind yourself why you're following the path. Often times, when mired in complacency, we've lost sight of our intention. The weather in the mind has turned murky, cloudy; the mind is afflicted by delusion.

In the service of renewing your intention, you might ask some pertinent questions:

Why am I following the path?

What is my intention for practicing the dharma?

What is my purpose in developing skillful qualities, concentration, insight?

Is there suffering in my life?

What do I want for myself in my life?

It may be useful, in renewing your resolve, to reflect on the truth of your suffering (of course, this must be done calmly, objectively). In reflecting, recognize that there's suffering in your life, the suffering that comes from wanting what you don't have and not wanting what you do have. In other words, the suffering in the mind, the mind infected with desire and aversion. Reflecting, open to the truth: the truth of your suffering. Put your attention on your body. Feel the truth in your body, in your heart. Recognize that you're not yet where you'd like to be. There's still suffering. There's still work to do. As you acknowledge your suffering, connect to the wish that you have to be free from it. Feel compassion for yourself.

In the final analysis, you move beyond complacency, you move forward, out of compassion for yourself.

In confronting your complacency, you may recognize that you need to increase your effort. You need to put more time into abandoning the unskillful and developing the skillful.

At times, when you've fallen into the rut of complacency, you may perceive that you need to make changes in your practice. You may perceive that there are elements of the path that you haven't given enough attention to, haven't developed. You may determine that you need to build your skill in these areas.

You may decide that there are certain skillful qualities that you need to cultivate, that you need to fortify, strengthen.

You may decide that you need to strengthen your breath meditation practice.

You may recognize that you need to make a deeper commitment to keeping the breath in mind in all postures, while engaging in the activities of your householder's life.

There have been various times when, realizing my practice was stalled, I've decided to make changes. Sometimes I've made small shifts. Other times I've made significant changes in my dharma practice.

After practicing the dharma for about ten years, I realized I'd reached a plateau. I wasn't moving forward. I was struggling with certain forms of suffering that I wasn't able to transform. Eventually I decided that I was going to have to learn to cultivate stronger concentration. I was going to have learn to cultivate jhana. I wasn't going to be able to move forward, end suffering and find true happiness if I didn't learn to develop much better concentration.

I began to learn to practice mindfulness of breathing, anapanasati, in the manner the Buddha suggested. Following Ajaan Lee's instructions for practicing mindfulness of breathing, I began to learn to cultivate jhana. It took a great deal of effort. I had to learn a new method for practicing breath meditation. But gradually, with the help of my teacher, I began to learn the method. And, of course, I'm still learning. (In learning breath meditation, we engage in an ongoing process; there's no room for complacency. It's said that Ajaan Lee himself, one of the foremost masters in Thailand, was still developing his practice right up to the time of his death.)

In the years that have followed, I've been able to develop much stronger concentration. I still have a ways to go, to be sure. But I'm getting there.

The important thing is, I'm moving forward. I'm continuing to grow.

Of course, as we move forward we don't want to move too quickly. We have to be careful not to try too hard to get further down the road. We have to be careful not to make too much effort.

The Buddha, asked how he crossed over the flood (a metaphor for attaining awakening), captured the essence of determined effort.

"Tell me, dear sir, how you crossed over the flood."

"I crossed over the flood without pushing forward, without staying in place."

"But how, dear sir, did you cross over the flood without pushing forward, without staying in place?"

"When I pushed forward, I was whirled about. When I stayed in place, I sank. And so I crossed over the flood without pushing forward, without staying in place."
(SN 1.1)

This pretty much says it all. We don't stay in place. If we stay in place, we'll sink, we'll never cross over the flood.

At the same time, we don't push too hard.

I can't help but think of my grandmother when I consider the skillful quality of determination. She was somebody with many good qualities. She wasn't familiar with the Buddha's teachings; her goodness shined through effortlessly. I lived with her for a while when I was an adolescent. It was a difficult period. I was riddled with anger and depression. I wasn't easy to be around. But my grandmother related to me, unfailingly, with kindness, compassion.

She lived to be 100 (an act of determination in itself). At the party celebrating her 100th birthday, I had the privilege of offering the "keynote speech." I explained that it was a blessing to have had her in my life. I talked about my grandmother's unswerving goodness. After I made my speech, others made comments. They all spoke about my grandmother's remarkable character. Finally my grandmother stood up and, in her wholehearted way, made her own speech (she was sharp as a tack, right to the end). As she went on, she remarked, "I really do appreciate what Peter said, and what everybody said. But I have to say, I'm not always that nice to the people in the nursing home. I get persnickety sometimes. I say things I shouldn't. I realize I've got to do better. It's something I'm going to work on."

Now that's determination! After 100 years, my grandmother wasn't going to rest on her laurels. She was still willing to grow. She was determined, after a century of life, to continue to develop her good qualities.

LAZINESS

An appreciation for the concept of entropy is helpful in understanding how we might develop the qualities of effort and determination. Entropy is defined as "a measure of the energy in a system or process that is unavailable to do work." As human beings, we're blessed with a certain amount of energy, but that energy dissipates, burns off, as we partake in the "work" of our lives, carry out our various tasks. The energy doesn't disappear, per se, but rather takes another form, and, alas, is no longer available to us. For most of us, I doubt this comes as a revelation; as the days and years go on, we realize we don't have access to the same fountains of energy, we don't have the same get-up-and-go we had when we were teenagers. More and more, we're prone to tiredness; scientifically speaking, entropy is increasing.

The challenge for dharma students faced with increasing entropy is to avoid succumbing to laziness. Each of us is confronted with entropy and each of us will have to learn to combat laziness. There may be a tendency, as you recognize your lessening energy, to think that you don't have what it takes, that you don't have the energy you need to do what you have to do. Assessing your energy level, you may be inclined to think: "I can't do it." "I have to back off." "I need to rest." Often times, there's a movement in the mind toward giving in, giving up.

In making an effort to move along the Buddha's path, you're asked to observe the thoughts your mind is generating, the thoughts you're chasing after. You're asked to question your assumptions ("I can't do it"), the preconceived notions you have about what you can and can't do. Just because your mind, reacting to a diminished energy level, is saying you can't, doesn't mean you're not capable of making effort. As a dharma practitioner, you're asked to separate out what's true and not true. Just because your mind is saying you don't have sufficient energy doesn't mean you don't. Just because your mind is telling you to kick back, take the day off, doesn't mean you should.

Laziness is a potent force in the mind. It's a mental state that prevents us from moving forward. It's an obstacle to ending suffering, finding greater happiness. It's important, therefore, that you're vigilant, that you watch out for laziness.

The Buddha, in his wisdom, suggests certain tendencies to watch for, ways that laziness typically manifests. In the sutta, "The Grounds for Laziness & the Arousal of Energy," he provides a template we can use to recognize laziness, the guises it takes. He identifies eight forms of laziness, actually four sets of paired expressions of laziness.

He begins the teaching this way:

> "There is the case where a monk has some work to do. The thought occurs to him: 'I will have to do this work. But when I have done this work, my body will be tired. Why don't I lie down?' So he lies down. He doesn't make an effort for the attaining of the as-yet-unattained, the reaching of the as-yet-unreached, the realization of the as-yet-unrealized. This is the first grounds for laziness."
> (AN8.8)

This is one of the grounds for laziness we're apt to claim, the Buddha says. It's one of the reasons we give ourselves for not making effort, not attending to dharma practice. In this scenario, we reason that because we have to work, we can't put time and energy into meditating or participating in other aspects of the practice. We don't possess the wherewithal, we think. We don't have an adequate supply of energy.

This mode of thinking may be familiar. You get up in the morning, you've got to go to work, and faced with the demands of the looming workday, anticipating a trying nine-to-five, you decide to bypass your regular morning meditation.

The second type of laziness follows on the first:

"Then there is the case where a monk has done some work. The thought occurs to him: 'I have done some work. Now that I have done work, my body is tired. Why don't I lie down?' So he lies down. He doesn't make an effort for the attaining of the as-yet-unattained, the reaching of the as-yet-unreached, the realization of the as-yet-unrealized. This is the second grounds for laziness." (AN 8.8)

This may also be a familiar scenario. After completing a full day at your job, or after finishing a task that required a good deal of effort, you might find yourself thinking, "I don't have any energy left for anything else." You might find yourself trying to convince yourself that you don't have enough energy to meditate, or to go to your dharma class, or to work on developing the skillful qualities. You might find yourself telling yourself that you need to take a break, relax, vegetate, watch TV, do absolutely nothing.

In developing determination, you're asked to observe your mind when it offers up grounds for laziness. You're asked to question your thinking. Is it accurate? Is it true? Is it true that you don't have enough energy? Is it true that you need to chill out? Is that the most beneficial route you can take?

Perhaps it is true. Perhaps you need to take a break. But you'll never know what the truth is if you don't ask, if you don't look for yourself.

The next form of laziness we should watch out for is described by the Buddha in this way:

"Then there is the case where a monk has to go on a journey. The thought occurs to him: 'I will have to go on this journey. But when I have gone on the journey, my body will be tired. Why don't I lie down?' So he lies down. He doesn't make an effort for the attaining of the as-yet-unattained, the reaching of the as-yet-unreached, the realization of the as-yet-unrealized. This is the third grounds for laziness."
(AN 8.8)

There are different situations when you might be apt to slide into this pattern of laziness. Maybe you've got plans to visit a friend and you're going to have to drive a good distance or take a long train ride. Daunted by the effort it'll take, you decide to cancel your daily period of sitting meditation.

I sometimes grapple with a variation on this theme on days when I've got a "full schedule." Perhaps I've got several appointments, several tasks to accomplish, several places to go. I'll start to think that I shouldn't bother to meditate that morning. I've got too much to do, I'll think, I don't have that much energy. I'll start to build an aversion to the whole idea of sitting down, closing my eyes, practicing breath meditation. Over time, however, I've learned to recognize this tendency toward laziness. I've learned to observe the thinking and to question it. I've learned not to be swayed.

In most cases I realize that, in fact, I have the energy to practice. And I practice.

The matching tableau looks like this:

"Then there is the case where a monk has gone on a journey. The thought occurs to him: 'I have gone on a journey. Now that I have gone on a journey, my body is tired. Why don't I lie down?' So he lies down. He doesn't make an effort for the attaining of the as-yet-unattained, the reaching of the as-yet-unreached, the realization of the as-yet-unrealized. This is the fourth grounds for laziness."
(AN 8.8)

After completing a "journey" you might be inclined to slack off. Returning home, you might think about taking the day off, suspending your practice for a day, or maybe two days, or maybe three days. You might think you're "too tired" to practice the dharma. But is it true? Are you too tired? Do you have to take a break?

Sometimes students show up at class the day after returning to the city after a lengthy trip. They're exhausted from their journey. They're jet-lagged. But they show up. They make an effort to be there. From my perspective, this is a noteworthy demonstration of determination. Somebody who puts forth this kind of effort is somebody who's developing skillful qualities.

The Buddha describes the next form of laziness like this:

"Then there is the case where a monk, having gone for alms in a village or town, does not get as much coarse or refined food as he needs to fill himself up. The thought occurs to him: 'I, having gone for alms in a village or town, have not gotten as much coarse or refined food as I need to fill myself up. This body of mine is tired & unsuitable for work. Why don't I lie down?' So he lies down. He doesn't make an effort for the attaining of the as-yet-unattained, the reaching of the as-yet-unreached, the realization of the as-yet-unrealized. This is the fifth grounds for laziness."

(AN 8.8)

And its complement is:

"Then there is the case where a monk, having gone for alms in a village or town, does get as much coarse or refined food as he needs to fill himself up. The thought occurs to him: 'I, having gone for alms in a village or town, have gotten as much coarse or refined food as I need to fill myself up. This body of mine is heavy & unsuitable for work, as if I were many months pregnant. Why don't I lie down?' So he lies down. He doesn't make an effort for the attaining of the as-yet-unattained, the reaching of the as-yet-unreached, the realization of the as-yet-unrealized. This is the sixth grounds for laziness."

(AN 8.8)

Not having eaten, you may conclude that you're too weak to attend to dharma practice. Having just eaten, you may claim that you're feeling weighed down, dull.

As dharma students cultivating determination we have to pay heed to the ways in which we relate to sense pleasure. We have to be wary, in particular, of the propensity we may have to forsake dharma practice in favor of partaking in some form of sense pleasure.

In giving in to laziness, we may be disposed to go down the road of desire; we may choose to bypass our practice and instead indulge in sense pleasure, whether it's cheesecake, television or the internet. As we've discussed, in addition to actual food there are many sense pleasures which we "feed on."

After taking in a certain amount of sense pleasure, we may be inclined to shun meditation and other facets of the practice. After feeding on sense pleasure, our energy level may be diminished and, consequently, we may tend toward laziness. We might experience lethargy after eating (in a common scenario, we decide to postpone our morning meditation until after we've eaten breakfast, and then, after eating, we feel too sluggish to practice) and we might experience lethargy, dullness, after staring at the television or computer for several hours. These activities contribute to a loss of affect. They cause weariness. They're a set-up for laziness.

The final pair of situations in which we might tend toward laziness are:

"Then there is the case where a monk comes down with a slight illness. The thought occurs to him: 'I have come down with a slight illness. There's a need to lie down.' So he lies down. He doesn't make an effort for the attaining of the as-yet-unattained, the reaching of the as-yet-unreached, the realization of the as-yet-unrealized. This is the seventh grounds for laziness.

"Then there is the case where a monk has recovered from his illness, not long after his recovery. The thought occurs to him: 'I have recovered from my illness. It's not long after my recovery. This body of mine is weak & unsuitable for work. Why don't I lie down?' So he lies down. He doesn't make an effort for the attaining of the

as-yet-unattained, the reaching of the as-yet-unreached, the realization of the as-yet-unrealized. This is the eighth grounds for laziness."
(AN 8.8)

In these passages, the Buddha presents a pair of dilemmas that every
dharma student will sooner or later confront. At times you might have a
"slight illness." You might have a cold or might be struggling with seasonal
allergies, something like that. And at times you might be getting over a
"slight illness." As the Buddha suggests, you may be apt to use the slight
illness as an excuse, a reason for not participating in dharma practice.

In developing determination, it's important to recognize the tendency
you may have to balk at making effort when you don't like the way your
body feels. As you travel the long road you'll find, on many occasions, that
you're subject to physical discomfort, subtle physical pain. Your body may
not feel one hundred percent. And, accordingly, you may be inclined to
put off practicing. This is problematic, given that the body rarely feels one
hundred percent. The fact is, the body, by its nature, is imperfect, fragile,
vulnerable, likely in any moment to be effected by unpleasant sensations.
There's often something going on in some part of the body. Aches and
pains, major and minor discomforts, are simply part of the deal, what you
signed up for when you took the human form. As years go on the body is
more and more susceptible to afflictions and tiredness.

All things considered, you have to be mindful of the tendency to resist
making effort when your body isn't feeling quite up to par. You have
to learn to keep on, make skillful effort, despite the way your body feels,
despite the unpleasant sensations. (As we follow the path, we learn to practice with unpleasant sensations; establishing refuge in the breath, being
able to put the sensations to the side is the first line of defense in working
with unpleasant bodily experiences.)

You'll note that the Buddha in this teaching uses the term "slight illness." He's not indicating, in any way, that we should attempt to make effort when we're seriously ill or in significant pain. By inserting the modifier "slight," the Buddha offers a compassionate guideline for making determined effort.

In teaching about laziness, the Buddha gives us a map, the locations where we might fall prey to laziness clearly marked.

In avoiding the traps of laziness, our task is to pay attention, to notice when the mind is offering up "grounds for laziness." Recognizing that we're thinking about abandoning our practice, we question our reasons. Are they valid? Is it true that we don't have sufficient energy? Is it true that we'll be better off if we don't make an effort to practice?

There will be times when you'll come to the conclusion that you don't have the energy, or that you don't feel well enough, and that, accordingly, the most compassionate tack you can follow is to back off, soften your effort.

More often than not, however, you'll come to see that you do have sufficient energy, and that, in fact, it would be good for you to practice, it would be the most compassionate thing to do. A good portion of the time, when we look we see that what the voices in the mind are telling us isn't accurate, isn't in our best interests. We see that, in fact, we have what it takes. We see that we can do it.

Relinquishing the grounds for laziness, deciding to practice, we develop skillful intention: we assert the intention to keep to the path, to practice, out of compassion for ourselves.

There will be times when you set out to practice when you won't have a terrific amount of energy. In these instances, it helps to acknowledge that you don't have an optimal amount of energy, that you might not be able to practice at the level at which you'd prefer, but that you'll still be able to practice. It helps to remember that even though things might not go spectacularly, you'll still benefit, you'll receive rewards, you'll move toward a greater happiness.

In the second half of the sutta, the Buddha suggests ways to skillfully approach dharma practice when faced with the eight scenarios he's just laid out. He explains how we might "arouse energy" when circumstances may not seem ideal.

In the case of the practitioner who has work to do, who's anticipating an effortful day at his job, the Buddha suggests the practitioner reflect on the fact that when he's working, plying away, he's not going to be able to practice, at least not on a full-scale level, and that, consequently, he should practice before he heads off to work. He should practice, meditate, while he has the opportunity.

> "There is the case where a monk has some work to do. The thought occurs to him: 'I will have to do this work. But when I am doing this work, it will not be easy to attend to the Buddha's message. Why don't I make an effort beforehand for the attaining of the as-yet-unattained, the reaching of the as-yet-unreached, the realization of the as-yet-unrealized?' So he makes an effort for the attaining of the as-yet-unattained, the reaching of the as-yet-unreached, the realization of the as-yet-unrealized. This is the first grounds for the arousal of energy." (AN 8.8)

If you're going on a "journey," the Buddha recommends you remind yourself that when you're on your journey you're not going to be able to make the same effort to practice the dharma that you'll be able to make before you go to where you're going. Therefore, you should make the effort before you go, while you have the chance.

"Then there is the case where a monk has to go on a journey. The thought occurs to him: 'I will have to go on this journey. But when I am going on the journey, it will not be easy to attend to the Buddha's message. Why don't I make an effort beforehand for the attaining of the as-yet-unattained, the reaching of the as-yet-unreached, the realization of the as-yet-unrealized?' So he makes an effort for the attaining of the as-yet-unattained, the reaching of the as-yet-unreached, the realization of the as-yet-unrealized. This is the third grounds for the arousal of energy."
(AN 8.8)

If you haven't yet eaten, or haven't yet engaged in feeding on some other sense pleasure you're thinking about feeding on, you might note that you're in good position to practice: you're not weighed down, you're not burdened by food or some other "food source."

When you've got a mild illness or when you've just recovered from a mild illness, you might engender skillful mental fabrication, reminding yourself that there may very well come a day when you're seriously ill, when you won't be able to practice. While you're still relatively healthy, relatively strong, while you're still capable, you should make an effort to practice. Later on you might not be able to. When applied skillfully, compassionately, this is a useful line of thinking.

Reflecting on the fact that someday you might be seriously ill, that someday you'll be old and infirm, that someday you'll die is an effective way to bolster your motivation to practice the dharma. The truth is, there's a very small window in which you can develop skillful qualities, concentration, insight. The time is short. The time to practice, accordingly, is now. Right now, while you have the chance.

In "arousing energy" we apply thinking in a skillful manner. We fabricate useful thoughts. We generate lines of thinking that support our efforts to find true happiness in our lives.

When faced with the prospect of a busy day or a journey of some sort, I often remind myself that if I take time to meditate, I'll be much better prepared to tackle the rigors of the day. I reflect on the fact, proven by my experience, that if I put some effort into developing mindfulness of breathing, I'll be able to attend to my tasks in more productive, more joyful fashion.

In our community there are quite a few students who have children. Being a parent, needless to say, is a time-consuming, energy-tapping endeavor. There may be a tendency for parents, given the effort required to assume the role of mother or father, to think they should put their dharma practice on hold while they're raising their kids. There isn't time. It's not possible. When the kids get older, I'll return to the practice. The thinking may go something like that. Many of the parents in our community, however, have learned to take a different view. They've learned to accept the fact that they won't be able to put as much time into the practice as students who don't have kids. At the same time, they've learned that they can find time to practice. They've learned, in fact, that they have to practice. They've come to realize that if they practice, if they do whatever they can to abandon the unskillful and develop the skillful, it will greatly enhance their ability to be good parents. They've learned that if they practice, it will have a tremendously positive impact on their children's lives. Instead of thinking that they can't practice because of their children, they take the view that they can't possibly not practice.

As we cultivate the skillful quality of determination, we begin to realize the benefits in staying with it, in moving forward, in getting beyond laziness, in making an effort even though it's difficult.

We strengthen determination, we learn, by moving through laziness. We strengthen determination by not taking the easy way out. We strengthen determination by meeting resistance, by moving through it. Moving through it skillfully, of course.

We build the muscle of determination the way a weightlifter builds muscle, by increasing the weight she lifts, by moving through the force of resistance. Strength builds when we extend ourselves, when we challenge our perceived limitations, when we transcend laziness. Like a weightlifter who doesn't attempt to lift more than she's capable of lifting, we don't push ourselves, we don't take on more than we can handle. But the truth is, we can often handle more than we think. Recognizing resistance as resistance, we don't back off simply because there are voices in the mind telling us we should. We don't back off because it seems like it's going to be hard to move ahead.

Realizing we have what it takes, we keep going.

As dharma students, we view the occasions when resistance emerges, when there's potential for laziness, as opportunities for developing determination.

There have been times in the years since we began DMC when there was a snowstorm on a night when a class was scheduled. Determined to get to class, students trudged the city streets in the falling snow. On these nights I've made it a point to remind the students that they've displayed extraordinary determination, that in coming to class they've strengthened their skillful qualities. When we look at a snowstorm on a night when we're meant to go to a class as an opportunity to develop the quality of determination, we're assuming the "right attitude." Students interested in developing skillful qualities learn to view these sorts of situations as opportunities, rather than nuisances, problems, hassles. Going to a class when there's bad weather, meditating when we're facing a jampacked workday, making an effort to be mindful of the breath in daily life when we're not feeling "so good" provides opportunity. It gives us a chance to develop determination. When we look at things this way, we align ourselves with the dharma; we find ourselves right where we need to be, on the path.

MORE JOY

It's important to take joy in your determined effort.

It's important to take joy in the fact that you've stayed with it for as long as you have. I try to take a moment, every now and again, to recognize that I've been practicing the dharma for more than 20 years. I take joy, acknowledging this indisputable fact, acknowledging the blessing of my determination.

However long you've been following the path, if it's been twenty years, ten years, five years, five months, five weeks, five days, you can take joy, acknowledging the blessing of your determination.

You can do it right now.

Pause.

Bring your attention in to your heart center.

Recognize that you've been practicing the dharma for however long it's been. Recognize that it's a blessing to have been able to follow the path for this long.

Connect to a feeling of gratitude.

Take joy. Connect to the quality of joy, the brightness in the heart.

Some students have difficulty with this practice and others similar to it. They think it's self-indulgent. But it's essential that we recognize our accomplishments. Our capacity to recognize ourselves and take joy will lead us toward true happiness in our lives, and when we begin to experience greater happiness, the other people in our lives will benefit significantly. In other words, everybody benefits.

It's said that dharma students, in making an effort to abandon the unskillful and develop the skillful, are "doing what has to be done." It's said we can take joy, knowing we're doing what has to be done. This is a classic Buddhist reflection, another way to cultivate joy.

Taking a step back, you can reflect, recognizing that you're doing what you've got to do, in order to end your suffering, in order to make the most of the time you have in this life, in order to find a greater happiness.

Dharma practice is often difficult. The road will have many ups and downs, twists and turns. You'll hit all kinds of barriers. But when you struggle, you can take joy, realizing that you're on the path, that you're doing what has to be done.

In contemplating that you're "doing what has to be done" you can acknowledge that, in following the Buddha's path, you're helping to alleviate the suffering in the world. You can reflect on the fact that you're helping to create a better world, a more compassionate world, a more peaceful world. You might hesitate to accept this view. You might think it's a bold notion. You might think it's farfetched. But the truth is, it's the truth. In practicing the dharma, you're doing something profound. What you're doing is important. It's meaningful.

As a dharma student you can take joy, recognizing the role you're playing in carrying forth the Buddha's teachings. In following the path, you're perpetuating the Buddha's message, you're keeping the dharma alive. Again, you might think this is an exaggerated or immodest claim. But again, it's the truth. It's how the dharma is passed on. It's the day-to-day effort made by sincere practitioners that enables the dharma to remain alive and vibrant. It's the determination of individuals, like you, that keeps the dharma going. The truth is, you're doing an extraordinarily important job in walking the Buddha's long road. Your efforts will have an effect on others for years to come.

In teaching dharma students to develop determination, I often talk about "seeing things through to the end." I encourage students to finish what they've started, if it's a period of sitting meditation, a six-week course, an eight-day retreat. When you see things through to the end, you cultivate determination. When you see things through, you come to know a sublime dharma joy. It's joyful to see things through.

Many people suffer from a tendency to quit before they get to the end. In dharma practice, this is highly problematic. There are considerable drawbacks in not seeing things through. We foster a habit of unskillful effort. We condition laziness. We lose respect for ourselves. We feel something rather antithetical to the joy that we know when we see things through.

Having participated in many day-long retreats as teacher, organizer and student, I'm aware of the tendency that students have to leave early. At DMC we hold day-long retreats every month. In teaching day-longs, I emphasize the importance of staying to the end. I explain that there's much joy in finishing what you've started.

I'm glad to report that our students almost never leave before a retreat ends (actually, I can't remember the last time somebody left early). During years of practice, the students in our group have learned to develop the quality of determination. They've learned to take joy in their persistent effort.

At the end of retreats, we bring the day to a close by reflecting on the blessing of our effort, our determination, the fact that we've seen things through to the end. We take joy.

After completing any dharma-related task, it's always a good idea to acknowledge that you've seen things through. It's always a good idea to take joy.

This is how your practice grows.

It's been noted that western dharma students participating in silent retreats tend to bring a grimness to the practice. This sort of grimness, however, isn't a pre-requisite for meditation practice. Far from it. The fact is, it's an impediment. According to the Buddha, it's essential to approach meditation practice with a bright heart. It's essential to practice joyfully.

There must be joy in your heart, in your mind, for concentration to develop and strengthen. This might seem paradoxical. We might assume that we develop concentration so that we can find joy. But the Buddha is very clear about the cause and effect process. There must be joy, he says, if we're going to build concentration, if we're going to cultivate jhana. There must be brightness in the mind. If you think about it, it makes sense. If you don't feel good about yourself, if you're downhearted, you're not going to want to spend time alone with yourself, sitting in silence, in meditation; you're going to want to get as far away from yourself as you can possibly get. If, on the other hand, you feel pretty good about yourself, if there's joy in your heart, you won't mind hanging out, in the present moment, with yourself.

In writing a chapter on "Effort & Determination," I'd be remiss not to talk about the pivotal role that community plays in developing ongoing, persistent effort. As you move along the Buddha's long road, you're going to need support. Without the support of others you're not going to get very far along the path. In years of teaching, I haven't yet met anybody who's been able to continue forward in dharma practice without being part of some sort of community.

You're going to need help. It's the way it is. It's the way the path is. It's the way life is. You're not meant to go through it alone. After deciding to teach, the Buddha immediately formed a sangha, a community of monks. He knew that community was necessary. Without community, people weren't going to be able to stay with it, weren't going to be able to make progress.

We need the support and guidance provided by teachers. We need teachers to instruct us in the basic skills, to teach us to develop skillful qualities, concentration, insight. We need teachers to tell us when we've veered, to show us how to get back on the road, to help us overcome complacency and laziness.

We need teachers to alert us to the long term consequences of our actions. When we take certain unskillful actions, the results of these actions may not be immediately apparent. We might not experience the drawbacks of our unskillfulness until we're further along the road. Teachers, having studied the long term consequences of their own actions, having learned from their own experience, are able to indicate to us that there are drawbacks in particular actions that we might be apt to take.

We need the support of our peers, the wise beings who are traveling the same road we're traveling. Our fellow students lift us up, give us strength. In undertaking any demanding task, like practicing the dharma, we need companions who are involved in the same undertaking, who speak the same language, who understand the process and are willing to share their experience of going through the process. It's extraordinarily helpful, as we engage in the different stages of dharma practice, to know that there are others who are engaging in a similar process, encountering the same sorts of trials and difficulties, the same joys and wonderments. To put it simply, we need others to talk to about what we're going through, as we're going through it.

As anybody who's meditated in a group knows, when we meditate with others we find we're more capable, more able to develop concentration. When we practice with others, our practice thrives. Beginning students notice this right away; they find they're able to meditate for longer stretches, with greater effectiveness, when they meditate with others.

There's a simple explanation as to why concentration strengthens when you practice with others: when you practice with others, your mind brightens. Your heart opens. Joy emerges. It's a blessing to be able to practice the dharma with others. Recognizing this, you experience joy. In turn, your meditation flourishes. The joy is what makes it possible.

There's joy in doing it together. It's one of the great joys you'll come to know as you practice the dharma.

PRACTICE SUGGESTIONS

REFLECTION:

Where am I in terms of the effort I'm making in my dharma practice? Is my effort unskillful? Skillful?

REFLECTION:

Looking at the quantity of your effort on the broad scale, the macro level, assess where you are in terms of the time and effort you're putting into dharma practice. Where do you need to put in more time and effort? Where are you putting in too much?

PRACTICE:

Be mindful of the quantity of your effort on the micro scale, while you're practicing breath meditation, while you're engaging in other facets of dharma practice. Notice when you're not making enough effort. Notice when you're trying too hard. Adjust your effort when necessary, bringing it into balance.

REFLECTION:

Look at the quality of your effort on the macro level. What is the quality of your resolve? What is the quality of your intention for practicing the dharma? Is it unskillful, imbued with desire, aversion, delusion? Is it skillful, driven by love, compassion?

PRACTICE:

Cultivate skillful effort. Before making an effort to practice, see what your mind is like. Develop skillful intention, the intention to practice out of compassion. While practicing, be mindful of your intention, making sure it's skillful.

PRACTICE:

Before practicing breath meditation, develop skillful intention.

PRACTICE:

Recognize the benefits in making skillful effort.

PRACTICE:

Take joy in your skillful effort. Recognize the blessing of your effort. Connect to a feeling of gratitude. Connect to the heart quality of joy.

REFLECTION:

Do I understand the importance of cultivating joy?

REFECTION:

Is my practice joyful?

PRACTICE:

As you develop the skillful qualities, take joy. Acknowledge the blessing of your goodness. Connect to gratitude. Connect to the quality of joy.

PRACTICE:

In preparation for practicing breath meditation, take a few moments to "brighten the mind." Cultivate joy, reflecting on the blessing of your skillful qualities.

PRACTICE:

After meditating, take a moment to reflect. Recognize the blessing of your effort and determination. Take joy.

PRACTICE:

Acknowledge the effort you're making to keep the breath in mind in all postures, during all parts of the day. Take joy.

REFLECTION:

Where am I in terms of the skillful quality of determination?

REFLECTION:

How do I tend to veer off the path?

REFLECTION:

When I veer off the path, how do I respond? Do I become discouraged? Do I engage in self-judgment?

PRACTICE:

Be mindful of the times when you veer off the path. See the drawbacks in not staying with it. Have compassion for yourself, given that you've veered off. Return to the path with compassion, remembering that you practice the dharma because you have the wish to be free from suffering.

REFLECTION:

Am I complacent in my dharma practice? What do I need to do to get myself moving forward?

REFLECTION:

Reflect on the truth of your suffering. Reflect objectively. Reflecting, develop compassion for yourself.

REFLECT:

In what ways do I succumb to laziness?

PRACTICE:

Be mindful of the occasions when you incline toward laziness, when you claim "grounds for laziness." In deciding whether to practice, see if you have sufficient energy. If you decide to practice, establish the intention to practice out of compassion for yourself. See the benefits in practicing when you might have taken the easy way out. Take joy in your determination.

PRACTICE:

When you feel an inclination toward laziness, assert grounds for the "arousal of energy." Use skillful fabrication in forging the impetus to practice.

REFLECTION:

Acknowledge the length of time that you've practiced the dharma. Recognizing the blessing of your determination, take joy.

REFLECTION:

Reflect on the fact that in following the Buddha's path you're "doing what has to be done." In reflecting, take joy.

REFLECTION:

Do I "see things through to the end"? Do I tend to quit before I get to the end? Do I understand the importance of seeing things through?

PRACTICE:

Make an effort to see things through to the end. When you see things through, take joy.

REFLECTION:

Do I have wise friends, teachers and peers who support me in my practice? Where am I in terms of my involvement in a dharma community? Do I understand the importance of community in developing the path?

PRACTICE:

Recognize the blessing it is to have people in your life who support you as you travel the path. Take joy.

CHAPTER FIVE

DISCERNMENT & LOVINGKINDNESS

HEEDFULNESS

What's the quality of the action you're taking right now as you begin to read this chapter? Is it skillful or unskillful? Is your mind afflicted with aversion? Is there a disinclination to put effort into reading these words? Is there delusion in the mind? Dullness? Blankness?

When you study your actions in this way, you're being heedful.

The skillful quality of discernment is cultivated by practicing heedfulness.

There are two components to practicing heedfulness: (1) being mindful of our actions, and (2) discerning whether our actions are skillful or unskillful.

Practicing heedfulness, we pay attention to our actions as we participate in our householder's lives, as we traverse the landscape of our days and nights, as we move from moment to moment.

Practicing heedfulness we observe our physical, verbal, mental actions.

Observing, we ask:

Is this action unskillful or skillful?

Are there drawbacks in taking this action?

Is this action leading to suffering or the end of suffering?

Is this action informed by unskillful intention, intention imbued with desire, aversion, delusion?

Is the intention skillful, motivated by love, compassion?

We've already talked about practicing heedfulness. As we've explained, the development of generosity, ethical conduct, and the other skillful qualities depends on our capacity to be heedful, to discern whether our actions, as we cultivate these qualities, are skillful or unskillful. In developing generosity we pay attention to whether our giving is skillful, driven by compassion, or whether it's influenced by an unskillful factor, by desire, aversion, delusion. For instance, as we're attempting to practice generosity, we may perceive that our giving is informed by desire, the desire, perhaps, to get something in return. It's heedfulness that enables us to notice our propensity to act unskillfully; it's heedfulness that enables us to refrain from acting unskillfully. It's heedfulness, accordingly, that enables us to take skillful action. If we don't practice heedfulness, we're not going to be able to develop skillful qualities. "All skillful qualities," the Buddha says, "are rooted in heedfulness."

Developing discernment, we expand the field: we make an effort to be heedful of all our actions, physical, verbal and mental. It's not enough, as I'm sure you can appreciate, to be heedful only when practicing generosity, ethical conduct, renunciation, etc.; we have to be heedful of all our actions. Our happiness depends on it.

As he travelled from town to town, as he taught monks and nuns, lay men and women, the Buddha constantly stressed the importance of practicing heedfulness. He was often emphatic in instructing his disciples to be heedful. He often ended his dharma talks by exhorting his followers : "Practice jhana, monks. Don't be heedless. Don't later fall into regret. This is our message to you."

The Buddha's last words were: "Bring about completion by being heedful." It's safe to say that, in uttering his final words, the Buddha wouldn't choose to make a less-than-significant statement.

It's also useful to note that all the monks in attendance when the Buddha gave his final instructions had attained at least the first stage of enlightenment: stream-entry. They'd all reached a high level. But they still needed to watch their actions. Don't stop making an effort to be heedful, the Buddha said.

Heedfulness, obviously, is an important skill. It's important simply because our actions are important. Our actions, the Buddha indicated, determine our happiness. All dharma students, he said, should frequently reflect:

"'I am the owner of my actions, heir to my actions, born of my actions, related through my actions, and live dependent on my actions. Whatever I do, for good or for evil, to that will I fall heir.'"
(AN 5.57)

As dharma students, we have to come to understand that our actions are what decide whether we find happiness in this life. We cultivate this all-important insight by paying attention to our actions, by seeing for ourselves that every action we take is meaningful, that every action plays a part in deciding what our lives will be like. As we foster this insight, we develop a strong desire to practice heedfulness.

In practicing heedfulness, we strive to be mindful of our actions, realizing we're not going to be able to be mindful every time we act. We do the best we can. We're heedful to the best of our ability. Over time our ability will grow. As we cultivate the skill over weeks, months, years we'll find that we're able to practice heedfulness with greater regularity and consistency.

Some examples of how we practice heedfulness:

You're a small business owner and you're about to talk to one of your employees about an assignment he messed up. You check yourself before speaking. Is the action you're about to take going to cause affliction for your employee, for yourself? What's the quality of your intention? Is it unskillful? Is it infused with anger?

You're a married man. You're talking to your neighbor, a married woman. You feel sexual desire for her. You flirt with her. Then you pause. You consider your verbal action. Is it unskillful? Is it going to bring about suffering?

After an upsetting telephone conversation with a family member, you replay the conversation in your mind. You fabricate streams of aversive thinking, manufacturing a strong resentment. Then you notice what you're doing. You're heedful of your mental action. You question it. Is this thinking skillful? Is it useful? Is it serving you? What will the consequences be if you continue to fabricate these thoughts?

In practicing heedfulness, we observe our actions. We take the position of the observer. We step back, look at our actions, as the Buddha says, like one person looking at another person. It's imperative in cultivating heedfulness that we develop the capacity to observe.

Taking the posture of the observer, we look objectively at our actions. Objectivity is critical. It's critical that we study our actions in an impartial, non-judgmental manner. The dharma student, developed in discernment, simply observes her actions, simply discerns whether her actions are unskillful or skillful. When she recognizes her unskillfulness, she doesn't criticize herself. She doesn't condemn herself. She doesn't react emotionally. The recognition of unskillfulness, it's important to understand, is not subjective; it's an acknowledgment of what is. It's an acknowledgment of the unadulterated truth.

Actions are either unskillful or skillful. They're either imbued with desire/aversion/delusion or love/compassion. It's pretty cut and dry.

As we observe our actions it's important, of course, that we practice truthfulness. It's important that we look truthfully at our actions. We've talked about being truthful with ourselves about ourselves. As we've said, we might be inclined to lie to ourselves about our actions. When we take an unskillful action, we might try to convince ourselves that it wasn't unskillful. We might rationalize our unskillfulness. We might downplay it. We might tell ourselves that what we did wasn't "that bad."

We might try to ignore the truth, protect ourselves from the painful reality.

In observing our unskillfulness, we might attempt to produce a "positive spin." In our culture, coming up with the right spin is practically an art form. But it's definitely not what the Buddha teaches. In practicing heedfulness, there's no room for shading the truth, for manipulating our perceptions.

In the Rahula sutta, the Buddha puts forth the basic instructions for practicing heedfulness. At the very beginning of the sutta he uses the metaphor of a mirror to explain how we should look at our actions:

"What do you think, Rahula: What is a mirror for?"

"For reflection, sir."

"In the same way, Rahula, bodily actions, verbal actions, & mental actions are to be done with repeated reflection."

In practicing heedfulness, we recognize "what is." Like a mirror, which reflects only what's in front of it, we recognize the pure truth. We don't distort the truth. We don't alter it. We don't add anything to it. We don't take anything away from it. We don't analyze, interpret, explain. We observe our actions exactly as they are: unskillful or skillful. If an action is unskillful, we acknowledge that it's unskillful. That's it.

At times, it may be difficult to look truthfully at our actions. It may be hard to see the truth. In such cases, it helps to talk to a teacher.

A good teacher helps us gain a clear view of the truth. A good teacher tells us the truth. In the most evolved teacher-student relationship, the teacher indicates where the student is acting unskillfully, he doesn't hold anything back, and the student, in turn, is utterly willing to listen, to hear every last bit of the truth. This sort of vigorously honest exchange, of course, can occur only when the relationship is well-established, when there's a high level of trust.

Sometimes students, when beginning to practice heedfulness, find it's difficult to tell whether certain actions are unskillful or skillful. This is understandable; as with all the skillful qualities, it takes time to develop discernment. Our ability to discern whether an action is leading to suffering or the end of suffering will mature as we continue to practice and cultivate sensitivity to the subtle distinctions between what's unskillful and what's skillful. Practicing heedfulness requires sensitivity. You may not find it difficult to discern whether a more blatant action is unskillful. If you speak in a loud angry manner to your child, you may not have any problem discerning that your verbal action is unskillful. But many movements of unskillfulness are subtle. For instance, when talking to your kid your speech may be infected with a slight irritation, an unskillful quality that may be rather subtle. It's the subtle actions that may present a challenge when learning to practice heedfulness; it requires a degree of sensitivity to tell if certain subtle actions are fueled by unskillful or skillful intention.

Sensitivity to the quality of our actions, to the movements of desire and aversion, develops as we become attuned to the body, as we establish embodied awareness. As we deepen in our capacity to perceive a felt sense of our mental qualities, we're able to pick up subtle dissonances, subtle indications of desire, aversion. We're more able to tell if our intentions are driven by unskillful factors.

As you can tell, it's very important to develop an "embodied awareness." If we're going to move further along the path we're going to have to learn to be in touch with the body, connected to the body. We're going to have to learn to "tune in" to the body. (Many students have difficulty connecting to the body; body-related practices such as yoga, body scanning, tai chi, qui gong, etc. are often helpful in cultivating embodied awareness.)

The story of Sona the monk offers a good picture of what it means to be sensitive to the quality of our intentions/actions. As you'll recall, the Buddha, using the simile of the vina (lute, guitar), taught Sona to discern whether he was making too little or too much effort. In the same vein, the dharma student practicing heedfulness discerns when her intention/action is unskillful or skillful. Like a musician who's able to detect when her guitar is out of tune, the student detects when her intention/action is out of tune. She "hears" the dissonance that arises when her intention/action is unskillful, imbued with desire, aversion, delusion. She feels the dissonance in her body. As she develops in heedfulness and becomes more sensitive to her body, she "hears" more acutely, she becomes more sensitive to when she's out of tune.

As we cultivate the skill of heedfulness, we purify our actions. We refrain from taking unskillful actions. We begin to take actions that are an expression of love, compassion. We change the way we live. It's a transforming skill.

And again, it's a skill we can learn. We can learn to follow the Buddha's injunction to be heedful. It requires learning the method. It requires practice. And it requires concentration, which is what we'll talk about in the next section.

NATURAL MEDITATION

We develop concentration by practicing mindfulness of breathing. It's the same method the Buddha used. When you see statues of the Buddha sitting, meditating, he's practicing mindfulness of breathing.

In practicing mindfulness of breathing, according to the Buddha's design, we establish the breath in formal meditation and maintain it throughout the remainder of the day. At DMC, where the students are householders, we place great emphasis on maintaining the breath in our daily lives. We call this facet of dharma practice "natural meditation."

In natural meditation we're mindful of the breath, as the Buddha says, in all four postures: sitting, standing, moving, and lying down. We keep the breath in mind when we're engaging in all the activities of our life, when we're working, when we're involved in interpersonal interactions, when we're eating, when we're walking down the street, when we're riding the bus, riding the subway, when we're shopping, scrubbing the kitchen floor, vacuuming, taking out the trash, when we're showering, brushing our teeth, putting on our coat, when we're opening a door, when we're closing a door. We make an effort to remain centered, mindful of the breath, wherever we are, whatever we're doing.

Let's try it.

Right now, as you're reading, put your attention on your breath.

Feel your breath somewhere in the area of your abdomen.

As you continue reading, keep your attention to some degree on your breath.

It may seem awkward; it may seem difficult to be mindful of the breath while you're reading, while you're talking to somebody, while you're eating lunch. But if you practice, you'll learn to do it. Gradually, you'll learn to do it. Students new to the skill frequently report that it's a challenge to maintain the breath and, at the same time, perform a certain task. But invariably, after putting effort into it, they become proficient at the skill. It becomes something they're able to do with a degree of facility, fluidity. It becomes natural.

In practicing natural meditation, your objective is to keep the breath in mind as you participate in all the different activities of your life. When involved in certain activities, you'll have to dedicate a good portion of your attention to the activity. Even so, you can maintain an awareness of the breath.

When you're walking down the sidewalk in Manhattan, you'll have to pay attention to your walking, you'll have to notice where you're going, you'll have to make sure you don't run into other pedestrians or step into traffic. But you can maintain at least some awareness of the breath.

When you're involved in an in-depth conversation with a work colleague, you'll be able to be mindful of the breath to some extent, although probably not to the same extent as when strolling along the sidewalk. Often times, when in the throes of a more involved activity such as a conversation your mindfulness of the breath will comprise feeling the breath every now and then. At intervals, you'll connect to the breath. Even if you feel just two or three breaths during the conversation with your colleague, it will help greatly. It will enable you to be heedful, to watch your verbal action, to recognize whether your speech is unskillful or skillful.

As you're practicing natural meditation, feel the breath at a point, a place, in the middle of the body, somewhere in the area of the abdomen. If you put your attention on a spot in the middle of the body, you'll be more apt to stay centered. Your attention, as you move through life, will be less likely to fly off.

Allow your breath to be easeful, pleasurable. If you've been cultivating an easeful breath in formal meditation practice, you'll be able to touch into an easeful-ness when practicing natural meditation. You'll be able to find an easeful, pleasurable inner refuge.

As you put your mind on your breath, notice your body in the background; notice the flow of easeful energy in the body.

Again, try it.

Feel your breath.

Connect to an easeful breath.

As you read, keep the breath in mind.

If you're able to maintain an easeful breath as you go about the business of your daily life, it will help you stay calm, composed. It will help you stay centered.

It's important as you learn to practice natural meditation to understand how the process works. It's important to understand that you won't always be able to maintain mindfulness of the breath. You won't be able to do it all the time. There will be times when you'll forget to be mindful of the breath. You'll neglect the breath. There will be times when you'll go for long stretches without noticing a single breath. That's normal. That's how the process works. It's a slow, gradual process.

In practicing natural meditation we make a wholehearted effort to be mindful of the breath; at the same time we understand that as we go through the day we won't always be able to keep the breath in mind.

As you make an effort to maintain the breath, you have to watch for self-judgment, discouragement, impatience, doubt. It's not an easy practice. Not by a long shot. You'll frequently lose the thread. You'll forget the breath. It's essential, therefore, that you guard against self-judgment and other less-than-useful reactions you might have to how the practice is going. It's essential that you learn to replace the unhelpful mental patterns with understanding and acceptance. It's essential that you have compassion for yourself. Motivated by compassion, you'll continue forward. If you engage in self-judgment when you fail to keep the breath in mind, you'll cripple your efforts to practice natural meditation. You'll eventually quit the practice.

Understanding that it's a gradual process, circumventing the potholes of self-criticism and discouragement, you just keep practicing. You stay with it, even though it's difficult. You stay with it out of compassion for yourself. You just stay with it. If you stay with it, you'll eventually become adept at maintaining the breath. At the start you might connect to the breath just a few times a day. Some days you might not connect to a single breath. After a while, though, you'll be able to keep the breath in mind with more frequency. As time goes on, you'll begin to put the mind on the breath rather naturally. If you stay with it, the practice will become somewhat effortless. It will become natural.

When we keep the breath in mind, we're in position to practice heedfulness. This is the most significant benefit in natural meditation. The truth is, we're usually not in position to practice heedfulness. That's because we're usually lost in thought. We're lost. When preoccupied with our thinking, we're obscured; we're not able to see clearly. We're not able to be heedful. We're not able to observe, to discern whether our actions are unskillful or skillful. Conversely, when we maintain the breath we're able to practice heedfulness. When we're centered in the breath we create space, separation from our intentions/actions. We're able to observe. The breath is akin to a tower, a vantage point from which we're able to observe our intentions/actions. Think of a forest lookout. High in his perch, with an expansive view of the trees, he can see if there's smoke, fire, danger, and he can ascertain if all is calm, peaceful. When we reside in the breath, we have that kind of perspective. We have the ability to observe.

Let's say your partner criticizes you. Historically, you don't respond well to criticism. In the past when she's criticized you, you've reacted angrily. Now, as she's speaking, you feel that familiar anger, rising up, through your body. You feel inclined to lash out. But you're centered, connected to your breath. Before you say anything, you pause. You assess the situation. You recognize your anger. You recognize your intention to speak in an angry manner. You understand that if you follow through on this intention, it will lead to affliction. For you. For your partner. Understanding the drawbacks in speaking harshly, you refrain from offering any angry, abrasive retorts.

Keeping our awareness in the body, centered in the breath, we remain somewhat removed from what's going on, the different movements of our lives. We watch what's going on. When there's potential for taking action, physical, verbal or mental, we consider the action, we discern whether it's unskillful or skillful. If we see that it's unskillful, we refrain from acting. If we see that it's skillful, that it will lead to happiness, we act.

So once again be mindful of your breath.

Let your breath be easeful.

Notice your body. Notice the pleasant energy in the body. Let it spread.

Keep the breath in mind.

Typically, western dharma students are taught to practice some form of breath meditation in the formal "closed eyes" posture, but they're not taught to maintain the breath throughout the day in the "open eyes" posture. As a result, you'll often hear students lament that despite years of meditation practice, despite attending countless retreats, they still struggle mightily in their everyday lives. They find themselves acting unskillfully in the work context, in relationship. Again and again, they slide into painful habitual patterns. For these students, things will continue in this vein until they learn to maintain present moment awareness, until they learn to practice heedfulness.

I can attest to this. My own practice was revolutionized when I learned to keep the breath in mind, when I learned to practice heedfulness. My life was revolutionized.

After practicing natural meditation for a while, students often say something along the lines of: "Now I understand what meditation is all about."

Students consistently report that as they've learned to practice natural meditation and heedfulness, they've witnessed significant changes in their lives.

Time and again, students describe how their relationships with their partners, kids, parents, friends, co-workers have been transformed by developing these skills. A few days before writing this, I was speaking with a student who told me that her relationship with her husband had been resurrected and rejuvenated due to her ability to maintain the breath and practice heedfulness. Her marriage had seemed destined to fall apart. But as she brought her skills to bear on the relationship, things began to change. She began to heal the marriage. Making a determined effort to stay connected to her breath, to be heedful of her actions, she began to refrain from interacting with her husband in habitually unskillful ways. She began to act with more kindness, compassion. As she began to effect changes, her husband, too, began to change. He began to treat her with more kindness.

This is what it's all about.

Developing skillful qualities is life-changing.

In this section I've outlined some of the fundamental principles of natural meditation, maintaining the breath in the "open eyes" posture. It's a skill, of course, that you'll develop over a period of time. You have to be willing to be in it for the long haul, to continue to practice, to cultivate the skill over months, years. Here, I want to emphasize the importance of developing this skill, of keeping the breath in mind. If you can do this, the path will unfold for you.

TWO SORTS OF THINKING

It's an indication you're moving forward when you're able to refrain from acting unskillfully with your body and mouth. There's much benefit in abandoning unskillful physical and verbal action. But when it comes to developing skillful qualities, abandoning unskillful physical and verbal action isn't the whole path. It's good, but it's not good enough. The Buddha asks that you go further, that you purify not only physical and verbal action, but mental action as well.

Mental action is thinking; specifically, the thinking you purposely fabricate. Thoughts constantly enter the mind. They arise unbidden. There's nothing you can do about it. But you have an opportunity to do something once the thoughts arise. You can pursue the thoughts. Or not. You take mental action when you pursue the thoughts that enter the mind. You take action when you grab on to the thoughts, when you take the thoughts and fabricate more thoughts, when you construct narratives, stories.

"Pursue" is a word the Buddha frequently uses in describing the manner in which we take mental action. Thoughts arise, we pursue them. We chase after them, like cops chasing a getaway car, like a dog chasing a squirrel in the town park.

The fact is, we spend a lot of time, a good portion of our lives, pursuing thoughts. We engage in mental action much more frequently than we engage in physical action and verbal action. Every now and then we take a physical or verbal action. But we're constantly taking mental actions. We're constantly thinking. And, unfortunately, most of our thinking isn't skillful. It brings about affliction, suffering.

Doesn't it?

The fact is, our unskillful mental action causes us an enormous amount of suffering. Think about the suffering, blatant and subtle, that you've experienced in the last twenty-four hours. In all likelihood the majority of it was the product of unskillful mental action.

All things considered, it's extremely important to learn to be heedful of your mental actions.

In the sutta, "Two Sorts of Thinking," the Buddha describes the strategy he employed as a Bodhisatta, in an effort to be heedful of his mental actions.

"The Blessed One said, "Monks, before my self-awakening, when I was still just an unawakened Bodhisatta, the thought occurred to me: 'Why don't I keep dividing my thinking into two sorts?' So I made thinking imbued with sensuality, thinking imbued with ill will, & thinking imbued with harmfulness one sort, and thinking imbued with renunciation, thinking imbued with non-ill will, & thinking imbued with harmlessness another sort."

(MN 19)

The Buddha divided his thinking into two categories: unskillful and skillful. Under the heading of unskillful he included thinking imbued with sensual desire (sensuality) and aversion (ill will, harmfulness). Skillful thinking comprised mental action informed by renunciation, love, goodwill, compassion.

Having made his categories, the Buddha paid attention to his mental actions.

> "And as I remained thus heedful, ardent, & resolute, thinking imbued with sensuality (desire) arose. I discerned that 'Thinking imbued with sensuality has arisen in me; and that leads to my own affliction or to the affliction of others or to the affliction of both. It obstructs discernment, promotes vexation, & does not lead to Unbinding.'
>
> "As I noticed that it leads to my own affliction, it subsided. As I noticed that it leads to the affliction of others... to the affliction of both... it obstructs discernment, promotes vexation, & does not lead to Unbinding, it subsided. Whenever thinking imbued with sensuality had arisen, I simply abandoned it, destroyed it, dispelled it, wiped it out of existence." (similarly, with ill will, harmfulness....)
> (MN 19)

The Buddha practiced heedfulness. And as you can see, he didn't go about it in a lackadaisical manner. He was "heedful, ardent & resolute." He made steadfast effort. He watched his thinking closely, scrupulously. He noticed when his thinking was informed by unskillful qualities (sensual desire, aversion). He noticed the drawbacks in this sort of thinking. He saw that it led to affliction. Recognizing the damaging consequences of involving himself in unskillful thinking, he sought to abandon it.

As the Buddha studied his unskillful thinking he recognized that "it leads to my own affliction." Here the Buddha gives a critical strategic instruction: in practicing heedfulness, you have to discern that your unskillful mental action causes you affliction, suffering. It's important to see that your unskillful thinking causes you harm. There may be a tendency, when you fabricate thinking imbued with sensual desire and aversion, to minimize the potential effects, to tell yourself that your thinking "isn't hurting anybody." It may very well be that the angry thinking you're generating with regard to another person isn't hurting that person. But you have to realize that you are hurting somebody: you're hurting yourself. In being heedful of your unskillful mental actions, this, largely, is what you're asked to see: you're hurting yourself.

The Buddha recognized that thinking driven by sensual desire and aversion "obstructs discernment" and "promotes vexation." Following the Buddha's lead, you're asked to see that when you take unskillful mental action you experience agitation, dis-ease. You're prevented from following the path, from finding true happiness. When you engage in this sort of thinking, you suffer. That's the bottom line. You suffer.

In being heedful of your mental actions, you're asked to see that thinking informed by desire and aversion leads to painful consequences, consequences you suffer in the short term and long term as well. You're asked to see that you experience pain, agitation, dis-ease as time goes on as a result of your unskillful thinking. The repercussions when you pursue unskillful thinking are far-reaching. You feel the effects in the ensuing hours, days, weeks, months, years.

When you chase after certain kinds of thinking, you condition your mind, you create grooves in your mind. Your thinking becomes habitual. Over time, the grooves in your mind grow deeper; your thinking travels the same tracks, again and again, with the regularity of suburban commuter trains.

If you indulge in angry thoughts on Monday, you'll probably indulge in the same kind of angry thoughts on Tuesday. That's basically how it works.

This is a primary drawback of unskillful thinking. It leads to more unskillful thinking. And more unskillful thinking. And more. And more.

In the sutta, the Buddha describes the process of conditioning:

"Whatever a monk keeps pursuing with his thinking & pondering, that becomes the inclination of his awareness. If a monk keeps pursuing thinking imbued with sensuality, abandoning thinking imbued with renunciation, his mind is bent by that thinking imbued with sensuality. If a monk keeps pursuing thinking imbued with ill will, abandoning thinking imbued with non-ill will, his mind is bent by that thinking imbued with ill will. If a monk keeps pursuing thinking imbued with harmfulness, abandoning thinking imbued with harmlessness, his mind is bent by that thinking imbued with harmfulness." (MN 19)

Your mind, the Buddha says, is "bent" by your thinking. Like Superman, who bends steel in his bare hands, you bend your mind when you pursue different lines of thinking. This is something to consider when you're proliferating thoughts of sensual desire and aversion. What kind of mind do you want? Do you want a mind bent toward sensual desire? Toward aversion?

Sometimes while traipsing the sidewalks of New York I'll notice that I'm fabricating unskillful thoughts, aversive thoughts, about people walking on the sidewalk, talking on cell phones. (People talking on cell phones in public places is one of my pet peeves. We've all got our pet peeves.) Centered in the breath, practicing heedfulness, I'll notice my mental action. Usually I'll notice that I'm thinking something along those lines of: You jerk! Why are you talking on that cell phone! Put that thing away!

Recognizing that I'm feeding on aversive thoughts, like a hungry teenager scarfing fastfood burgers, I'll assume the role of the observer. Like a person standing looking at somebody sitting on a chair, I'll observe my mental actions. I'll question my actions: Is it useful to feed on these thoughts? Is it serving me? Is it in my best interests?

Looking at my thinking objectively, truthfully, compassionately, I might ask: What are the consequences in doing what I'm doing? How is this thinking affecting me? This is the pivotal question. How is it affecting me? Forget about the guy gabbing on the cell phone. What am I doing to myself? Am I hurting myself?

I'll make an effort to investigate what's happening in my body. Acquiring a felt sense, I'll discern the consequences of my thinking. I may notice an inner dissonance, the sure sign of suffering.

I might try to gain insight into the long term consequences of my thinking. I might ask: If I chase after these aversive thoughts, how is it going to affect me going forward? How is it going to affect the rest of my day? How is this thinking going to affect my ability to teach the dharma later this evening? How is it going to affect my efforts to find true happiness in my life?

I might ask: What kind of mind am I shaping? How am I bending my mind? Is a mind bent by aversion the kind of mind that I want?

In drawing this scenario I'm describing different strategies I might use in an attempt to comprehend the drawbacks in my unskillful mental action. In most cases I wouldn't use all these strategies. Taking that into account, the reader might still wonder if this method of looking at mental action isn't extreme, excessive. Really, it isn't. It's important to remember that when it comes to the state of your mind, there needs to be a sense of urgency. Your thinking is incredibly important; you have to pay close attention to it; you have to make every effort to understand the drawbacks in unskillful thinking.

In the sutta the Buddha depicts the ardent effort we should apply in abandoning unskillful mental action.

"Just as in the last month of the Rains, in the autumn season when the crops are ripening, a cowherd would look after his cows: He would tap & poke & check & curb them with a stick on this side & that. Why is that? Because he foresees flogging or imprisonment or a fine or public censure arising from that [if he let his cows wander into the crops]. In the same way I foresaw in unskillful qualities drawbacks, degradation, & defilement...."
(MN 19)

You have to make sure to take care of your mind, the Buddha says. If you allow yourself to become involved in desirous and aversive thinking, you're going to pay a stiff penalty, you're going to put yourself at risk. You're going to suffer.

The Buddha realized that if he abandoned unskillful mental action and developed skillful mental action, he would move toward ending suffering, finding true happiness. The strategy of being heedful of "Two Sorts of Thinking" is one you can apply. So, apply it. Learn to look at your thinking in this manner.

It's a strategy that worked for the Buddha. If you put effort into it, it will work for you, too.

SKILLFUL ACTION

Discernment is seeing what we have to do to fulfill our wish to be happy.

Lovingkindness is doing it.

As dharma students developing lovingkindness, we strive to take action, physical, verbal, mental, that's motivated by the heart, by love, good will, compassion. We strive to act straight from the heart.

In this book we've learned that as we develop qualities such as generosity, ethical conduct, renunciation, in order to be skillful our actions must be driven by love, compassion. Now we're broadening the range of our actions to include all of our actions. As we cultivate lovingkindness, we make an effort whenever we take action to act skillfully, heartfully, with love, good will, compassion. We make an effort, whenever we act, to establish skillful intention.

Lovingkindness is a translation of the Pali word "metta." It doesn't, however, quite capture the essence of metta. Metta encompasses many qualities, including lovingkindness, love, kindness, friendliness, good will. It includes a range of heartful attitudes. It's often useful to think of metta as an attitude of good will. In cultivating metta, the dharma student seeks to relate wholeheartedly to all beings, including himself. It's not possible, realistic, or appropriate to expect that we'll be able to take loving action toward all beings, but we can learn to extend our good will to them. In doing so, we're not implying that we're going to spend time with them or take care of them, but rather that we wish them well. As Thanissaro Bhikkhu says, an attitude of good will is often more skillful for us than an attitude of lovingkindness.

Metta is the baseline quality of the heart. When the heart is open, it shines with metta. Metta is boundless, limitless. It shines everywhere. It doesn't have preferences, doesn't pick favorites, doesn't decide to shine in one place but not another.

In cultivating metta, we seek to extend good will to all beings. As the Buddha says:

> With good will for the entire cosmos,
>   cultivate a limitless heart:
> Above, below, & all around,
>   unobstructed, without enmity or hate.
> Whether standing, walking,
>   sitting, or lying down,
>   as long as one is alert,
> one should be resolved on this mindfulness.
> This is called a sublime abiding
>   here & now.
> (Sn 1.8)

In our culture when we talk about love we're referring for the most part to romantic love. This romantic love, glorified in movies, popular songs and novels, is the product of desire, the often intense desire to engage with the other, to experience connection, to experience sense pleasure: the pleasure that comes when we're in the throes of relationship, the pleasure that derives from physical contact, sex. This romantic love is not boundless. It doesn't transcend preferences. Just the opposite. It's driven by our preferences. In pursuing romantic love, we purposefully limit our focus: we seek just one person, a single recipient of our love. We may even speak about finding "the one."

Romantic love is motivated by desire, clinging. It's a volatile emotion. It's impermanent. As we all know, it doesn't last. In fact, it usually dissipates rather quickly. Needless to say, romantic love isn't what the Buddha is talking about when he talks about love. Love, according to the Buddha, occurs in the place where there's release from desire, letting go of clinging.

When we take action informed by lovingkindness for ourselves we act in support of the wish that we have to be happy. We seek to fulfill our wish to be happy. When we take action informed by lovingkindness for others, we act in support of the wish they have for true happiness.

Lovingkindness and the other heart qualities (compassion, joy, equanimity) are sometimes known as "sublime attitudes." It's a good way to think about these qualities. They're attitudes. Skillful attitudes. Most of us probably haven't gone through life with a very skillful attitude. Speaking for myself, for a good part of my life I went about my business with a fairly suspect attitude, a rather cynical, negative attitude. In developing lovingkindness, we relinquish our former attitudes, our old ways of going about things; we relate to ourselves and others with an attitude of lovingkindness, good will. We act with this sublime attitude.

It's all about action. As you follow the path, your heart will open, you'll feel lovingkindness. As dharma practitioners, however, we don't simply feel lovingkindness. We don't simply immerse ourselves in the warmth of lovingkindness. We don't luxuriate in this pleasant feeling, like somebody taking a warm bubble bath. We take action.

We have to act.

The fact is, when the heart is open we don't have any choice but to act. The Buddha knew this. In the days following his awakening, his heart was wide open, effusing love, compassion. He realized, accordingly, that he had to express his love. He realized that he had to engage in a full encounter with the world. He decided, therefore, to teach the dharma. And he spent the next 45 years doing that, acting in a completely loving, compassionate manner.

Sometimes new students worry that practicing the dharma will result in a sort of passivity. They hear about cultivating qualities like generosity, ethical conduct, renunciation, lovingkindness, equanimity, and they worry that if they follow the Buddha's path they'll turn into soft, mushy, motivationless people. They're afraid they won't accomplish anything. This is a grave misconception. We have only to look at the example the Buddha set to see that it isn't true. The Buddha, acting strictly out of love and compassion, accomplished a lot. He accomplished a hell of a lot. If anybody's life is a demonstration of accomplishment, it's the Buddha's. The fact is, when we act from a place of lovingkindness, we put ourselves in a much better position to accomplish something in our lives.

When you act from the heart, you act from a place of strength. Lovingkindness is your greatest strength. If you think about anything of great significance that's been accomplished by human beings, it's been done by people who've been propelled by love, compassion. The Buddha. Ghandi. Martin Luther King, Jr. They're people we're still talking about, years after they lived, because their actions were motivated by the heart. The idea may not align with the belief structures of many people in today's world, but the fact remains: the heart is by far the source of your greatest strength.

In previous chapters we've talked about paying attention to the "blatant and subtle." The principle applies here. Cultivating lovingkindness, we consider the big stuff and the small stuff. All of our actions are important. They're more important, undoubtedly, than we think.

In developing lovingkindness, we take heartful action with regard to the most significant aspects of our lives, our work, our relationships with our partner, children, parents, friends. We also cultivate lovingkindness when taking subtle actions. We bring heartfulness to the so-called small moments: getting out of bed in the morning, buying a quart of milk in the corner grocery, checking email, walking across the parking lot. I find walking a good activity in which to cultivate lovingkindness. As I'm walking along the street, I'll ask myself: How am I walking? Am I walking with lovingkindness? Walking along the concrete sidewalk, I'll cultivate skillful intention, the intention to walk with an attitude of lovingkindness. As St. Francis of Assisi said: "It is no use walking anywhere to preach unless our walking is our preaching."

All your actions ask for your attention, your care, your lovingkindness. Every action you take represents an opportunity to develop your heart, to meet the world and yourself with lovingkindness and good will.

When you take action imbued with lovingkindness, you condition lovingkindness. Lovingkindness is conditioned action by action, intention by intention. Each heartful action that you take, even the smallest action, contributes to the opening of the heart, the inclination to act heartfully going forward. The capacity to act with lovingkindness grows drop by drop. Each action is like a drop in a bucket; gradually the bucket fills up. Gradually you develop the habit of taking action, physical, verbal, mental, that's motivated by lovingkindness and good will.

Every time you take skillful action, you bend your mind in the right direction.

Cultivating lovingkindness, of course, is a skill. We develop the skill when we follow the five-step process for developing skillful intention/ action.

Before acting, you see what your mind is like. If there's unskillful intention in the mind, you abandon it.

Perhaps you're about to talk to your fourteen-year-old son. You check your mind. You notice some aversion. You really don't feel like talking to him. Observing the aversion, refraining from feeding on it, you leave it to the side.

You set a skillful intention: the intention to act, to speak with your son, with lovingkindness.

You assert directed thought. You tell yourself: I'm going to speak with kindness. Or something along those lines (it's important to find your own way of verbalizing intention).

You connect to your heart, to a felt sense of your heart. You feel lovingkindness for your son.

Now, you speak with him.

While you're interacting with your son, you pay attention. You're heedful. If you begin to feel the aversion you'd experienced before, you notice it, put it to the side. You re-assert your skillful intention. You re-connect to your heart.

(If you realize, while you're in the midst of an action, that you've neglected to set an intention, you can set a skillful intention right then, right there, wherever you are. You can bring in the intention to act with lovingkindness. You can connect to a felt sense of your heart. You can change your course at any point. You're not condemned to unskillful action.)

After speaking with your kid, you acknowledge that you've acted skillfully. You recognize the benefits of taking heartful action. You pause for a moment. You reflect. You get a felt sense of the truth: the truth of the benefits in acting with lovingkindness.

There are extraordinary benefits in taking action driven by lovingkindness. It's important to recognize the benefits. It's important to recognize the power of lovingkindness. The Buddha said that the tiniest bit of lovingkindness has a powerful effect. You have to see that.

Lastly, there's step five: you take joy. Acknowledging the blessing of your skillful qualities, your lovingkindness, you take joy. You connect to the feeling of joy that arises in the heart when you act skillfully.

Most of us aren't in the habit of meeting the experiences of our lives with lovingkindness and compassion. It's not the way we've gone about things. For most of our lives we've acted from a place of desire and aversion and delusion. But the Buddha's teachings, the step-by-step instructions for developing skillful intention/action, provide a means for changing our habitual way of doing things.

You may believe on some level that you can't change. But it isn't true. You can. You can develop new habits. You can learn the necessary skills.

You can learn to meet life with an attitude of lovingkindness. You can learn to relate to yourself, to others, with lovingkindness. You can learn to adopt the sublime attitude of lovingkindness.

Even as you're reading this, you can cultivate lovingkindness. You can assert your intention to read these words with an attitude of lovingkindness, recognizing that you're taking care of yourself, that you're doing something that's going to help you in your efforts to find true happiness.

Try it.

Feel your breath.

Bring your attention in to your heart center.

Assert directed thought.

"I'm going to read with lovingkindness."

Connect to a felt sense of the heart, your wish to be happy, the quality of lovingkindness.

Read this sentence with an attitude of lovingkindness, connected to your wish to be happy.

And this sentence.

And the next sentence.

As you continue forward, in reading, in doing whatever you're going to do after reading this part of the book, cultivate a sublime attitude, an attitude of lovingkindness.

TAKING CARE OF YOURSELF

In developing lovingkindness we have to learn, first and foremost, to develop lovingkindness for ourselves. We have to learn to take action that's an expression of lovingkindness for ourselves. We have to learn to take good care of ourselves.

In any given day, we're faced with countless decisions about what to do, what actions to take. In cultivating lovingkindness, we seek to make decisions that are in accord with our wish to know true happiness.

It might not be that easy. The person most of us have the hardest time relating to, being kind to, is ourselves. When it comes to taking action informed by lovingkindness, there isn't anybody who presents quite the same challenge.

Typically, unskillful intention motivates the actions that we take with regard to ourselves. Self-aversion frequently influences the way we treat ourselves. Most of us aren't connected to feelings of lovingkindness for ourselves. As a result, we're not inclined to take actions that are good for us, that are in our best interests. We're not inclined to take good care of ourselves.

In teaching students to cultivate lovingkindness, I suggest they purposefully take one action every day that's an expression of lovingkindness for themselves. It doesn't have to be a big action. It might involve making a healthy dinner, or going for a walk, or exercising, or reading. I remind the students to use the five-step process. Before acting, see what your mind is like. Develop skillful intention, the intention to act out of lovingkindness for yourself. While acting, be heedful, make sure you're staying to your intention. After acting, see the benefits, take joy. Sometimes when explaining the exercise, I say, "This will probably be the hardest assignment I ever give you." I say it jokingly. But, in fact, most students find the activity challenging. They struggle with it. Often times, students follow the assignment for a couple of days and then drop it. It's nearly impossible for them to stick with it.

Most students, in trying this exercise, are entering uncharted territory. They're taking action that's radically different from the kind they normally take. They're attempting to adopt an altogether different attitude, an attitude of lovingkindness.

It's often a difficult exercise. But if students put some effort into it, things begin to shift. Even if they take a heartful action just once or twice during the week, things begin to shift. They begin to move in the right direction. They begin to learn to take care of themselves.

If you're going to find a reliable, lasting happiness, you're going to have to learn to take actions that are in support of the wish you have to be happy. It seems obvious. But unfortunately, many of us don't know how to do this. For this reason, developing lovingkindness for yourself should be a priority. It should be a primary theme in your dharma practice.

You have to resolve to develop lovingkindness for yourself.

As you approach your life you have to learn to ask:

What do I have to do in order to fulfill my wish to be happy?

What actions can I take that are an expression of lovingkindness for myself?

In studying your actions you have to learn to ask:

Is this action motivated by lovingkindness for myself?

Is this action in alignment with my wish to know true happiness?

You have to grasp the importance of developing lovingkindness for yourself. As you foster this understanding, you'll deepen your resolve to take action that's in support of your wish to be happy. Explaining the criticalness of taking care of ourselves, the Buddha offers the parable of the two acrobats. One acrobat sits atop a bamboo pole. The other acrobat sits on his shoulders. The acrobat sitting on the pole says to the acrobat sitting on his shoulders: "I'll look after you, and you look after me, and we'll be alright." The acrobat sitting on his shoulders disagrees. She says: "No. I'll look after myself. And you should look after yourself. Then we'll be okay." The Buddha sides with her. The Buddha says you should look after yourself. If you maintain your center, keep your balance, you'll be able to support others. If however you don't keep your balance, you'll bring others down. If you take care of yourself, the Buddha says, you'll be able to take care of each other. "When watching after oneself," he declares, "one watches after others." In the Buddha's scheme, this is a basic law. Take care of yourself properly and you'll be able to take care of others. You have to take care of yourself. That's your first priority. You have to take actions that are a reflection of lovingkindness for yourself. If you do that, you'll put yourself in position to help others. If you treat yourself with kindness, you'll be equipped to treat others with kindness. You'll be able to love others.

Think about relationships you've had with people who didn't love themselves, didn't take care of themselves. Think about this kind of person. Is this the kind of person who's going to be able to support you? Is this the kind of person from whom you want to receive help? Is this the kind of person you'd want for a dharma teacher? For a therapist? What's it like to have an interaction with somebody who doesn't act in a loving, compassionate way toward him or herself? What's it like to interact with somebody who's riddled with self-loathing? What's it like to have a relationship with somebody who's chronically unhappy?

The bottom line is you can't have a loving relationship with another person unless you have a loving relationship with yourself. It's just not possible.

As we've noted, if a parent is making an effort to take care of herself, it will have a positive effect on her kids. On the other hand, if the parent isn't doing what she needs to do to take care of herself, if she isn't taking actions that are an expression of lovingkindness for herself, her children will suffer. It's hard to imagine a worse scenario for a child than to have a parent who's unhappy, who's besieged with self-loathing. It's a set up for a lot of pain.

As we've indicated, a parent who's attending to her dharma practice, who's developing skillful qualities, is in good position to help her kids. She's taking care of herself, and consequently, she's going to be able to take care of her kids.

People often object when it's suggested they develop lovingkindness for themselves. Some people believe it's a "selfish" pursuit. Some people think it's "wrong." But the Buddha's teachings certainly don't suggest this. It's helpful to remember that, according to the Buddha, we're as deserving of our lovingkindness as anybody else.

There are any number of arguments that people put forth in an attempt to explain why it's "wrong" to practice lovingkindness for themselves. These arguments, in general, are manifestations of resistance. Most of us resist, to some degree, taking action that supports our wish to be happy. The notion that we should act in the service of taking care of ourselves runs counter to our habitual patterns of belief and behavior. In many ways, at the core of our resistance is the simple fact that it's hard to change. In taking action toward ourselves that's informed by lovingkindness and compassion we're effecting change. And change is hard.

As always, we have to be heedful: we have to recognize our resistance. We have to question it. Is it useful? If we're going to learn to take care of ourselves, if we're going to change, we have to work skillfully with our resistance.

As you make an effort to take action in support of your wish to be happy, you'll experience resistance. That's okay, as long as you work skillfully with it, as long as you remember to look at it as a doorway. Meeting resistance and learning from it is an integral part of the process of bringing about change.

We can change. If we develop the skills the Buddha teaches, there's no doubt we can change. We can learn to take good care of ourselves.

One of the most important ways that we cultivate lovingkindness for ourselves is by practicing breath meditation, following the Buddha's instructions for mindfulness of breathing. The first task in being mindful of the breath is finding a place to put our attention, a place where the breath feels good. In selecting a place where the breath is comfortable, we learn to take care of ourselves. When I first learned to meditate, I wasn't given this key instruction. I was told to focus on the breath at a specific spot and stay with that spot no matter what. Every time you meditate, I was told, be mindful of that same spot. The problem was, that spot wasn't always comfortable. The spot I used was located in the abdomen, but there were many times when I sat down to meditate when there were unpleasant sensations in that region of my body. There were times, for instance, when I was stricken with indigestion. Diligent student that I was, I stayed with that spot. What I was doing, of course, was reinforcing a pattern of putting myself in painful situations, not taking good care of myself. Fortunately, I learned another way of doing things: I learned to put my attention on the breath at a place where the breath was comfortable, easeful. If I typically felt the breath in my abdomen, but on a certain day I had a stomach ache, I shifted and felt the breath at my nostrils. Practicing in this way, I learned to care for myself. It may seem like a small thing. But small things, as we've noted, often yield big results. For me, learning to choose a comfortable place at which to feel the breath led to a significant shift in the way I related to my experience, the way I made decisions about what actions to take as I travelled the roads of my householder's life.

In the phase of breath meditation known as "evaluation," we continue the process, we build a further understanding of what's good for us, what we need to do to take care of ourselves. In this step, we take a close look at the breath, we scrutinize every breath, in-breath and out-breath; we discern where in the breath there's dis-ease, where there's ease. Observing the breath, we learn to recognize dis-ease and ease, to differentiate between the two. This isn't a skill many of us have learned. We've never learned to cultivate this kind of sensitivity, this kind of insight. In evaluating the breath, we learn to be sensitive to our experience. We learn to comprehend what's good for us.

Gradually, as we evaluate the breath, we focus our attention on the easeful part of the breath. We allow the easeful breath quality to unfold, expand. We cultivate the ease. We let ourselves breathe in the most easeful, pleasurable way. We let ourselves reside in this easeful place.

In cultivating the easeful breath, in putting our mind on the easeful breath, we choose to act toward ourselves in a way that's loving, compassionate. We take good care of ourselves.

As for myself, it's been through practicing breath meditation in the manner described that I've been able to make the most strides in learning to take actions that are in my best interests, loving, compassionate actions. I've learned to choose what's good for me. Developing the ability to discern the ease in the breath, and, in turn, to put my attention on the ease, has been pivotal in my journey.

As I've developed the ability to choose to abide in an easeful, pleasurable breath, I've developed the ability to choose what's good for me in other areas of my life. I've begun to incline toward acting in a more loving way toward myself in other parts of my life, in work, in relationship, and so on.

It wasn't something at which I had much, if any, skill. I didn't know how to take actions that were an expression of lovingkindness for myself. It wasn't my habit. I worked at the same job for 20 years. It wasn't a terrible job, but I didn't particularly enjoy it, didn't find significant fulfillment in it. It certainly wasn't something I should've been doing. Working at this job, I wasn't in harmony with my wish to find true happiness. But I just kept doing it. I didn't know any better.

Most of us don't know how to take good care of ourselves. We put ourselves in all kinds of situations that aren't good for us. We engage in work that isn't good for us. We get involved in relationships that aren't good for us. We develop habits that aren't good for us. We take lots of actions that aren't a reflection of lovingkindness for ourselves.

But we can change. We can learn to develop lovingkindness for ourselves. And one of the most important ways we can learn to take good care of ourselves is by practicing mindfulness of breathing, by learning to build an easeful, pleasurable refuge in the breath.

As we develop the quality of lovingkindness, we learn to change the habits of a lifetime. We learn to look at our actions with a discerning eye, the same way we learn to look at the breath. We learn to take actions motivated by lovingkindness for ourselves.

In developing lovingkindness, we learn to take care of ourselves. We learn to love ourselves.

Like it or not, it's something we've got to do.

METTA MEDITATION

It's helpful to take time every day to practice metta meditation.

In and of itself, metta meditation is beneficial. It's calming. It's healing. Practicing metta, we experience pleasant, blissful states. But we should remember that metta meditation isn't meant to be a stand-alone practice; the main purpose of the meditation is to help us strengthen our ability to take actions that are an expression of lovingkindness and good will. As always, it's all about action.

There isn't much point in practicing metta meditation if, after getting off the cushion, we don't take skillful actions.

Try to practice metta meditation every day. That's the recommendation. Practice every day for at least five or ten minutes.

You might practice at the beginning of your daily period of sitting meditation, before you practice breath meditation. Or you might do the metta meditation after practicing breath meditation. Or both. Or you might do it at some other juncture during the day.

Here are some basic instructions:

Find a comfortable sitting posture. It's helpful in metta meditation if you're able to maintain a comfortable posture; you don't want to have to put much, if any, effort into dealing with physical pain.

Close your eyes. However, if you begin to feel dull or sleepy, keep your eyes slightly open. There needs to be a degree of energy in order to get the most out of the meditation. Without sufficient energy, it's going to be difficult to connect to the heart.

Take a few moments to center yourself in your breath. Then enlarge your awareness. Be mindful of your entire body.

Then bring your attention to your "heart center," the place, probably somewhere in the upper body, where you connect to the feelings of loving-kindness, good will. Put your focus there.

If you like, place your hand on your heart center.

Keeping your attention on your heart, begin to see if you can get a felt sense of your wish be happy.

As I've said, we all have the wish to be happy. Deep inside, we wish true happiness for ourselves. This is the most foundational statement of metta. It's an expression of self-love.

We have the wish to be happy. It's innate. But we're usually not connected to it. We're cut off from it. We've lost the signal, the way we might lose our internet connection. Our primary task in metta meditation is to connect to this wish.

As you connect to your wish to be happy, remember that in using the term "happy," you're not alluding to the happiness that people seek in following the ways of the world, the temporary happiness that derives from sense pleasure, gain, status, praise. You're referring to a greater happiness. True happiness. The happiness of the heart.

It's very important to learn to connect to a felt sense of your wish to be happy. You want to learn to feel this wish. Actually feel it. In the body. In the heart. You want to learn to know it. The same way that right now you know the feeling of this book in your hands, the feeling of your body against the chair you're sitting in.

I learned to connect to a felt sense of the heart from the meditation teacher Michele McDonald. The suggestions I'm offering in this section are largely a reflection of what I've learned from Michele. Her teachings have made an extraordinary difference in my capacity to connect to my heart, to open my heart, to encounter life with an open heart. As Michele says, we want to learn to practice wordlessly. Or at least as wordlessly as possible. It will be necessary to apply some thinking in order to guide yourself toward your wish to be happy, the felt sense of the wish. But it will be to your advantage if you keep thought fabrication to a minimum. You might think of thought fabrication as scaffolding. You'll need some scaffolding in order to connect. But you don't want to mistake the scaffolding for the building. Your objective is to enter the building of metta. The scaffolding, the thought fabrication, just helps you get there.

Metta meditation, Michele McDonald says, is all about learning to connect. As spiritually-minded people, we might be interested in talking about things like love and compassion, but we might not be able to connect to these qualities. Practicing metta meditation, we learn to move beyond the thinking realm to the felt sense. We learn to get out of the head, into the body, into the heart.

It may be hard at first to connect to a felt sense of the heart. The felt sense may seem elusive. Going inside, being sensitive to what's inside may seem alien, incongruous, like finding yourself in room with people who are speaking a foreign language. But it's definitely something you can learn to do. Like everything, it takes practice. Practice, practice, practice. I've seen many students, at first unable to get in touch with their wish to be happy, eventually able to connect with great facility to the felt sense.

If it's hard to connect, simply incline yourself toward knowing a felt sense of your wish to be happy. Orient yourself toward the felt sense, like somebody looking toward the horizon, watching for the sun to rise. Develop the intention to connect. It all begins with intention.

Connected to a felt sense, put your attention right there. Focus on the felt sense of your wish to be happy. This is how we cultivate any quality, by focusing on it, shining the light of awareness on it.

Connected, let the felt sense unfold, expand. Deepen into it. Absorb into it.

As you cultivate the felt sense of your wish to be happy, you'll begin to feel lovingkindness. You'll begin to feel the love you have for yourself. The feeling may be characterized by a warmth, a tenderness. As you connect to this feeling, put your attention on it. Allow the feeling of lovingkindness to suffuse your heart.

As the feeling of lovingkindness radiates, let it radiate, let it flow out, into your body. Let it move, out, beyond your body.

This is precisely the Buddha's instruction for cultivating the heart.

"That disciple of the noble ones — thus devoid of covetousness, devoid of ill will, unbewildered, alert, mindful — keeps pervading the first direction (east) with an awareness imbued with good will, likewise the second, likewise the third, likewise the fourth. Thus above, below, & all around, everywhere, in its entirety, he keeps pervading the all-encompassing cosmos with an awareness imbued with good will — abundant, expansive, immeasurable, without hostility, without ill will."
(AN 10.208)

Metta is a real thing. It's something you can feel. It's not just an idea. It's not just conceptual. For many of us, love is a concept. A fairly abstract concept. But when you cultivate a felt sense of the heart, in the manner described here, you come to know that it's a real thing.

Your ability to connect to the heart will develop, slowly, over time. If you keep making an effort, the results will begin to show. But you can't force the results. You have to watch out for the desire to make things happen too quickly, to obtain fast results. You have to be careful not to push too hard. Remember the simile of the lute. The key, as ever, is to apply the right amount of effort. If you don't make enough effort, you won't be able to connect to your wish to be happy. If you make too much effort, you'll foil your attempts to connect. You'll create dis-ease. You'll give rise to something quite the opposite of lovingkindness. If you become disappointed in your progress, if you become frustrated, impatient, you'll jam the signal, you'll sabotage your capacity to connect.

In practicing metta meditation, it's sometimes helpful to use "metta phrases." As we've said, we want to practice as wordlessly as possible. We want to put up as little scaffolding as possible. But at certain times saying phrases may support our efforts to connect.

Phrases might include:

"May I be happy of heart."

"May I have true happiness."

"May I be safe and protected."

"May I be healthy and strong."

"May I live with ease and well-being."

In general you'll want to begin the meditation by following the guidelines we've set forth: put your attention on your heart, connect to a felt sense of the wish that you have to be happy. If it's difficult to acquire a felt sense, you might want to try using some phrases. If you think that saying phrases will facilitate your ability to connect, by all means try it. With your attention on your heart, say the phrases softly, silently. You may want to use just one phrase.

"May I be happy of heart."

Say the phrase. Maybe once. Maybe twice. Then let the phrase go, let it drop, as though you're letting it drop down, into your body, into your heart, as if you're dropping a stone into a pond. The stone drops, down, into, through, the water. Ripples form, spread out.

As you say the phrases, see if you begin to detect a felt sense of your wish to be happy. If you notice a felt sense, put your attention there. If you're not able to connect to a felt sense, that's okay. You're developing intention. You're planting seeds. Sooner or later, they'll sprout and blossom.

In using phrases, you may want to say the phrase every now and then. You'll want to experiment, find a suitable pace, a rhythm. You may decide to say the phrases at certain intervals. You may choose to use just one phrase, such as "May I be happy of heart." Or you may choose to use several phrases. See what works for you, what supports your efforts to connect to a felt sense of your wish to be happy.

There may be times when you'll decide to repeat the phrases, again and again, perhaps in synch with your breathing. This strategy is often useful when the mind is dull, sleepy; saying the phrases may help you to rouse energy, stay alert.

When using phrases, pay attention to the way you're saying the words. Sometimes there's a tendency to say the phrases in a dull, monotonous fashion. Be careful of sliding into this sort of affectless pattern. Try instead to say the words with a degree of wholeheartedness, earnestness.

Try to have an appreciation for what the phrases mean. When you say, "May I be happy," know what that implies. Understand the subtext. Understand that when you're speaking about happiness, you're referring to the Buddha's happiness, you're not alluding to the sort of "happiness" that comes when you scarf down a piece of cake or buy a new cell phone. You're talking about true happiness.

Begin the meditation by connecting to your wish for true happiness. Then develop your wish for true happiness for people you love, family members and friends for whom your heart is open, people who support you in your life. Begin to connect to the wish you have for these people. Put your attention on the felt sense.

If you like, you might try using some phrases, such as, "May you have true happiness."

As you practice, certain people will appear in your mind's eye; when that occurs, focus on the person. Connect to your wish for them that they have true happiness.

It often will help to have a visual image of the person.

During a meditation, several people who are dear to you may come to mind. Wish each of them well. Connect to the heart.

It's important to remember that cultivating the wish that somebody find true happiness doesn't necessarily mean that they'll find it. In the final analysis, whether somebody discovers true happiness depends on what they do, the actions they take. We cultivate metta for others so that we might strengthen our ability to relate to them with greater skill, greater kindness. We cultivate metta so that, in interacting with others, we might support the other's efforts to know true happiness.

Next, you can develop metta for other people you know. There are, of course, many people with whom we have relationships, with whom we engage, with whom we cross paths as we travel the days and nights of our lives. With some people, such as co-workers, we might have a more involved relationship; with others, such as the cashier in the local super-market, our relationship may be less involved. But in practicing metta, in cultivating the heart, it's important to remember all the people we come into contact with, all those we know, regardless of how well we know them.

In developing metta for others, it's very useful to think of the practice as one in which we're extending good will to the other. While it may be a challenge to open to the notion of loving a broad spectrum of people, we may find it not-so-difficult to offer them our good will. When we extend good will to others, we're not saying that we're going to take care of the other, be there for them no matter what; we're simply wishing them well, we're wishing them inner peace, ease, well-being in their lives. In many situations, for many of us, extending good will will be more realistic, more truthful, than seeking to extend love. Many students find it far easier, in practicing with others, to extend good will.

As you continue, bring to mind people you find difficult, people for whom you feel aversion. This is often a challenging part of the practice. It's always wise to move slowly through this rough terrain. Don't take on more than you can handle. Don't over-do it. In each meditation, you may want to choose one "difficult" person to work with; each time you practice, you can choose a different person.

And you don't have to choose the person who's most difficult for you; as you begin practicing metta meditation, you're probably better off if you don't choose to work with your arch-enemy.

It's always helpful to remember that in cultivating good will for a so-called difficult person, we're not condoning any unskillful behavior they might engage in, behavior that may have caused us to dislike them. We're wishing that they find true happiness, the happiness inside, the happiness of the heart. After all, if these hard-to-deal-with people find an inner happiness, they'll be much less likely to act in unskillful, harmful ways; they'll almost certainly be much easier to interact with.

Lastly, you can develop good will for all beings. In extending your good will to all beings, you might let your awareness radiate out, to the east, west, north, south, above, below, as you attempt to include all beings in your thoughts.

One of the benefits of metta meditation is that it helps us learn to connect to our wish to be happy. As we've noted, we tend to be cut off from this elemental wish. When I was child, I had a keen awareness of my wish to be happy. But as the years went on, I lost my connection to it. My wish to be happy was gradually covered over, obscured, like a kitchen wall covered with numerous layers of wallpaper. As we journey along the Buddha's path, we strip off the old wallpaper. We re-awaken to our wish to have true happiness. As I began to practice the dharma, I began to remember my wish to be happy. Metta meditation helped me strengthen my ability to be in touch with this wish, to open my heart to myself.

As you practice metta meditation, you'll gradually be more able to connect to your heart as you go through the day, as you engage in your daily affairs; you'll be more able, when taking action, to connect to your heart. As you become more connected to your wish to be happy, you'll be more able to recognize the wish that others have to be happy. You'll be more able to interact skillfully with others. You'll be more able to meet life with a sublime attitude.

THE KEY OF COMPASSION

Compassion, we might say, is a subset of lovingkindness. It's the quality in the heart that responds to suffering. If lovingkindness is a broad expansive light shining everywhere, compassion is a spotlight zeroing in on suffering.

Compassion is expressed, in its essence, by the wish to find freedom from suffering.

In cultivating compassion for ourselves, we connect to our wish to be free from suffering (when we develop compassion for others, we connect to our wish that they be free from suffering). Like the wish that we have to be happy, the wish to be free from suffering is elemental, innate. It's a wish we all have.

Describing lovingkindness, the Buddha provides the example of the heartfelt action that a mother would take toward her infant child. In the same vein, compassion is exemplified by the concerned, caring action that the mother would take when her child is sick.

Like a doctor diagnosing an illness and prescribing treatment, the dharma student recognizes suffering and, in turn, prescribes compassion. It's important to cultivate compassion when it's called for. In other words, when there's suffering. If you try to cultivate lovingkindness when the situation calls for compassion, your efforts will be thwarted. Let's say you're struggling with loneliness. You're suffering. The right prescription, given that you're suffering, is compassion. If you try to cultivate lovingkindness, to connect to the wish you have to be happy, you'll hit barriers. It will be like trying to fit a square peg in a round hole.

In cultivating compassion, we recognize that we're suffering (or that another is suffering). The word "suffering" is an awkward translation of the Pali word "dukkha." Like many Pali words, "dukkha" has multiple meanings. Generally when we use the term "suffering" we're referring to mental suffering, the suffering we bring about by taking unskillful actions. The root of this mental suffering, as explicated in the teaching on the Four Noble Truths, is clinging, the way we hold on to desire, aversion, delusion. As the Thai master Ajaan Maha Boowa puts it, when we're in the throes of mental suffering there's a "squeeze on the heart." In developing compassion, we're asked to notice when we're afflicted with this form of dukkha, mental suffering.

We're also asked, in developing compassion, to notice when we're subject to another kind of dukkha: the dukkha that's an unavoidable aspect of being human, the dukkha inherent in sickness, aging, death, separation.

Recognizing suffering, we turn to it, face it, look at it. We open to the truth of our suffering (or another's suffering). This isn't, of course, how we typically relate to suffering. Our tendency, when confronted with suffering, is to avoid it, run from it. Here we're doing something radically different.

In order to open to our suffering, we have to be able to calmly, objectively observe it. We have to be able to observe our suffering like a person sitting on a chair looking at a person lying on the floor. We have to be able to move from "I'm suffering" to "there's suffering." We're able to create this kind of spacious relationship to suffering when we have a degree of concentration, equanimity. If we don't have sufficient equanimity, we'll get knocked off balance by our suffering, we'll get thrown by it.

We shouldn't try to open to suffering for too long. Otherwise, we'll get overwhelmed by it.

Recognizing suffering, opening to it, we cultivate compassion. We assert directed thought. We fabricate a simple intention: Let me have compassion for myself. Or: Have compassion. Something like that.

Bringing our attention to the heart, we connect to a felt sense of our wish to be free from suffering. We feel compassion for ourselves (or another).

When specific physical or verbal action is called for, we act, motivated by the heart, by compassion.

Let's say you've separated from your partner. You're anguished. You're in pain. Taking a step back from what's going on, you acknowledge that you're suffering. For a moment, you open to this truth. You establish the intention to have compassion for yourself. You say: Let me have some compassion for myself. Putting your attention on your heart center, you connect to a felt sense of compassion for yourself. You have compassion for yourself.

If you like you can try it right now.

Center yourself in your breath.

Allow your breath to be easeful, pleasurable.

Think about an area of your life in which there's suffering. Maybe you have a difficult physical condition. Maybe there's a form of mental suffering that you're battling. Maybe you're angry with a family member. Maybe you're dissatisfied with the way your job is going.

If it's helpful, bring up a visual image pertaining to your experience of suffering.

Acknowledge that there's suffering in your life.

See if you can open to truth of your suffering. Be with the truth of your suffering for a moment. Just for a moment.

Now cultivate compassion for yourself.

Assert directed thought.

"Let me have compassion for myself."

Bring your attention to your heart. Incline toward your wish to be free from suffering. Connect to a felt sense of compassion for yourself.

Stay with the heart, with the feeling of compassion, for a few moments. Then return to your breath.

It's very important to learn to develop compassion for ourselves. Why? Because we suffer. It's that simple. We suffer. We suffer a lot. The Buddha, well aware of the extent to which we suffer, puts it like this:

"From an inconstruable beginning comes transmigration. A beginning point is not evident, though beings hindered by ignorance and fettered by craving are transmigrating & wandering on. "What do you think, monks: Which is greater, the tears you have shed while transmigrating & wandering this long, long time — crying & weeping from being joined with what is displeasing, being separated from what is pleasing — or the water in the four great oceans?"

"As we understand the Dhamma taught to us by the Blessed One, this is the greater: the tears we have shed while transmigrating & wandering this long, long time — crying & weeping from being joined with what is displeasing, being separated from what is pleasing — not the water in the four great oceans."

"Excellent, monks. Excellent. It is excellent that you thus understand the Dhamma taught by me.

"This is the greater: the tears you have shed while transmigrating & wandering this long, long time — crying & weeping from being joined with what is displeasing, being separated from what is pleasing — not the water in the four great oceans." (SN 15.3)

It's imperative that you learn to respond skillfully to your suffering, that you learn to have compassion for yourself. If you're not able to develop compassion for yourself, you'll find it difficult to get further along the Buddha's path. Conversely, if you learn to open to your suffering and have compassion for yourself, you'll continue to advance in your dharma practice.

A phrase I like is: "the key of compassion." Compassion is the key to the door to the place of healing. It opens the door, leads us to the path to the end of suffering.

It's compassion that brings us to the path. We're suffering and we have the wish to end our suffering. Out of compassion for ourselves, we make an effort to follow the path.

As we continue forward, it's compassion that keeps us going. We stay with it, we keep practicing, day after day, year after year, out of compassion for ourselves.

As we've noted, there will be times when you'll veer off the path. There will be times when you'll fail, when you'll mess up. You'll set out to cultivate generosity, but you'll stumble into ruts of greediness. You'll intend to speak skillfully, but you'll end up speaking harshly and divisively. You'll vow to observe the uposatha, follow the eight precepts, but, failing to meet your objectives, you'll spend hours in front of the TV watching meaningless programs. You'll make a commitment to meditate every day but you'll go several days, or longer, without getting on the cushion. You'll sit down to practice breath meditation, but you'll find yourself constantly wandering off, going down dubious alleyways.

There will be times when you'll act unskillfully. You'll have the intention to practice heedfulness, to act with lovingkindness. But instead you'll act from a place of desire, aversion.

You're going to make mistakes. The Buddha knew this. He was a human being. He knew what it was to be human.

In the "Instructions to Rahula," the Buddha gives strategies to employ before taking action, while taking action, and after taking action. The third part, after taking action, is extremely important. In this phase, we review our actions. When we act unskillfully, we look at our unskillfulness. We respond with wisdom and compassion.

The Buddha includes this third set of instructions because he knows that making mistakes is part of the process. He knows that if we're able to respond wisely and compassionately to our mistakes, it will have a profound effect on our ability to move forward along the path.

After you've acted unskillfully, there are two ways to go, two roads from which to choose. One is the road of self-judgment. This may be the road you're most familiar with, the road you're most apt to go down. You may have a long history of judging yourself harshly when you fail. For dharma students this is problematic. The problem is, when you go down the road of self-judgment you move further from the path.

If you disparage yourself after acting unskillfully, you compound your unskillfulness. You compound your suffering.

The road of self-judgment leads to suffering. As a dharma student, you have to see this, understand this.

When you're in the habit of engaging in self-judgment, you foster a climate of self-aversion in your mind; you incline yourself toward taking actions informed by self-aversion, actions that aren't in your best interests, actions that are harmful to you. There isn't any advantage in self-judgment. It's the wrong road.

The Buddha's road leads to the end of suffering. It leads to true happiness. When you've taken an unskillful action, the Buddha instructs, make it a learning experience. Acknowledge that you've taken an action that's brought about suffering for yourself and for others. Calmly, objectively, see the drawbacks in your unskillful actions. Think about how you might act differently in the future. In this spirit, you might ask: As I go forward, is this the sort of action I want to take? Do I want to continue to take actions that bring about this kind of suffering? What can I do differently next time?

Establish a resolve. Vow to make an effort to act skillfully.

Then have compassion for yourself.

As dharma students, we don't ignore or condone unskillful actions. We don't turn away after we've taken an unskillful action. In a misguided attempt to practice acceptance, we don't tell ourselves, "It's okay." No. We confront the truth. We confront our unskillfulness. We acknowledge that we've caused suffering.

Acknowledging our unskillfulness, we have compassion for ourselves.

The interesting thing is, if we don't open to our unskillfulness, we're not going to be able to develop compassion for ourselves.

Recognizing our suffering, having compassion for ourselves, we do what we have to do, to end our suffering, find true happiness.

It's compassion that puts us back on the path.

Compassion is the key.

The changes we make, in dharma practice and in life, come from responding to our mistakes with wisdom and compassion. When we attend to our mistakes with wisdom and compassion, they become the starting point for making changes in our lives.

For most people the movement toward compassion goes fiercely against the grain. Students often note that when they're suffering, compassion is the "last thing" they think about. When they make mistakes, compassion is the last place they think to go. For most of us, the place of compassion is remarkably far-off. We just don't go there. But we have to learn to go there. We have to learn to develop compassion for ourselves.

We have to make it a habit.

Consider the plight of the dharma student who's veered off the path. It's been weeks since she's practiced breath meditation. She feels sharp resistance whenever she contemplates the prospect of getting on the cushion.

How does she respond to this predicament?

She might judge herself, condemn herself for being a wayward student. She might doubt her ability to practice the dharma.

She might conjure up different schemes, ways she might "fix" the problem. She might think about going on a retreat.

But the most useful response is to develop compassion. Recognizing that she's involved in a painful process, the dharma student should have compassion for herself.

It will be compassion for herself that will drive the student's efforts to renew her practice. Remember, compassion is what compels us to practice. The student's relationship to her practice, the resistance she's grappling with, will never be cured by self-aversion; it will only be healed by love, compassion.

When we hit obstacles, the skillful response is compassion, compassion for ourselves.

Let's say you've had an argument with a friend. You've spoken unskillfully. You've used some harsh words. Afterwards, you reflect on your actions. You look truthfully at what you've done. You acknowledge that your speech has caused harm, suffering. You vow to speak more skillfully in the future.

Then you have compassion for yourself.

In cultivating compassion, you set the wheels in motion for bringing about change, for taking verbal action driven by the heart, for taking action in support of your well-being and the well-being of others.

There are many ways in which we might relate to our unskillfulness, our difficulty, by using the key of compassion. When students talk about problems they're having, struggles they're going through, I invariably suggest they have compassion for themselves.

A young woman in our group was involved in a painful dynamic with some family members. Apparently they'd chosen to ostracize her. The student was hurt. And she was angry. Trying to assume the posture of a model dharma student, she tried to let go of her anger. She tried to forgive her family members. But she wasn't able to do any of that. She felt awful; she felt like she wasn't being a very good student.

In talking to the student, the diagnosis I made was: she was suffering.

The prescription: she had to have compassion for herself.

She had to have compassion for herself because she was suffering. She had to have compassion for herself because she was afflicted with anger, resentment. She had to have compassion for herself because she wasn't able to forgive.

She had to have compassion for herself because she was being hard on herself, judging herself.

She had to have compassion for herself because her relationship with her family members had fractured.

She had to cultivate compassion. Her heart was closed, tightly; by having compassion for herself, she'd begin to open it.

Another student had lost his job. He had to look for work. But he wasn't able to take action. He was stricken with inertia. He was sleeping a lot, watching a lot of TV. He wanted, understandably, to know how he might overcome his lethargy. I suggested, first things first, that he have compassion for himself. He was suffering. He had to have compassion for himself. It was going to be compassion, the opening of his heart, that would inspire the student to move ahead, instigate a job search.

We have to remember to use the key of compassion.

Motivated by compassion, we take the actions we need to take to end our suffering. Motivated by compassion, we make the path.

PRACTICE SUGGESTIONS

REFLECTION:

Do I understand what it means to practice heedfulness? Do I understand the importance of practicing heedfulness?

PRACTICE:

Practice heedfulness. Be mindful of your physical, verbal, mental actions. Discern whether your actions are unskillful or skillful. Practice to the best of your ability, understanding that you're not going to be able to be heedful of all your actions, right from the start.

PRACTICE:

Pick one specific action that you take regularly; for instance, speaking with your partner or your child. Make an effort to be heedful when taking this action.

REFLECTION:

Am I truthful in looking at my actions?

REFLECTION:

Am I able to look calmly, objectively at my actions?

PRACTICE:

Practice natural meditation. As described in the chapter, keep the breath in mind, to the best of your ability, during the course of the day.

REFLECTION:

How do I relate to natural meditation? Do I understand how the process works? Do I hold the practice with patience, compassion? Or do I become frustrated, discouraged? When I'm not mindful of the breath, do I judge myself?

REFLECTION:

Do I understand the importance of being heedful of mental actions?

PRACTICE:

Practice being heedful of mental actions, according to the Buddha's teaching on "Two Sorts of Thinking." Notice when your thinking is unskillful, imbued with sensual desire or aversion. See the drawbacks in unskillful thinking. Notice when your thinking is skillful, imbued with lovingkindness, good will, compassion. See the benefits in skillful thinking.

PRACTICE:

Choose a line of thinking, a "narrative" that you frequently pursue. Practice heedfulness, paying attention to when you become involved in this pattern of thinking.

PRACTICE:

Practice taking action driven by lovingkindness. Apply the five-step process for developing skillful intention/action. Practice developing lovingkindness with regard to both "blatant and subtle" actions.

PRACTICE:

Pick an action that you take on a regular basis. It can be an action that you take with regard to yourself or another person. In performing this action, cultivate intention/action informed by loving-kindness.

REFLECTION:

Do I take actions that are an expression of lovingkindness for myself? Is it difficult for me to take actions that are motivated by lovingkindness for myself?

PRACTICE:

Take one specific action every day that's an expression of lovingkindness for yourself. Generally, it should be an action you don't engage in on a regular basis. It can be something very simple, very ordinary, like making a healthy meal or reading a poem. In taking this action, follow the five-step process for developing skillful intention/action.

PRACTICE:

In practicing breath meditation, cultivate an easeful breath. Allow yourself to breathe in the most comfortable way.

PRACTICE:

Practice metta meditation following the guidelines provided in the chapter. Practice every day for at least 5 – 10 minutes.

PRACTICE:

Practice developing compassion for yourself. Recognize when there's suffering. For a moment, open to the suffering. Asserting directed thought, establish the intention to have compassion for yourself. Connect to a felt sense of your heart, the quality of compassion.

Practice when there's an opening, when you're able to be with suffering with calmness, equanimity.

PRACTICE:

Think about an area of your life in which there's suffering. Recognize your suffering. Open to it. Have compassion for yourself.

CHAPTER SIX

PATIENCE & EQUANIMITY

ENDURING THE DISAGREEABLE

I've always found it surprising that patience is considered one of the most important skillful qualities, that it's given such lofty standing in the Buddha's scheme of things. I guess I undervalued patience. I guess I didn't think it was that important. But it is. It's extremely important.

I think it's fair to say that, as a culture, we don't put much value on the quality of patience. We're not disposed to cultivate patience. To put it kindly, it isn't our forte. The truth is, we're an impatient lot. We want immediate results. We demand instant gratification. We don't like to have to wait. If we can't get it quickly, with a click, it's hardly worth getting.

We live in a technological culture, and much of the technology is designed to provide different phenomena with greater and greater speed. More and faster. That's the prevailing direction. That's the way of the world.

Laptop computers, tablet computers, smart phones, cell phones, portable media devices make it possible to garner sense experience, receive entertainment forms, procure information, interact with others whenever we want, wherever we are.

The cell phone, now ubiquitous, allows us to make contact with others almost instantaneously, at any moment. If we study the habits of cell phone users, we find that the technology exacerbates the cultural impatience. In New York City, it's not uncommon to encounter somebody walking on the sidewalk, cell phone pressed to the ear, talking to a companion with whom, apparently, he's just about to meet. "I'm down the block from your place," he says. "I see your building. I'll be there in a minute." We have an increasing inability to endure gaps. We can't tolerate unfilled space.

The computer is the perfect apparatus for an impatient world. High-speed internet connections enable us to tap into all manner of sense experience, access vast amounts of information, and make transactions in a matter of moments.

I'm somewhat astounded when I notice impatience arising in my mind while I'm waiting for a website to appear on my computer screen. It wasn't all that long ago, after all, that the primary means of communication across any distance was the Pony Express. It's a fast moving world, and we'd like it to move even faster.

As dharma students, it's imperative that we develop a willingness to go against the stream, to cultivate patience. We have to recognize the critical-ness of developing this decidedly countercultural quality. We have to give it priority, as the Buddha did.

If you're going to follow the Buddha's path, you're going to need patience. If you're going to go through life in a truly awake, joyful way, you're going to need patience. You're going to need a ton of patience. You're going to need the sort of patience the poet Adrienne Rich refers to when she speaks of "a wild patience."

In developing patience, we learn to "endure the disagreeable." A good definition for patience is "The ability to skillfully endure what's disagreeable."

Three categories of experience that we may find disagreeable or unpleas-ant include:

1-human beings
2-hardships
3-dharma practice

The first category is human beings. There will be times when people will act in ways that you'll find disagreeable, unpleasant. You may become impatient when interacting with certain human beings.

The second category is the hardships you encounter, the difficulties that occur in your life, the adversities, dilemmas, obstacles. The road isn't always wide open. There will be times when the traffic isn't flowing smoothly, and, in response, you may become impatient.

There will be times when you'll be asked to endure blatant hardships. A long, cold bitter winter. An oppressively hot, humid summer. A storm knocks out electrical power. Having to wait to find out if you've been accepted for a certain position. Your job is a struggle, you'd like to retire, but you've still got a few years before you're eligible for a full pension. You break your leg and you're laid up, in a cast, for six weeks. You're afflicted with severe physical pain. You're stricken with a debilitating illness.

Most days you'll confront subtle hardships: a common cold, inclement weather, a long line in the post office, a traffic jam, a flat tire. You misplace your keys. You can't find an email. You accidentally delete an email. Your internet connection is on the fritz. The train is late. The train breaks down.

The third category is dharma practice. There will be times when you'll find dharma practice disagreeable, unpleasant. There will be times when you may become impatient with the way it's going. Or not going.

Dharma practice develops gradually, and for many of us that's a disagreeable fact. Many of us become impatient, wanting to get further down the road, wanting results, wanting to attain certain levels of concentration and insight.

Like everything in life, dharma practice will have its ups and downs. We'd like, no doubt, for the arc of our progress to resemble a smooth, ever-upward line on a graph. But that's not how it works. The line on the graph is going to be jagged. There will be peaks and valleys. And we may find the valleys disagreeable, unpleasant. We may become impatient when we struggle to practice breath meditation. We may become impatient when we try to act skillfully but act unskillfully. As we've said, it's going to take a while to change the habits of a lifetime. But when we hit low points or slide into habitually unskillful patterns, we may become impatient. It's very important, in these situations, to notice our impatience. If we don't make an effort to put impatience to the side, we may very well descend into doubt. If our doubt increases, we may forsake the practice. We may quit.

Progress along the Buddha's path is generally incremental. We change, we move forward, step by step, action by action, intention by intention. If we keep practicing, if we follow the Buddha's instructions, we'll make progress. There's no question about it. But we may not always be able to see the progress we're making. Explaining the way growth presents itself, the Buddha uses the example of a brand new axe. You take the axe, chop some wood. Afterwards, you look at the axe but don't notice any wear and tear. The blade looks exactly the same. During the next week, you chop wood every day. But still you don't perceive any change in the axe blade. It's changed, of course. There's some wear. But you can't see it. It's the same with dharma practice. Progress is often imperceptible. Often times you're not able to see the changes that are taking place.

After using the axe for a year, chopping wood every day, you don't have any trouble seeing that the blade has worn down. You can see the change. Again, that's how it is with dharma practice. Eventually you're able to see that change has occurred.

But, of course, you may find the process unpleasant. You may become impatient, wanting to see results.

In developing patience, we're asked to cultivate a skill. Developing patience is a skill. It involves a step-by-step process. The Buddha doesn't say, "Be patient," and leave it at that. He provides a method. He teaches a skill.

The first step in cultivating the skill is to recognize when you're impatient.

You develop patience by seeing impatience.

You're heedful. You notice when you're impatient. You notice your impatient thinking. You notice your impatient actions. You notice when you're having difficulty enduring what's disagreeable, whether it's dharma practice, a hardship, or another person.

Recognizing your impatience, you see the drawbacks in it. At this stage you might ask: Is this impatience useful? Is it serving me?

In seeing the drawbacks in impatience, you might, for a moment, notice the body, the dissonance in the body, the dis-ease.

This is the second step: seeing the drawbacks in impatience.

Seeing the drawbacks in it, you leave the impatience to the side, the same way you'd forsake that chocolate cake sitting on the kitchen table. You distance yourself from it. You don't feed on it. And you put your mind someplace else. You find an agreeable place to put your mind. This is the third step: finding an agreeable refuge, a place to reside while enduring what's disagreeable. You find a comfortable dwelling, someplace where you can weather the storm. Usually this means putting your mind on your breath. You reside in the calm, easeful breath.

So these are the three steps for developing the skill of patience:

1-seeing impatience.

2-seeing the drawbacks in the impatience.

3-putting the attention on the breath.

Let's say you're waiting on line in the supermarket. The line is inordinately long. And it's not moving. Or at least it's not moving very quickly. Or at least not as quickly as you'd like.

You find the situation distasteful.

You feel impatient.

You begin to fabricate a stream of aversive thinking. This is terrible, you think. This is awful. I don't have time for this. What's going on here? Why is this line so long? Why isn't it moving?

Then you're heedful.

You recognize your impatience. You make a mental note: Impatience.

At this juncture you take the role of the observer. Instead of involving yourself in the impatient thinking, you observe the thinking. You watch the thoughts flow through your mind, as if you're sitting in a cafe, looking through the window, watching the cars flow down the street.

You ask: Are there drawbacks in this impatience? What are the consequences of engaging in this sort of impatient thinking? Is it useful? Is it in my best interests?

Exploring your body, you get a felt sense of the drawbacks of the impatience. You notice the suffering that impatience brings about. You notice that your body is contracted, ill-at-ease.

You put the impatience to the side. It's still there, in the mind, but you don't give it any weight. You don't engage with it. You don't feed on it.

You put your mind in a calm, easeful, agreeable place. You put your mind on your breath. You reside there.

If you follow these steps, you'll find freedom from impatience. You'll be able to skillfully endure the disagreeable. This is how you develop patience. The key is the first step, being heedful, seeing your impatience. You've got to notice your impatience; you've got to be on the look out for it.

When you have an opportunity, an opening, you may want to take some time to further investigate impatience. The more insight you acquire into impatience, the less likely you'll be to become enmeshed in it. In investigating impatience, we deconstruct it, we take it apart, the way a watchmaker might take apart a watch in order to learn more about it.

Thankfully, impatience doesn't have quite as many parts. In examining impatience, we're asked to discern that impatience has three component parts: (1) the experience: the person, hardship, or slow pace of the practice; (2) the movement in the mind that registers the experience "disagreeable;" and (3) our aversion to what's disagreeable, our "disliking."

Let's use the example of a dharma student who's attempting to complete a work project. She's hit some barriers. She'd thought the project would take about a week to complete, but several weeks have passed and she's not close to being finished. She's feeling impatient. She's obsessing about the project, the fact that it isn't going the way it's supposed to be going, the fact that it isn't finished.

She decides at some point to take a deeper look at her impatience.

Investigating her impatience, the dharma student recognizes that she's dealing with a particular hardship.

She recognizes that there's a movement in her mind that, responding to the hardship, registers: "disagreeable." She acknowledges, in other words, that she finds her experience, what's going on with the project, disagreeable, unpleasant. She makes a mental note: Disagreeable.

She recognizes her aversion. She discerns that she dislikes the disagreeable experience. Sensitive to the quality of her mind, she perceives the mental movement of "disliking." She makes a note: Disliking.

Scrutinizing her impatience, the dharma student recognizes that the mental movements of "disagreeable" and "disliking" are two entirely separate events. Typically, we don't understand this. Typically, we mush "disagreeable" and "disliking" together. We think they're one thing, a thick loathsome mass of impatience, pain. But the Buddha's teachings indicate that, in fact, they're two discrete movements. Investigating impatience, cultivating insight, we're asked to see this.

Separating the "disagreeable" and "disliking," the dharma student takes a close look at the "disliking." She investigates it. Her investigation comprises, at heart, seeing the drawbacks in the "disliking." To this end, she asks: Is this disliking useful? Is it serving me? Is it necessary? What would it be like if I let it go?

Aware of her body, she notices the consequences of participating in "disliking." She notices the dis-ease, suffering.

Continuing her investigation, the dharma student asks: Can I simply be with what's disagreeable?

The teachings suggest that if we don't add the "disliking," and simply endure what's "disagreeable," there's no problem, no suffering. There's no impatience.

Accordingly, the dharma student asks: What's it like when I don't engage in the "disliking?" What's it like when I'm just with what's "disagreeable?"

She centers herself in the breath. She remains focused right there, on the breath, in that pleasant abode. She takes refuge.

It's essential in developing patience, in enduring the disagreeable, to have an agreeable place to put the mind. The fact is, it's not possible to endure what's disagreeable if we don't have an agreeable place to reside in. If the only experience that we know is disagreeable, we won't have a chance. We'll collapse under that heavy, burdensome weight. We won't be able to endure.

In developing patience, the breath is an essential refuge. It gives us a good place to put the mind. As Ajaan Lee says, the breath provides a "home for the mind." A comfortable home.

Recognizing impatience, developing patience, we put the mind on the easeful, pleasurable breath. We reside there. We connect to the happiness inside.

In this way, we skillfully endure the disagreeable.

ACTIVELY SEEKING THE PRESENT MOMENT

When we're suffering impatience, we're averse to our experience. We dislike it. We want some other kind of experience. We want to be somewhere else.

We may tend, when impatient, to look toward the future; when we're not happy with things as they are, we may be apt to look toward the future in an attempt to locate a place of happiness there. This is an unfortunate habit, given that the future isn't real. It manifests strictly in the mind. It's a concept.

In disliking what's disagreeable, we may be apt to think: I don't like what's going on right now but at some point in the future I'll be happy.

Happiness, we may believe, lies somewhere in the distance.

For a good part of my life, I've subscribed to this view. When I was growing up on Long Island I figured I'd find happiness in the future, when I fled the suburbs. After college I moved to the city, to Queens. It wasn't long, however, before I became dissatisfied with the way things were. I figured I needed to move to Manhattan; when I get to Manhattan, I thought, I'll be happy. Eventually, I took up residence in Manhattan. But after a while I began to think that happiness lay somewhere in the distance, beyond Manhattan. By then, Brooklyn had become popular. Everybody was heading to Brooklyn. I began to think that if I moved, if I got a place in Brooklyn, I'd find happiness. Needless to say, this kind of thinking isn't consonant with what the Buddha taught. As far as I know the Buddha didn't say that happiness is found in Brooklyn. What he said, of course, is that happiness is found right where you are, wherever you are.

Cultivating patience, we recognize impatience, see the drawbacks in it, center ourselves in the breath. In connecting to the breath, we bring ourselves into the present moment. As dharma students we put much effort into finding the present moment, living in the present moment. But it can be a challenging task. The present moment isn't a place we have much familiarity with; we haven't spent much time there. The truth is, we've spent most of our lives looking to escape the present moment. We've made it a central purpose to avoid the present. We've lived at a distance from the present moment, traveling in thought worlds, anticipating various forms of sense pleasure that we might attain in the future. As a result, when we put our attention on the breath we may find it difficult to stay there. We may find ourselves moving, rather automatically, away from the present moment. We may be stricken by a fierce desire to be somewhere other than where we are. We may find ourselves casting our gaze toward the future in an attempt to identify a place where happiness might lie.

Given our inclination to shirk the present, to look toward the future, it's helpful in developing patience to actively seek the present moment. It's helpful to purposefully, and perhaps emphatically, assert an intention to center ourselves in the present moment.

How do you do this? It's actually rather simple. Putting your mind on your breath, you plunge yourself into the present moment by fabricating a firm, straightforward directive: you state your aim. To yourself, you say:

Present moment.

Or you might try another clear, sharp, no-frills verbalization.

Some examples:

Be present.

Be here.

Right here.

Right now.

This moment.

In actively seeking the present moment, you're urging yourself, exhorting yourself. Your intention, it's important to remember, is informed by compassion. Compassion for yourself. It's the kind of compassion you'd exhibit if you were walking on the sidewalk with your three-year-old daughter and she ran into the street, into traffic, and you grabbed her, pulled her to safety.

When we employ skillful fabrication, when we assert the intention to connect to the present moment, we create new pathways in the mind. Like somebody digging a trench in hard sun-baked earth, we dig new grooves. It's important to do this, because the old grooves run deep. We typically slide automatically into those old grooves. I don't want to be in this moment. Anywhere but here. I want to be somewhere else. I want to be somewhere in the future.

If we don't dig new grooves in the mind, we'll invariably slide into the old grooves. We'll relate to the present moment the same way we've always related to it: with aversion. We'll continue to evade the present moment. We'll continue to look to find happiness in the future.

Sometimes, walking to my apartment in the evening, I'll notice I'm feeling impatient. I want to be home. My experience, I'm finding, is disagreeable. After a long day, my body doesn't feel great; there's weariness, fatigue. Perhaps it's one of those hot humid New York City summer nights. I don't like the way I feel. I don't want to be walking. I don't want to be where I am. All I can think about is getting back to my place.

Heedful, I'll recognize my impatience. I'll see the drawbacks in it. I'll put my mind on my breath. But I may not able to stay with the breath; I may not able to stay there, in the present moment. I might keep thinking about getting home, how much better it's going to be when I get to my apartment. At this point, I'll actively seek the present moment. Re-placing my attention on my breath, I'll fabricate a resolute intention. Softly, but firmly, I'll tell myself: Present moment.

It's a good strategy. When it's difficult to stay present, to stay with the breath, actively seek the present moment. Make a forthright assertion. Encourage yourself to be present.

In actively seeking the present moment, you're invoking a sense of urgency. The fact is, it's an urgent matter. It's imperative that you learn to dwell in the present moment. This, after all, is where life is lived, truly lived.

This moment, the moment you're in right now as you're reading this sentence, is what's important. This is where happiness is found. It's the only place. You may be holding on to the idea, even as you're reading this, that you'll discover happiness in some other place, in the future. Maybe after you finish this chapter. Maybe after you put down the book. Maybe later on today. Maybe tomorrow. Maybe when you go on vacation. Can you perceive your tendency to think like this? Can you release this way of thinking? Can you assert your intention to be present, to be right here, right now?

Try it.

Put your mind on your breath.

Now actively seek the present moment.

Make a strong assertion.

"Present moment."

Keep your attention on your breath.

"Present moment."

Be here. In this moment. Right now.

The fact is, this moment is all you've got. This is it. The past is past. The future is an idea, a non-reality, a fantasy, a dream.

The fact is, it isn't guaranteed you'll make it to tomorrow. The fact is, you don't know what's going to happen. You don't know when your life will end. You don't have any idea what day will be your last.

Several years ago I stayed for a lengthy stretch at a monastery in California. At times I found my experience disagreeable. At times I felt impatient. Every now and then I found myself thinking about going home, returning to New York. When I told my teacher about my impatience, he reminded me that it wasn't guaranteed I'd even make it back to New York. There'd been a fairly resounding earthquake while I was at the monastery. There might be another. Anything might happen. Given that the future wasn't promised, there was only one reasonable course of action to take: I had to focus on the moment I was in, the present moment. I had to stay there. Right there.

As the Buddha notes:

You shouldn't chase after the past
　or place expectations on the future.
What is past
　　is left behind.
The future
　　is as yet unreached.
Whatever quality is present
you clearly see
　　right there, right there.
Not taken in,
unshaken,
that's how you develop the heart.
Ardently doing
what should be done today,

for — who knows? — tomorrow
    death.
There is no bargaining
with Mortality & his mighty horde.

Whoever lives thus ardently,
    relentlessly
      both day & night,
has truly had an auspicious day:
so says the Peaceful Sage.
(MN 131)

As the Buddha indicates, you have to make a wholehearted effort to put your attention on the present moment. You have to strive "ardently, relentlessly" to live in the present moment.

This is where happiness is found.

Every now and again, as you strive to reside in the present moment, you might want to guide yourself toward recognizing the happiness that's found only in the moment. It's another good strategy. As you ground yourself in your breath, you might ask:

Where is happiness found?

Can I find happiness in this moment?

As you incline to the happiness that exists potentially in every moment, you may begin to get intimations of that happiness. You may begin to detect it. The happiness that's right there. The happiness that's always there.

When I lodge myself in the present moment, I'm often at least slightly stunned to find happiness right there. Walking to my apartment on a hot summer night, recognizing my impatience, centering myself in my breath, shifting inward, into my body, into my heart, I find that happiness is right there.

When faced with disagreeable experience, you can still know happiness, the happiness inside, the happiness of the heart. You might suppose, when confronted with disagreeable experience, that all your human experience is disagreeable. You might believe that you don't have any choice except to be unhappy. But it's not so. Our existence is comprised of many different experiences. The world is wider than our view of it. When things like the weary body, like the weather, are disagreeable, you can still find an agreeable refuge in the breath. You can still find happiness. Happiness is there. If you look, you can find it.

As we move forward, we learn to appreciate the paradoxes of dharma practice. The practice requires extraordinary patience, wild patience. We're asked to accept that the path unfolds gradually, slowly. At the same time, we're asked to pay close, urgent attention to the present moment; we're asked to find happiness right here, in the moment we're in.

A MIND LIKE THE EARTH

The culminating skillful quality is equanimity. In the Buddha's dharma, it's a profoundly significant quality. We might call it the "crowning" skillful quality.

Equanimity is imperturbability, unshakableness.

Thanissaro Bhikkhu defines equanimity as "An attitude of even-mindedness in the face of every sort of experience, regardless of whether pleasure and pain are present or not."

Developed in equanimity, we keep our balance. When confronted with agreeable and disagreeable experience we don't get knocked off stride; we remain calm, composed, steady. In stressful situations, we're not flustered. We keep our cool.

We develop equanimity through concentration practice, by practicing mindfulness of breathing. Equanimity is one of the primary jhana factors, one of the most important results of practicing breath meditation.

In fostering equanimity there are four basic steps that we follow:

1-recognizing when experience is agreeable or disagreeable.
2-cultivating insight.
3-inclining to the quality of equanimity.
4-centering in the breath.

It may seem like dharma practice is inordinately structured. It may seem like there are lots of "steps." But there are good reasons why we teach a step-by-step approach. For one thing, it makes it a lot easier to remember what to do. It's especially important for householders, with fast-paced lives and myriad responsibilities, to utilize step-by-step instructions. To offer an analogy, let's say you're going shopping. You have to buy a large amount of groceries, so it's a good idea to make a list. That way, you'll remember what to buy. In the same way, a step-by-step approach helps us remember what to do, how to practice, how to move toward a greater happiness.

In that spirit, let's take a look at the four steps for developing the skill of equanimity.

First, you recognize when your experience has turned agreeable or disagreeable.

Agreeable experience takes many shapes. You get a promotion. You enter into a romantic relationship. You think about an upcoming vacation. You reminisce about beloved high school companions. Your kid does well on his report card. You have an enjoyable conversation with a dear friend. You dig into a pint container of your favorite ice cream.

And, of course, disagreeable experience takes many forms. You're ill. You lose your job. Your job isn't bringing you any satisfaction. You have a difficult relationship with a co-worker. Your teenager is experimenting with drugs. You have an argument with your partner. The washing machine ruins your most cherished pair of pants. You buy a pint of ice cream but when you get home you realize you bought the wrong kind.

In practicing this step, you're heedful. You pay attention to your experience. You notice when your experience is agreeable or disagreeable. It's always useful, in perceiving your experience, to make a mental note: "agreeable" or "disagreeable."

The second step is "cultivating insight." At this stage in the process, you're asked to discern that your experience is impermanent, inconstant.

All conditioned experience, the Buddha teaches, is impermanent. In translating the Pali word "annica," Thanissaro Bhikkhu prefers the term "inconstant." Most scholars translate "annica" as "impermanent," but "inconstant" gives us a more accurate, descriptive picture of the nature of our experience. The dictionary defines "inconstant" as "changeable; likely to change frequently and unpredictably." Our experience of body and mind is just like this; it's forever changing. It's always in flux. It's always vacillating, sometimes unpredictably, from agreeable to disagreeable, from disagreeable to agreeable. What this means is you'll always have to contend with disagreeable experiences; you'll never be able to avoid the disagreeable. It also means that agreeable experiences will always pass; you'll never, ever, be able to hold on to agreeable experience.

In cultivating insight, you're asked to recognize the drawbacks in wanting to latch on to what's agreeable and wanting to eliminate what's disagreeable.

The drawbacks, to put it succinctly, are that you cause yourself suffering.

The next step is "inclining to the quality of equanimity." Equanimity is innate. It's part of the everpresent truth. You have equanimity. It may not be well-developed, but it's there, inside, the same way that generosity is there, lovingkindness is there. In this step, you bring your awareness to your body and choose to connect to a felt sense of the quality of equanimity.

It may help, in inclining to equanimity, to think of it as inner strength, the strength to remain balanced, no matter what your experience is like.

Let's say you've received bad news. You're going to need a lot of dental work. You begin to feel stress. Cultivating equanimity, you recognize that your experience is "disagreeable." You see clearly that this sort of disagreeable experience is an inevitable part of life. You ascertain that there are drawbacks in fighting disagreeable experience. Letting your awareness reside in your body, you incline toward the quality of equanimity. You assert: "Equanimity." You garner a felt sense of equanimity, inner strength.

When Rahula became a monk, the Buddha taught him to be "in tune" with the quality of equanimity. He provided the symbol the earth to help Rahula comprehend the nature of equanimity.

"Rahula, develop the meditation in tune with earth. For when you are developing the meditation in tune with earth, agreeable & disagreeable sensory impressions that have arisen will not stay in charge of your mind. Just as when people throw what is clean or unclean on the earth — feces, urine, saliva, pus, or blood — the earth is not horrified, humiliated, or disgusted by it; in the same way, when you are developing the meditation in tune with earth, agreeable & disagreeable sensory impressions that have arisen will not stay in charge of your mind." (MN 62)

The earth, the Buddha says, is subject to disagreeable experience, rain, snow, ice, cold, wind. People throw unclean things on it. But the earth isn't horrified. It doesn't get bent out of shape. It remains steady, unshaken.

When conditions are agreeable, when the weather is pleasant, when the air is warm and fragrant, when the sun shines gently on its surfaces, the earth doesn't get all juiced up, doesn't ask for more. It maintains its evenness, day after day, season after season.

Nature offers countless examples of equanimity. The trees and rivers exemplify steadiness, strength. The Buddha recommended dharma practitioners go into nature in support of their practice. When we go into nature, when we perceive the goodness in nature, we're reminded of our own goodness. We're reminded that we possess the quality of equanimity. When we commune with the trees and rivers, the mountains, the sprawling valleys, we get in touch with our own equanimity, our own capacity for inner strength.

As we develop in skill, we become more able to tune in to the quality of equanimity. The skilled practitioner, the Buddha says, attunes to equanimity as easily as he might "snap his fingers."

Inclining to the quality of equanimity, you center yourself in the breath. This is the fourth step. You put your mind on the breath. You keep it there. Right there.

Centered in the breath, in the body, you remained unmoved. You're not knocked off balance by agreeable or disagreeable experiences.

Your capacity to keep your mind on the breath, to remain steady, even, will depend on the degree to which you've developed concentration, jhana. You cultivate equanimity, inner strength, by practicing breath meditation. The potential for equanimity is there. But if you're going to stay centered in the face of every kind of experience, you're going to have to cultivate it. You're going to have to build your inner strength.

VICISSITUDES OF LIFE

Most people don't like change. They'd prefer things remain stable, steady. But the things of life will always be in flux, subject to constant change. Understanding that the conditions of life won't provide stability, the dharma student develops inner stability. He develops equanimity. Developed in equanimity, he skillfully meets the vicissitudes of life.

Webster defines "vicissitude" as: "1.a: the quality or state of being changeable: mutability. b: natural change or mutation visible in nature or in human affairs. 2. a: a favorable or unfavorable event or situation that occurs by chance: a fluctuation of state or condition (the conditions of daily life). b: alternating change: succession."

In a well-known teaching the Buddha delineates "eight vicissitudes" of life. The eight vicissitudes include four pairs of agreeable and disagreeable experience. They are: (1) pleasure and pain, (2) gain and loss, (3) status and disrepute, (4) praise and blame. The dharma student cultivating equanimity is encouraged to recognize when he's subject to these eight fluctuating circumstances. The eight vicissitudes are the "worldly conditions" we're most prone to become involved with, entangled with, enmeshed in, thrown by; when we get caught up with these conditions we bring about suffering. It's said we're going along with the "ways of the world" when we chase after pleasure, gain, status, praise, when we try to escape pain, loss, disrepute, blame. In following the Buddha's way, it's critical that we don't get sidetracked by these eight vicissitudes.

First, there's pleasure and pain. Experience that we take in through our sense doors may be pleasurable or painful. According to the teachings, there are six sense experiences: sights, sounds, smells, tastes, bodily sensations, mental impressions (thoughts, emotions). There will be times when our experience, received through the eyes, ears, nose, mouth, body, mind will be pleasurable; there will be times when it will be painful.

Cultivating equanimity, following the four-step process, we recognize when we're subject to pleasure and pain. We discern that our sense experience will change, fluctuate between pleasure and pain. There will always be pleasure. And there will always be pain.

During the course of any day we're subject to an array of pleasurable and painful sense experiences. You eat a delicious breakfast. A half hour later you've got indigestion. You leave your house, step outside to a beautiful warm spring day. Later it rains and you get soaking wet. Pleasure and pain. All day long your experience is in flux.

When practicing breath meditation, we often get a good picture of the manner in which bodily sensations vacillate. At the start of the meditation there's tightness in the body. After a while there's ease. Then there's a quality of bliss. Then your knee begins to hurt, you're stricken with sharp stabbing pain. Then the pain subsides and everything feels okay. And so on. It's the way it is. In life, there's pleasure and pain.

Sometimes there's a shift while you're experiencing a specific sensation. You go to a meditation class on a hot summer night. You take a position on the floor directly beneath the rapidly beating ceiling fan. At first the sensation of the air against the skin is rather pleasant; however after some time passes you begin to feel cold. The sensation is the same but the flavor is different. The experience of the air hitting the body is now unpleasant, painful.

Next, there's gain and loss.

Gain takes various shapes. You make money. Your business flourishes. You get a job. You sell some of your work. You buy a car. You buy a television. You meet a new friend. You get married. A child is born.

Then there's loss. You lose money. You lose your job. Your car is stolen. Your television breaks down. A dear friend moves to another city. You get divorced. A family member dies.

The dharma student notices when there's gain and loss.

She comprehends the truth: there will always be gain and loss.

Gain and loss, she discerns, are both part of life.

We'd like, of course, for there only to be gain. But it's not going to happen. Loss is inevitable. People are outraged when the economy takes a downturn, when the housing market suffers, when the stock market drops precipitously. As if it shouldn't happen. But, in fact, it's exactly what should happen. It's the way things are, the way things will always be. There will be gain and there will be loss.

The next pair of vicissitudes is status and disrepute. At times we'll enjoy status. Others will regard us highly. In our careers we'll assume a lofty position. We'll take certain actions for which we'll receive acclaim. And then there will be times when we'll fall into disrepute. We'll be held in low regard.

Recognizing when we're subject to status and disrepute, we apprehend the unalterable truth that for as long as we sojourn in the human realm, the way that people look at us, think about us, will fluctuate. At your job, for instance, there will be times when your co-workers will hold you in high esteem, times when they'll hold you in low esteem. How does the song go? Riding high in April, shot down in May. That pretty much sums it up. You receive tons of acclaim for your accomplishments, but then something goes awry and suddenly you're the object of condemnation. We frequently observe this kind of alteration in the lives of celebrities.

The movie star involved in a scandal is relegated from hero to villain with startling velocity.

Although you may not be a star of stage and screen, you'll experience status and disrepute.

Lastly, there's praise and blame. Sometimes we'll be praised. Sometimes we'll be blamed, criticized.

Recognizing when he's subject to the eight vicissitudes, the dharma student takes the position of the observer. With the objectivity of a scientist looking through a microscope, he notes: "there's praise" or "there's blame." Labeling is useful; it helps set up a spacious, non-attached relationship to the experience of praise or blame, pleasure or pain, gain or loss, status or disrepute.

Observing praise and blame, the dharma student realizes that, as a human being, he'll receive both praise and blame. It's an unavoidable truth.

When we take an action, some people may praise us, and some may blame us, criticize us. When I give a dharma talk, some people like it, other people don't like it. Although I'd prefer that everybody acknowledge the talk in glowing, highly complimentary terms, it's not a realistic expectation. There's always praise and blame.

When I've organized dharma programs, there've been occasions when, after a class with a teacher, somebody approached, told me how much they appreciated the program, how much they enjoyed the teachings, and while the person and I were speaking another person came over and expressed dissatisfaction with the event, distaste for the teacher. It was right there in front me. Praise and blame.

As dharma students, we may have the idea that when we achieve a level of proficiency we'll no longer experience pain, loss, disrepute, blame. We'll only know pleasure, gain, status, praise. But that's not how it works.

Everybody is subject to the eight vicissitudes.

Everybody encounters both the agreeable and disagreeable. Everybody. Even the Buddha had to deal with disagreeable experience. There were people who disparaged him. He had to manage quarrels amongst monks. In his later years the Buddha's closest friends died. The Buddha himself was wracked with severe back pain. Like all human beings, he met with sickness, aging, death, separation.

Everybody experiences pleasure and pain, gain and loss, status and disrepute, praise and blame. The difference between the skilled practitioner and the unskilled person is that the skilled practitioner isn't knocked off balance by the vicissitudes of life. The skilled practitioner isn't disrupted by the eight vicissitudes. As the Buddha puts it, he doesn't "welcome" what's agreeable and doesn't "rebel against" what's disagreeable.

"He doesn't welcome the arisen gain, or rebel against the arisen loss. He doesn't welcome the arisen status, or rebel against the arisen disgrace. He doesn't welcome the arisen praise, or rebel against the arisen censure. He does not welcome the arisen pleasure, or rebel against the arisen pain. As he thus abandons welcoming & rebelling, he is released from birth, aging, & death; from sorrows, lamentations, pains, distresses, & despairs. He is released, I tell you, from suffering & stress.

"This is the difference, this the distinction, this the distinguishing factor between the well-instructed disciple of the noble ones and the uninstructed run-of-the-mill person."
(AN 8.6)

The skilled practitioner understands the drawbacks in "welcoming" pleasure, gain, status, praise, in "rebelling against" pain, loss, disrepute, blame. He develops this understanding by paying close attention to the way he relates to the eight worldly conditions. With a keen, objective eye, he observes his unskillfulness. When he chases after the agreeable and opposes the disagreeable, he recognizes the painful consequences. He sees that when he becomes preoccupied with the eight vicissitudes, he suffers. In this way he gradually cultivates understanding, insight. Rooted in insight, he develops the skill of equanimity.

The Buddha puts it rather eloquently:

> Gain/loss,
> status/disgrace,
> censure/praise,
> pleasure/pain:
> these conditions among human beings
> are inconstant,
> impermanent,
> subject to change.
>
> Knowing this, the wise person, mindful,
> ponders these changing conditions. Desirable things don't charm
> the mind,
> undesirable ones bring no resistance.
>
> His welcoming
> & rebelling are scattered,
> gone to their end,
> do not exist.
> Knowing the dustless, sorrowless state,

he discerns rightly,
    has gone, beyond becoming,
    to the Further Shore.
(AN 8.6)

A HOME FOR THE MIND

If we develop equanimity we'll meet life's vicissitudes with steadiness, strength and grace. No matter what happens, we'll live joyfully.

Life, after all, is meant to be joyful.

Faced with the vicissitudes of life, we strive to remain centered; we strive to keep our spot, to refrain from chasing after pleasure, gain, status, praise, from rebelling against pain, loss, disrepute, blame. We strive to keep our attention on the body. We strive, when all is said and done, to keep our mind on the breath.

As I've said, our ability to keep the mind on the breath in the face of agreeable and disagreeable conditions depends on the degree to which we've developed concentration, jhana. We build equanimity through concentration practice.

Practicing mindfulness of breathing, in formal meditation and natural meditation, we cultivate equanimity. It's a practice. It requires determination. It requires patience. If we put in the effort, over a period of months, years, we'll build equanimity. We'll build inner strength.

The Buddha gave specific instructions for practicing mindfulness of breathing. In fact, they're the most detailed meditation instructions he gave during his 45 years of teaching. Following these instructions, we cultivate equanimity, the ability to keep the mind centered, steady, even, in every situation.

It's important to understand that if you're going to develop equanimity, the sort of equanimity that will enable you to remain steady, strong, in the face of pleasure and pain, gain and loss, status and disrepute, praise and blame, you're going to have to follow the Buddha's instructions. If you don't practice breath meditation in the manner the Buddha teaches, if you don't make an effort to cultivate jhana, if you decide to follow a less comprehensive style of meditation, you may develop some equanimity. But wouldn't you rather develop more than just "some" equanimity? The fact is, you're going to need more than "some" equanimity. You're going to need a lot of equanimity to skillfully meet the vicissitudes of life.

The bottom line is, if you don't follow the Buddha's instructions, you won't develop the equanimity you're going to need when confronted with the constantly changing experiences of life, the ups and downs, highs and lows, the "full catastrophe."

Practicing mindfulness of breathing, adhering to the Buddha's steps, we put the mind on the breath at one point, a point in the body where the breath feels comfortable. This step is "directed thought." The next step is "evaluation." In this step we pay attention to what the breath is like, where in the breath there's dis-ease, where there's ease. Gradually we cultivate an easeful breath. Then we allow the ease, the "breath energy," to spread throughout the body. The body is gradually suffused with ease, smooth flowing energy. This physical ease gives rise to mental ease, tranquility, pleasure. Experiencing pleasure, we're happy to be where we are; we're happy to stay put, to keep our attention on the body; we don't have a lot of interest in other phenomena, thoughts, sounds, sensations. When we return our focus to the breath at one point, the breath is remarkably smooth, easeful, pleasurable; the mind, for the most part, is willing to stay right there. We don't have to make much effort to keep it there. It just stays there. Right there.

In this way, we develop concentration, the ability to keep our attention on the breath, the ability to stay put. As we keep practicing, we foster our ability to stay put. We cultivate equanimity. We cultivate the strength to stay put no matter what, regardless of how agreeable or disagreeable our experience might be. As human beings, we possess a capacity for inner strength; in practicing breath meditation, we cultivate this strength, the same way we cultivate strength in the arms by doing lots of push-ups. (The reader should note that in this book we're not providing detailed instructions for practicing mindfulness of breathing. The serious dharma student interested in developing all the facets of the path should make an effort to seek out step-by-step instruction in breath meditation.)

The dharma student developing the skill of equanimity recognizes when her experience has turned agreeable or disagreeable. She sees the drawbacks in chasing after what's agreeable, opposing what's disagreeable. Inclining to the quality of equanimity, the inner strength she's built during many hours of practice, she puts her mind on her breath. She keeps it there. She stays put. She remains steady, even, imperturbable.

Ajaan Lee says that in practicing breath meditation we build a "home for the mind." The dharma student, in putting her mind on her breath, takes up residence in this home for the mind.

The breath is a place to put the mind. In the same way we'd situate ourselves in a safe, comfortable dwelling when there's a storm, we put our mind on the breath when confronted with the vicissitudes of life. We reside in this home for the mind.

It isn't a conceptual task, some sort of metaphysical gyration. We're putting our attention in a real place. This home for the mind is a real place. The breath is real. It's a real place in the body.

The home we construct when we make persistent effort to practice mindfulness of breathing isn't a flimsy structure. It's sturdy. It's strong. As we cultivate jhana, we're more and more able to keep the mind on the breath.

We're able to remain inside the home for the mind, in all situations, whether there's pleasure or pain, gain or loss, status or disrepute, praise or blame.

As we continue over the long haul to practice mindfulness of breathing, we strengthen the foundation of our home for the mind. It's as if we're driving steel girders deeper and deeper into the ground, the way they drive steel into the earth, into layers of rock, when they build skyscrapers.

Describing equanimity, strength of mind, the Buddha uses a similar metaphor:

'Just as if there were a stone column, sixteen spans tall, of which eight spans were rooted below ground, and then from the east there were to come a powerful wind storm: The column would not shiver nor quiver nor quake. And then from the west... the north... the south there were to come a powerful wind storm: The column would not shiver nor quiver nor quake. Why? Because of the depth of the root and the well-buriedness of the stone column. In the same way, my friend, even if powerful forms cognizable by the eye come into the visual range of a monk whose mind is thus rightly released... etc... his mind is neither overpowered nor even engaged.'
(AN 9.26)

If you put wholehearted effort into developing the breath you'll build a strong home for your mind, a place where you'll be safe, protected, comfortable in every kind of weather. But if you don't develop the breath, your shelter will be vulnerable, suspect. It will be like a brokendown shack. When there's pleasure and pain, gain and loss, status and disrepute, praise and blame, the room will leak, the walls will fall apart and you'll be exposed to the elements, the screaming wind, stinging cold, harsh rain.

Developed in equanimity, we remain steady, imperturbable, when our experience is blatantly agreeable or disagreeable. We remain even-minded when we lose our job, when we get the job we've always dreamed about, when we make a lot of money, when we lose a lot of money, when we begin a romance, when we go through a break-up, when we're ill, when we're dying. We keep our balance. We don't get carried away by currents of unskillful thinking. We don't obsess. We don't drown in turbulent emotional waters. We don't live "in the head." Instead, we reside in the body. We keep our mind on the breath. We keep it right there, in that well-built abode.

Recently a beloved member of our group died in a tragic biking accident. John was a quiet leader, an exemplary dharma student, a great guy. His death had a powerful effect on everybody in the community. The members of the community were shocked. They were deeply sorrowful. They had a profound experience of the "pain of separation." But they kept their balance. They remained steady. In the days and weeks following John's passing, the members of the group displayed great equanimity. It was, in my view, an indication of the strength of their practice, all the effort they'd put in over the years. This, I thought, is what it means to have developed equanimity.

Most days, of course, we're not subject to blatant expressions of pleasure and pain, gain and loss, status and disrepute, praise and blame. But every day we encounter subtle forms of agreeable and disagreeable experience. In developing equanimity, we make an effort to remain steady, balanced, when faced with both blatant and subtle conditions. It's important to recognize the subtle movements; as we all know, we can easily get knocked off stride by the small things, the so-called broken shoelaces.

In class one evening a group member described an incident when he remained equanimous when faced with a subtly disagreeable experience.

Walking to class, he got caught in a thunderstorm. He didn't have an umbrella and was forced to seek shelter in a nearby store. Realizing he was going to be late for class, he started to worry. He became anxious. Practicing heedfulness, he recognized that he was "rebelling against" what was happening. The situation, he realized, was disagreeable. These sorts of disagreeable experiences, he realized, were an unavoidable part of life. He comprehended the drawbacks in rebelling against what's disagreeable. Inclining to the quality of equanimity, he placed his attention on his breath. He kept his mind right there. Right there. Steady, balanced, he felt a contentedness. Looking through the store's plate glass window, he watched the thunderstorm. And, lo and behold, he was able to enjoy it.

The Buddha, of course, is the most profound example of a human being who developed the quality of equanimity. He was the picture of inner strength. Looking at statues of the Buddha we appreciate his extraordinary equanimity. He's steady, strong, utterly imperturbable.

You don't see statues of the Buddha off balance, teetering.

Many statues portray the Buddha sitting, meditating, on the night of his awakening. On that night Mara tried to prevent the Buddha from attaining awakening. He tried to knock the Buddha off his spot. He threw everything he had at the Buddha, the most alluringly agreeable phenomena, the most violently disagreeable phenomena. But the Buddha didn't move. He didn't waver. He didn't flinch.

That night the Buddha practiced mindfulness of breathing. He cultivated the breath.

Established in equanimity, the Buddha stayed put. Mara tried. He made every attempt to knock the Buddha off balance. But the Buddha didn't budge. He remained unmoved, imperturbable.

That's equanimity.

That's inner strength.

PRACTICE SUGGESTIONS

REFLECTION:

In what areas do I tend to become impatient?

REFLECTION:

Am I impatient when it comes to dharma practice?

PRACTICE:

Practice developing patience, following the instructions set forth in the chapter: (1) seeing impatience, (2) seeing the drawbacks in the impatience, (3) putting the attention on your breath.

PRACTICE:

Choose one specific disagreeable experience with which you have a regular habit of becoming impatient. It might be something rather ordinary, like waiting in line in the supermarket. Be heedful, paying close attention to the way you relate to this disagreeable experience. Recognize when there's impatience. Cultivate patience, following the above instructions.

PRACTICE:

Consider your dharma practice. Notice if there's impatience with regard to any aspect of your development along the path. Recognize the impatience, see the drawbacks in it, ground in present moment awareness.

PRACTICE:

When practicing breath meditation, notice if there's impatience. Cultivate patience.

REFLECTION:

Do I tend to think I'll find happiness somewhere in the future?

PRACTICE:

Practice actively seeking the present moment. Seeing impatience, centering in the breath, urge yourself to pay attention to the present moment. Make a firm assertion, such as: "Present moment" or "This moment."

PRACTICE:

When there is an "opening," investigate impatience. Deconstructing impatience, take the following steps: (1) recognize impatience; acknowledge that you're having difficulty enduring a particular experience, a person, hardship, some aspect of dharma practice, (2) recognize that you find the experience "disagreeable," (3) discern that you're "disliking" the disagreeable experience, (4) discern that the movement in the mind that registers the experience as "disagreeable" and the movement of "disliking" are two separate events; ask: can I simply be with the disagreeable experience without adding on disliking?

REFLECTION:

Where am I in terms of the skillful quality of equanimity? Do I maintain steadiness, even-mindedness, in the face of agreeable and disagreeable experience? In what areas, blatant and subtle, do I need to develop equanimity?

PRACTICE:

Develop equanimity. Utilize the four-step process: (1) see when your experience is agreeable or disagreeable, (2) cultivate insight, (3) incline to the quality of equanimity, (4) center in the breath.

PRACTICE:

Choose one specific agreeable experience that you have a tendency to "welcome." Practice developing equanimity with regard to this experience.

PRACTICE:

Choose one specific disagreeable experience that you have a tendency to "rebel against." Practice developing equanimity with regard to this experience.

REFLECTION:

Where am I in terms of how I relate to the eight vicissitudes: pleasure and pain, gain and loss, status and disrepute, praise and blame?

PRACTICE:

Develop equanimity, as above, when confronted with the eight vicissitudes.

PRACTICE:

Choose one experience of either pleasure, gain, status, or praise that you frequently "welcome." Make a point to develop the skill of equanimity with regard to this experience.

PRACTICE:

Choose one experience of either pain, loss, disrepute, or blame that you frequently "rebel against." Make a point to develop the skill of equanimity with regard to this experience.

REFLECTION:

Is my breath meditation practice developed to the point where the breath is a "home for the mind"?

CLOSING WORDS

WHERE YOU'LL FIND WHAT YOU'RE LOOKING FOR

For some time people have urged me to write a book describing the teachings I've been giving in New York City for the last number of years. I've been hesitant, largely because I'm keenly aware of the tendency people have when it comes to dharma books: They read the books, they read about the dharma, but they don't practice the dharma. I've been leery about contributing to this scenario by writing yet another dharma book.

Dharma practice, as we've said, is a practice. It's something you do. It requires taking action. It requires putting in effort.

As a dharma teacher, my job is to teach skills. I teach skills that students cultivate in the service of developing skillful qualities, concentration, insight. What it comes down to is, you have to cultivate the skills. You have to practice. You aren't going to develop skillful qualities simply by reading this book.

In these pages we've talked about how to cultivate the skills of generosity, ethical conduct, renunciation, truthfulness, effort, determination, discernment, lovingkindness, patience, equanimity. But you'll learn, truly learn, these skills only by making an effort to cultivate them, by practicing. Learning transcends intellectual knowing; learning is accomplished by doing, by engaging in an active process, by seeing for ourselves.

As we develop the skillful qualities we experience a greater happiness. This happiness, I think it's fair to say, is something we'd all like to know. But you won't know a greater happiness by reading this book. You'll only know it by taking action.

The Buddha's happiness is a happiness that depends on our actions.

Life in and of itself is meaningless. We give it meaning through our actions. We give life meaning by taking actions inspired by lovingkindness and compassion.

As you consider taking action, you might think: "Yes, I need to put these teachings into practice. I need to put an effort into developing these skills. And eventually I will. At some point in the future I'll do it."

You might tell yourself that you can't do it right now, but that at some future juncture you'll make an effort to develop the skillful qualities. You might come up with a timetable. You'll do it after your kids finish high school. You'll do it after you leave your job. You'll do it after you complete the project you're working on. You'll do it after you move to a new place.

You might think that if you could make a bold move you'd be more able to follow the path. If you could go to Thailand, spend time at a monastery. If you could visit India, make a pilgrimage to the very spot where the Buddha awakened. If you could take a year to meditate at one of those nicely polished western centers. If you could get out of the city, move to the country.

This sort of thinking is misguided. It isn't useful. As long as you hold on to the idea that you'll be able follow the path when things are different, when conditions are more suitable, you'll never get to where you want to get.

The only place you'll find what you're looking for is right here, right where you are, right now.

This is the time that you have in which to practice. This is the time to develop skillful qualities.

You have to begin now. In this moment. Not later today. Not tomorrow. Not next week. Right now.

Your life might not be what you'd like it to be. You might not be where you'd like to be. Really, though, it doesn't matter. You can begin to develop skillful qualities.

It's important to remember that this is something you can do. You can do it. If you learn the skills, if you practice, you can do it.

As the Buddha said:

"Develop what is skillful, monks. It is possible to develop what is skillful. If it were not possible to develop what is skillful, I would not say to you, 'Develop what is skillful.' But because it is possible to develop what is skillful, I say to you, 'Develop what is skillful.'"
(AN 2.19)

LIFE IS SHORT

In an effort to engender the desire to practice, to move forward along the path, there are certain reflections you might engage in.

One is the reflection on suffering. When you contemplate the truth of your suffering, you become more inclined to do what you have to do to end it. Acknowledging your suffering, you respond with compassion, and out of compassion you make an effort to abandon the unskillful and develop the skillful.

Another important contemplation is the reflection on death. In making this reflection there are three basic truths you might reflect on:

1-You will die.
2-Life is short.
3-The time of death is uncertain.

When we reflect on the truth of death, we're disposed to act accordingly, to make the most of our lives, to practice the dharma in the service of ending suffering and finding true happiness. Death is the great motivator. It strengthens our resolve. It instigates a sense of urgency.

The Buddha encouraged his followers to remember that life is short and that they should make an effort to find true happiness while they had the chance. He used vivid similes to describe the brevity of life.

"'Just as a dewdrop on the tip of a blade of grass quickly vanishes with the rising of the sun and does not stay long, in the same way, brahmans, the life of human beings is like a dewdrop....

"'Just as when the rain-devas send rain in fat drops, and a bubble on the water quickly vanishes and does not stay long, in the same way, brahmans, the life of human beings is like a water bubble....

"'Just as a line drawn in the water with a stick quickly vanishes and does not stay long, in the same way, brahmans, the life of human beings is like a line drawn in the water with a stick....'"

(AN 7.70)

The fact is, you've got just a brief amount of time in which to live, in which to find the happiness that's available to a human being. You don't want to squander the little time you've got.

You might think about it like this:

You take a trip to Paris. You've never been there, but you've always wanted to go. Finally you're there. You're going to be there for a week. You don't want to spend your time in your hotel room, reading magazines. You want to experience the city, see the sights. You want to go to the Eiffel Tower and the Louvre. You want to stroll along the Seine. You want to make the most of the limited time you have.

That's how it is with this life. It's just a brief stay. You're not going to be here very long. You've got just this small piece of time. You want to make the most of it.

It's easier, perhaps, to ignore the truth. It's easier, perhaps, to turn away from the fact that death is unavoidable. It's easier to forget. For this reason, we need to make it a practice to remember. The Buddha said that he reflected on the truth of death with every breath. Clearly, that's way too much for us; we don't have quite as much equanimity as the Buddha. The reflection on death must be practiced skillfully. We need to reflect with steadiness, strength. In other words, we need equanimity. Developed in equanimity, we're less likely to get knocked sideways by the reflection.

I generally recommend that students reflect on the truth of death once every day. There will be days, of course, when you won't have the necessary equanimity; if you don't feel up to it, you should bypass the reflection. You shouldn't reflect if you're not able to do it skillfully.

The reflection shouldn't take longer than a few moments. I usually suggest that students reflect for no more than ten seconds. Five seconds is probably long enough.

And in fact, you don't need to reflect for longer than that. If you reflect for a few moments every day, or almost every day, on an ongoing basis, you'll benefit significantly.

In reflecting, you're asked to remind yourself of the truth of death. The Buddha offers the basic reflection:

"I am subject to death. Death is unavoidable."

Other possible reflections include:

"Life is short. Shorter than I think."

"The time of death is uncertain."

"The days and nights are passing endlessly. How am I spending my time?"

As always, the reflection will be most effective if you find your own words, your own way of saying it, your own way of directing yourself toward an understanding of the truth.

Reflecting, keep your attention in the body. Connect to a felt sense of the truth, the truth of death, the truth of your own death. Feel the truth.

If you like, you can try it now.

Put your mind on your breath. Let the breath be easeful, pleasant.

Keeping your attention in your body, reflect on the truth of death.

Assert directed thought.

"I am subject to death. Death is unavoidable."

Allow the reflection to pervade your body, move through your body. Let it touch in to your heart.

Apprehend a felt sense of the truth.

After five or ten seconds, put the reflection to the side. Focus on your breath. Feel the easeful breath.

Some people protest when they're advised to reflect on the truth of death. They complain that it's a morbid, gloomy practice. But the reflection on death isn't meant to promote gloominess. To the contrary, it's meant to guide us toward the end of suffering. The reflection, when practiced skillfully, opens us to the truth. It motivates us to practice the dharma. It promotes a sense of urgency. It reminds us to have a sense of our true priorities and to stick to them. It points us in the right direction. It leads us toward a greater happiness.

A GREATER HAPPINESS

The purpose of dharma practice is simple. We follow the Buddha's path so that we might end our suffering, so that we might find a greater happiness.

There is a greater happiness. The Buddha found it. That's what he set out to do. He had a pretty good life. He was well-off. He had a lot of stuff. He had access to an array of sense pleasures. But he questioned the happiness this life offered. He figured there had to be a greater happiness. At any rate, he was going to find out. And he did. He discovered there was, indeed, a greater happiness.

As dharma students we resolve to know this greater happiness. This is why we develop the skillful qualities.

It's our habit to look for happiness where everybody else is looking for it. In many ways it's easier to do what everybody else is doing; it's easier to let the rapid current carry us off down the world's river. As I'm writing this book, one of the most popular, most desired forms of new technology is the flat-screen TV. Everybody, it seems, is buying one of these gigantic televisions. The prevailing message, dictated by the present-day culture, is that if you want to be happy you've got to get a flat-screen TV. This is the way of the world, the path the world suggests for finding happiness. Buy a new TV. Be happy.

At times I find myself listening to this message. Putting my eyes on one of these flat-screen televisions in a friend's home or in the window of an appliance store, I find myself wondering if I should buy a new TV. I find myself thinking that's what I need. That's the solution. If I buy a flat-screen TV, I'll be happy.

There is a kind of happiness that we obtain from material objects, from the sense pleasures they deliver. There is a "happiness" that we garner from pleasure, gain, status, praise. But it's a flawed happiness. It's a happiness that's intrinsically stressful, painful. The problem, as we've noted, is that it's inconstant, unreliable. It doesn't last. The flat-screen TV will provide only temporary happiness. After a while, probably not a long while, it won't offer the same jolt, it won't supply the same happiness it did when it was first plugged in. It probably won't be long, in fact, before the technology becomes outdated, before another technology take its place as the favored instrument for TV watching. As you're reading this, it might have already happened. The flat-screen TV might already be a dinosaur. And we know what happens when that happens: We become dissatisfied with what we have. We want the new and improved TV. We want the latest thing.

The fact is, if we look for happiness in things that can't provide a reliable happiness, we'll always suffer. We'll go through life perpetually dissatisfied.

The Buddha discovered that there's a happiness that's quite different from the happiness offered by things like flat-screen TVs. There's a happiness more satisfying than the happiness we gain by subscribing to the ways of the world. There's a greater happiness.

It's a true happiness. It doesn't let us down. It doesn't falter. It's always there. It's inside. It's the happiness inside. The happiness of the heart.

It's a happiness, it should be noted, that's extraordinarily sublime, to the point where it can't really be described.

And make no mistake, it's a happiness that's available to you. It's a happiness that, as a human being, you can know.

On the night of his awakening, the Buddha was assailed by Mara. When the Buddha didn't succumb to the forces of desire and aversion, when he remained unmoved, Mara, in frustration, asked the Buddha what he thought he was doing, who did he think he was, looking for true happiness. The Buddha, in response, simply touched his hand to the earth. It's a pose depicted in many statues. The Buddha, essentially, was saying that he had a right to a true happiness. It was his birthright. Living on earth, as a human being, he had an opportunity to know a greater happiness. And he was seizing it.

As a human being, you have a right to a greater happiness. It's up to you to seize the opportunity, to make the most of your life.

The effort you make in developing the qualities we've talked about in this book will bring you to the heart. It will open your heart. Like many rivers leading to the sea, you'll move, in developing the skillful qualities, toward a province of vast heartfulness, lovingkindness, good will, compassion, joy, equanimity, acceptance, peace.

You'll know a greater happiness.

ACKNOWLEDGMENTS

I first learned meditation in 1975, from my college roommate, Edward "Woody" Spiegel, who passed away while I was writing this book. Thanks Woody!

I want to express my thanks to the teachers who've showed me the Buddha's path, including Eugene Cash, Christina Feldman, Michele McDonald, and Thanissaro Bhikkhu.

The Skill of Living is inspired by the teachings of Ajaan Lee and Thanissaro Bhikkhu. I have extraordinary gratitude for the lineage of Ajaan Lee and all those who've helped to keep it going. Much gratitude to Thanissaro Bhikkhu for his careful and expert reading of the manuscript, wise guidance, and many spot-on suggestions. This book is much better thanks to Than Geoff.

My thanks to Thanissaro Bhikkhu for letting me use his brilliant translations of the Buddha's suttas.

I have to give major thanks to Leslie Maslow for her superb writerly counsel and generosity. Many thanks, also, to Mary Talbot for her help and support with this book and many other things through the years. Several people offered the gift of their time and attention in reading the manuscript, including Laura Berringer, John Corwin, Connie Hatch, Mary Ellen O'Boyle, Andy Stone, and Paul Weinfield. Thank you so much.

I am blessed to have a wonderful editor in Jillian Magalaner Stone. Gail Doobinin designed the cover; I am forever grateful to her. And thanks to Claudine Anrather for the beautiful painting of the lotus flower which forms in the mud and rises to know the light.

Finally, my gratitude to the members of Downtown Meditation Community whose wholehearted effort to develop the skillful qualities is at the heart of this book. Their goodness and love of the dharma brings me joy every day of the year

ABOUT THE AUTHOR

Peter Doobinin is the founder and guiding teacher of Downtown Meditation Community. He's also a co-founder of New York Insight Meditation Center. Through the years he's taught the dharma at many venues, including the New York City public schools. As a teacher in New York City, Peter's foremost interest is in helping people follow the Buddha's teachings within the context of their contemporary urban lives. His vision is to provide refuge for dharma students, a place where people can practice together and support each other in their efforts to find greater happiness in their lives. Peter also writes fiction. His most recent novel is *Suburban Boy*. He lives, downtown, in Manhattan.

TO FIND OUT MORE

For more information please visit these websites:
Peter Doobinin www.doobinin.com
Downtown Meditation Community www.dnymc.org
Theravada Buddhism www.accesstoinsight.org

ABBREVIATIONS

Pali Texts

AN   *Anguttara Nikaya*

Dhp   *Dhammapada*

Iti   *Itivuttaka*

MN   *Majjhima Nikaya*

SN   *Samyutta Nikaya*

Sn   *Sutta Nipata*

Ud   *Udana*

The suttas (discourses) contain the primary teachings of Theravada Buddhism. All of the translations in this book were done by Thanissaro Bhikkhu. You can find the complete translation of the suttas denoted in *The Skill of Living* at the Access to Insight website: www.accesstoinsight. org.